PUBLIC DIALOGUE AND PARTICIPATORY DEMOCRACY

THE CUPERTINO COMMUNITY PROJECT

THE HAMPTON PRESS COMMUNICATION SERIES
Communication and Participation
Thomas L. Jacobson, supervisory editor

PUBLIC DIALOGUE AND PARTICIPATORY DEMOCRACY

THE CUPERTINO COMMUNITY PROJECT

SHAWN SPANO

SAN JOSE STATE UNIVERSITY

 HAMPTON PRESS, INC.
CRESSKILL, NEW JERSEY

Printed in the United States of America

Library of Congress Cataloging-in-Publication Data

Spano, Shawn J., 1958-
    Public dialogue and participatory democracy : the Cupertino community project / Shawn Spano.
        p. cm. -- (The Hampton Press communication series. Communication and participation)
    Includes bibliographical references and index.
    ISBN 1-57273-358-6 (cl) -- ISBN 1-57273-359-4 (pp)
    1. Communication in community development--California--Cupertino--Case studies.
    I. Title: Cupertino community project. II. Title. III. Series.

HN80.C87 S63 2001
307.1'416--dc21

                                 2001016891

Hampton Press, Inc.
23 Broadway
Cresskill, NJ 07626

CONTENTS

FOREWORD

DON BROWN

CUPERTINO CITY MANAGER

One of the acid tests for a community is the way it responds to unexpected challenges. An unexpected challenge can take many shapes. It could be the response to a natural catastrophe such as flood, fire, tornado, hurricane, or earthquake. It could be the response to a major crime such as a mass murder. Or it could be in response to a major accident resulting in significant loss of life such as a plane crash or bus accident. These kinds of instantaneous calamities frequently bring a community closer together as people deal with the shared grief and ultimate recovery.

Sometimes unexpected challenges come more gradually and present a different kind of test to the fabric of the community and its citizens. It was this second kind of challenge that caused Cupertino, California to look at different ways of doing things.

Changes in this community's ethnic mix began during the 1980s. Cupertino's highly valued education system and high quality of life was attractive to a wide variety of immigrants. These newcomers arrived from Taiwan, Hong Kong, China, Iran and other eastern Euro-Asian countries. The dominant ethnic background has been Chinese. The predominant profile has been high education/high income with a preeminent value on education for the children.

who are these predominantly white Chinese.

As these changes accelerated into the 1990s, and became more and more evident to the "traditional" community, signs of discomfort and resistance were evident. The community was changing right before people's eyes and they were not sure what to make of it. As the "minority" cultures approached 40% of the total population of the community the sense of uncertainty increased.

As public officials, elected and professional staff alike, there is a public policy question when this kind of change occurs: "Do we have a responsibility to the community to strategically plan for these changes or just let them happen and deal with the consequences, whatever they may be"? We are not aware of examples of other communities that chose to be proactive and strategic in approaching gradual yet dramatic demographic changes.

Political leaders (elected city council members) and professional staff (city managers and department managers) come to their respective roles with a well established frame of reference based on a strong tradition of local government in California and other states. Neither of these traditional roles has prepared us to deal with the challenge described briefly above, and in greater detail in Shawn Spano's book.

Political leaders view themselves as representatives of the community. They rely heavily on their constituents for information on how things are going. For the most part they respond to finite and well-defined issues and problems and try to deliver solutions that sort out these issues and solve these problems. Much of what they deal with are physical in nature, i.e. how things look, and how they will look in the future.

Professional staff members view themselves as problem solvers and experts. They are trained to find "correct" answers that are based on a technical evaluation of information. They have a stake in continuity and keeping a lid on things.

Cupertino changed from a mono-cultural community to a multi-cultural community in a relatively compressed time period. Changes were manifested in ways that did not fit neatly into either of the above-described roles. Because race and ethnicity are sensitive topics, people find it difficult to discuss openly their true feelings. (There were a number of flare-ups that had at their core ethnic misunderstandings and suspicions of underlying motives.) How do political leaders deal with an issue that is generating strong community feelings but is not being openly talked about? How do professional managers tackle an issue that cannot be defined and any potential solution involves risks that could blow up in your face? Where do either of these groups go for examples of how other communities have approached these challenges?

In reviewing how other communities have dealt with similar issues it seems that most have taken the traditional approach of responding to problems after the fact with proposed actions. Examples include establishing human relations commissions that receive complaints and develop responses. These responses range from some form of mediation to legal prosecution for illegal discrimination or hate crimes.

The nature of how cities in California, and other parts of the country, conduct the public's business does not lend itself to a thoughtful dialogue on topics that have no clear solutions. City council meetings are formal proceedings. The agendas are posted and, by law, must be adhered to. These same rules apply to advisory bodies appointed by the city council. By their nature, sensitive and potentially volatile topics centering on race and ethnicity seem to have a better chance of a positive outcome in informal settings and with the guidance of skilled facilitators. For Cupertino to engage citizens in an ongoing dialogue about multiculturalism a new approach had to be developed.

The project described in this book was developed as an iterative process. I don't believe that in the early meetings between the Public Dialogue Consortium (PDC) and city officials, that any of us could have envisioned the activities and directions we would take over the next few years. As public officials, we learned that it is possible to have a robust public dialogue on a sensitive community issue. We also learned that there will be detractors, but that by encouraging their involvement you reinforce your commitment to open dialogue. One of the most rewarding concepts derived from our efforts thus far is that people are allowed to "stand their ground". We are not in the business of getting everyone to think the same way. Our aim is to provide a place where strongly held views can be given and received in a respectful manner. At the least, this will improve the clarity of our respective views. At the best, through this increased clarity, we may find that we share more common values about our community than we thought.

Having been in the city management business for nearly 25 years and having served five different communities, my initial reaction to this project was guarded. My initial reservations were based on two general concerns: First, does a communication theory developed in an academic setting by communication professors work in a real-world setting? Second, since discussions about race and diversity are fairly risky topics, do I want to put my own career at risk by pursuing this untested approach?

I overcame the first reservation primarily through a series of lengthy conversations with some of the key participants from the PDC. None of us had ever done this before and, as such, we understood the responsibility for a careful and sensitive approach. The "light bulb" moment for me came when I realized that this project was not about changing people's minds, but that it was about giving people a way to talk about tough issues. I also realized that people's fears and concerns are real and legitimate and that they need a way of talking about them without the fear of being branded a racist.

I overcame my reservation about the career risk in two ways. First, through self-assessment. My strengths were that I was viewed as a seasoned and experienced professional manager who had provided strong and positive leadership in the community over a span of seven years. I felt that by providing leadership in this arena the upside, potential gains for the community outweighed the downside risk of negative political fall out. I also felt that I could weather some negative results if the positive motivations of everyone involved were continually emphasized. I'm not sure if I would have come to this same conclusion at an earlier point in my career.

Second, it was vitally important that the city council understood and supported these efforts. I knew that in my role as city manager I could not move this effort forward without strong buy-in and visible support from the elected policy makers. As I talked through the issues and the approach with individual council members, it became clear that the political support for moving ahead was in place. Strong individual and consensus leadership emerged from the city council as the project began to take shape.

My personal and professional participation in this public dialogue project has been among the most rewarding activities of my career. I am very proud of the Cupertino community. In many ways the city is becoming the model for a multi-cultural community. My hope is that through this book and the continued work of the Public Dialogue Consortium the techniques developed in Cupertino will be seen as valuable and useful in other communities.

PREFACE

This book is a case study account of a community project designed to enhance the quality of public communication among and between residents and city officials in Cupertino, California. Its purpose is to convey the story of the Cupertino Project to academics, public professionals, and communication practitioners, and to assist them in developing community-building programs, action research projects, and other forms of social practice that foster collaboration, shared decision-making, and civic engagement.

The project is the brainchild of the Public Dialogue Consortium, a non-profit organization composed of communication teachers, researchers, and practitioners. As a member of the PDC, I was involved in the planning, facilitation, and assessment of each of the four phases of the project covered in this book.

Although it is situated within the boarders of one particular city, the Cupertino Project is driven by concerns that extend to communities across the United States. From Cupertino to New York City to Bismarck, North Dakota, communities are struggling to find ways to respond to rapid social change, to find ways for people with different backgrounds, ideologies, and abilities to live together peacefully and productively.

This is an enormously serious and complex challenge. It is widely recognized that the social problems that typically confront American cities—school safety, immigration, growth and development, affordable housing, lack of community—are bound up in larger networks of relationships and activities. As such, they do not lend themselves to easy answers or simple solutions. Elected officials, public professionals, and technical experts can and should help, but they cannot be successful if they act alone. Active citizen engagement, participatory democracy, is essential if we are to effectively manage our most pressing social problems. As it turns out, this is no easy task either.

To actually initiate a project in participatory democracy one has to be able to swim against some very strong political currents. The first is the common perception that citizens are passive, disengaged, and indifferent to civic affairs and political activities. Why bother to reinvigorate democratic participation if citizens are unwilling to get involved?

Projects in participatory democracy must also challenge the conventional belief that elected officials and public professionals cannot be trusted, and that political processes are inherently corrupt. According to this line of critique, powerful economic, bureaucratic, and legislative forces have managed to wrestle democracy away from regular citizens. Public decision-making processes are now so beholden to the private interests of a few that the public's voice is simply not strong enough to be heard. The system is corrupt. Why bother?

The final and most important challenge is at the heart of this book. It has to do with communication. Simply put, *projects in participatory democracy must be based in different forms or patterns of communication than what we normally see operating in public today.* Along with many others, we have observed that when people are divided on social issues and public problems they have difficulty expressing their differences constructively. All of us have some experience with loud, polarized, acrimonious conflict. We see it on political talk shows, in political campaigns, and at local city council meetings. While this type of negative conflict is certainly destructive, so too is avoidance. In Cupertino, for example, we found that there were some topics that people simply would not discuss in public. We suspect the same happens in other communities as well. Confrontation or avoidance? Participatory democracy demands that we find a better way.

The PDC initiated the Cupertino Project in order to create communication structures and processes that would allow residents and city officials to work together to identify concerns, articulate visions, and develop action plans that enhance, strengthen, and build community. As described in this book, the project locates the solutions to our most serious social problems at the intersection of public dialogue and participatory democracy, at the point where genuine human contact becomes the vehicle for achieving self-governance. It describes what can happen when citizens become actively engaged in the civic life of their communities, when they become partners with elected officials and public professionals in making decisions and deciding how they are going to make decisions. It shows how the quality of democratic participation is inexorably tied to the quality of public communication. It demonstrates in the most practical way possible that public dialogue is a useful and valuable response to the most serious and complex problems that confront us.

BRIDGING THEORY AND PRACTICE

The work of the PDC in Cupertino is guided by a social constructionist theoretical perspective and an eclectic set of interventionist practices adapted from other practitioner groups and organizations (see Chapter 2). This conceptual and methodological orientation leads us to view the expression of social problems not as objective statements depicting the true state of affairs, but rather as utterances in an ongoing, malleable, and ultimately incomplete process. The influx of Asian immigrants in Cupertino, for example, was defined as problematic by some because it was couched in a pattern of communication that made this interpretation possible. Our approach is to draw attention to the meanings that are being constructed around problems and issues, and to invite community members into different patterns of communication that will hopefully enable other interpretations and actions. It is a way of working that moves seriously in the direction of bridging theory and practice.

POTENTIAL AUDIENCES

This book has been written with three audiences in mind: (1) communication scholars, students, and teachers interested in the practical uses of social theory and action research methodology, (2) public administrators and elected officials interested in developing community-building programs that draw on principles of democratic participation, and (3) communication practitioners interested in case study descriptions, applied techniques, and reflective practice.

By situating public dialogue and participatory democracy around the particulars of a specific case study project, I hope that this book will serve as both a practical demonstration and a possible resource for each of the three potential audiences. Communication scholars are likely to concentrate on our application of social constructionist theory and our interventionist approach to social research. Public professionals will be interested to learn how city officials in one community participated in a collaborative decision-making process with residents to address a difficult and controversial social issue. Communication practitioners will want to focus on the facilitation techniques used and the way in which each of the events and phases of the project were developed and designed. Each of these aspects is not distinct, however. In fact, I hope that all readers will benefit from the way the various disciplinary interests depicted in the project are integrated and blended together.

ORGANIZATION OF THE BOOK

The book is divided into four parts. Part I provides a brief overview of the Cupertino Project and a theoretical framework for conceptualizing and practicing public dialogue and participatory democracy. The first chapter introduces the reader to the nature, scope, and purpose of the project, and delineates the community dialogue process model that developed as a result of our work in Cupertino. The second chapter describes the communicative foundations of participatory democracy, the essential characteristics of public dialogue, and the theoretical and methodological approach used in the Cupertino Project. These chapters together provide the framework for the case study example described in Part II.

The chapters that comprise Part II of the book describe in detail how the Cupertino Project developed over four interrelated phases. Here I provide both a description of events and a running commentary on how the PDC team and others in the project helped shape the nature and sequence of events. The chapters are written in a narrative style that involves a first-person plural "we" description of events, a second-person "meta-narrator" who provides PDC commentary and critical reflection about the events (choices we made, how we made them, why, and to what effect), and a third-person account of the project from the participants (actual excerpts of discourse). The purpose is to take the reader into the inner workings of the project, the subtle ways in which it unfolded, how each phase set the conditions for the next, and what project participants actually said and did. Given that the work of the PDC in Cupertino is still ongoing as of this writing, I conclude Part II with a brief epilogue on the current status of the project.

After completing Part II of the book, I invited colleagues from the three different audiences for the book (communication scholars, public administrators, and communication practitioners) to read what I had written and to offer their perspectives on the project. Their responses are included in Part III. This was an open invitation with few constraints or limitations on either form of content. The contributors were asked to simply respond to the project by offering their reflections and critical evaluations, and to compare the work conducted in Cupertino with their own professional activities and experiences.

The six contributions, along with an interview I conducted with Cupertino city council member Michael Chang, are grouped into four different chapters. Chapter 7 includes responses and critical evaluations from those who participated in the project. Chapter 8 includes reflections and evaluations of the project from the perspective of a group of dialogue practitioners known as the Public Conversations Project. The two contributions in Chapter 9 provide scholarly accounts of the project from intercultural and interpersonal communication theorists. The contributions in Chapter 10 examine the project from the perspectives of two public administrators, and includes comparisons of the Cupertino Project with other community dialogue initiatives.

In Part IV I offer a response to the contributors by grouping common themes and points of difference into three sections: (1) those that affirm and extend the work of the PDC and the community dialogue process in Cupertino, (2) those that critique and challenge the decisions, choices, and actions taken in the project, and (3) those that offer lessons for improving community dialogue processes.

As we shall see, Parts III and IV represent a departure from most academic texts and case study accounts. This is no accident. The Cupertino Project, and the practice of public dialogue more generally, is itself a departure from "business as usual." Books, like traditional forms of public communication, are almost always monologic. A writer or speaker holds forth, telling others the way things are and how they ought to be. To create something different, writers and speakers need to create opportunities to listen and respond to what readers and audiences have to say. No single individual can or should lay claim to the final word. In this book, as in the Cupertino Project, I hope to both describe and demonstrate how the creation of civil society and the answers to our most pressing social problems are made in public dialogue, in ongoing exchange between citizens as conversational partners.

ACKNOWLEDGMENTS

The Cupertino Project was (and is) a collaborative effort involving the support and insight of numerous groups, individuals, and organizations. As such, my role in writing this book is closer to narrator than author. The story I tell, after all, is not my own. I am especially indebted to my colleagues on the PDC team: W. Barnett Pearce, Kim Pearce, Stephen Littlejohn, Kevin Barge, Victoria Chen, Kathy Domenici, Ralph Banks, Claire Calcagno, Michael Leitao, and Rita So. My work with this group, both on the Cupertino Project and elsewhere, has been the most intellectually stimulating and rewarding experience of my career. This book would not have been possible without them. To simply say "thank you" does not seem like thanks enough.

I am also grateful to the contributors for reading early drafts of the manuscript and offering their responses in writing: Robyn Penman, Sallyann Roth, Robert Stains Jr., Richard M. Chasin, Rona Halualani, John Stewart, Joy Salmon, John Hiatt, and Mark Linder. Their provocative questions and insights have given this book a depth and perspective that I simply would not have been able to attain on my own. Thank you for joining the conversation.

Several people offered valuable feedback and critical commentary to the PDC throughout the course of the project. For their willingness to listen, ask tough questions, and offer advice, thanks to Sandy Acebo, Sarah Cobb, Pat Brown, Tim Hegstrom, Dennis Jaehne, Duane Kobo, Elaine Lee, Mark Linder, John Stewart, Kris Tetford, Betsy Vegso, and Mara Wold. For their help and assistance working on the project, we are grateful to Theresa Berry, Margaret Couch, Michele Demetras, Annabell Forbes, Eugene Fujimoto, Jeff Grant, Ann Ranch, and Alicia Testa.

Sandy Acebo and Martha Kanter made the initial contact with Cupertino city manager Don Brown, and later helped us secure grant funding. We are forever indebted to you.

We were fortunate to work with an outstanding group of public professionals and elected officials in Cupertino. First and foremost, a very special thank you to Don Brown for his willingness to take a chance on us and for his ongoing assistance and keen insights in moving the public dialogue process forward. We also want to acknowledge and thank Laura Domondon Lee for providing the organizational support necessary to sustain and grow the project. We are grateful as well for the support of the Cupertino city council members who served terms in office during the phases of the project described in this book: John Bautista, Don Burnett, Michael Chang, Wally Dean, Sandy James, Lauralee Sorenson, and John Statton. We are especially indebted here to Michael for his active participation and leadership, and John S. for helping recruit project participants from the business community when he was head of the Chamber of Commerce, before being elected to the council.

We are deeply and profoundly grateful to the thousands of Cupertino residents and community members who participated in the project. I regret not being able to acknowledge all of them here because it was their involvement that shaped and energized the project, ultimately transforming it into a richly textured communication mosaic. If it is indeed a thing of beauty, as Barnett might say, it is because community members have made it so. I do wish to thank the following community members, in particular, for their contributions to this book: Don Allen, Laina Raveendran Greene, Roberta Hollimon, Donna Krey, Joanne Laird, Piper McNulty, Fariba Nejat, Claire Omura, Zahara Pavlovic, Roger Peng, Jenny Purushotma, Janet Shannon, and Ann Woo.

Our work with the Sheriff's Department was greatly aided by Captain Bob Wilson, who helped us convene the law enforcement discussion groups and gave us access to his school resource officers: Janet Shannon, Linda Rios, and Ed Laverone. We also wish to acknowledge Sergeant Steve Angus for his contributions as community programs liaison.

A number of people were instrumental in helping the PDC develop public dialogue programs in the Cupertino public schools. Thanks to Joe Hamilton, Superintendent of the Fremont Union School District; Barbara Nunes, Principal at Cupertino High School; Mary Stone, Principal, and Joanne Laird, Vice Principal at Monta Vista High School. The students who participated were both gifted and inspiring. While there are too many to list here, we would like to acknowledge two students, Macy Armstrong and Bre Fowler, for going above and beyond the call of duty.

The Cupertino Telecommunications Commission and Cupertino Community Television at De Anza College provided invaluable assistance recording events and televising programs on the project. A well deserved thanks here to Bill Mannion. Thanks also to Marie Moore for coordinating our training with members of the Cupertino Emergency Preparedness Program.

The Cupertino Project was funded, in part, by grants from the David and Lucile Packard Foundation. Funding also came from the U.S. Department of Justice (Citizens Options for Public Safety or C.O.P.S. grants) through the City of Cupertino. I am grateful as well to San Jose State University, my home institution, for providing me the time and resources (sabbatical leave, research grant) necessary to initiate the writing of this book.

My personal thank you is to my wife, friend, and partner, Cristina, for challenging my ideas and for loving and nourishing me.

Finally, I dedicate this book to the memory of my father, Carmelo. He taught me to value work, to choose a profession I'm passionate about, and to always finish what I start.

I

THE THEORY AND PRACTICE OF PUBLIC DIALOGUE

1

INTRODUCTION

In 1995, Kim Pearce organized a group of professors, students, and practitioners interested in exploring how interpersonal communication principles and skills could be used to improve the quality of public communication. In our first year together, our group, known as the Public Dialogue Consortium (PDC),[1] conducted two public forums using an innovative approach to conflict resolution known as Kaleidoscope, sponsored a two-day international conference for communication practitioners and a national teleconference on alternative conflict resolution skills, attended workshops sponsored by other practitioner groups, and held extensive training sessions and simulations to refine our own communication abilities and skills. We emerged from these activities with a preliminary set of ideas and methods for promoting "good" communication around public issues. Our decision to continue working together was predicated on the idea that we could utilize these ideas and methods in a long-term, sustained community project.

ENTERING THE COMMUNITY

Approximately a year after coming together, the PDC approached the city manager of Cupertino, CA,[2] Don Brown, and volunteered to initiate a collaborative project in public communication. The goal, as originally conceived, was to link citizens and city officials together in on-going conversations about the city. By focusing on the form of these conversations, in addition to the content, the project was designed to create opportunities for people to identify community issues and problems and talk about them in productive and constructive ways. Don was initially skeptical, but he was also intrigued with the proposal and interested in exploring it further. For several months he met with members of the PDC team to talk about our theoretical approach to public communication, and how it might fit within the context of the Cupertino community. Convinced that there was merit in moving forward, he then arranged for the PDC to present its proposal to the five city council members.[3] The council, like the city manager, reacted initially with a mixture of interest and skepticism.

Support for the project at this point was tenuous and shallow. From the council's perspective, it was important that the work of the PDC not be formally sanctioned by the city. Inviting the public into an open-ended, community dialogue process can be a risky undertaking for elected leaders and city officials. For one thing, it is difficult to specify outcomes in advance. Moreover, the project, as we described it, called for collaborative forms of leadership and a decentralized approach to decision making. This no doubt posed something of a challenge to those leaders accustomed to exercising power and authority in a top-down fashion. Although the council decided not to fund the project or endorse it in any formal way, they did not object to letting the PDC go forward with the first phase. This tacit approval established a baseline level of support, which in turn created an opening for the PDC to enter the community.

In our initial interactions with city officials and residents, the PDC presented itself as an independent, volunteer organization. We have since come to see how critical this was in establishing our credibility with community members. As public communication facilitators, consultants, and researchers, we were careful to assume a nonpartisan stance relative to political issues in the city. Advancing a position of neutrality early in the process was essential for building trust and establishing relationships with city residents and the various stakeholder groups in the community. It would have been difficult, if not impossible, to develop the kinds of equitable relationships necessary for working collaboratively with community members had the PDC been perceived as an extension of city government or a political organization advancing a particular cause, issue, or agenda.

Box 1.1. A Healthy Level of Skepticism

The Cupertino Project would have never gotten off the ground without the city manager's early endorsement. Don Brown is truly one of the heroes of this story. It took awhile for him to fully embrace our ideas for doing public dialogue, however. For the first six or so months of the project he kept a wary eye on us, cautiously maintaining a healthy level of skepticism. At the conclusion of almost every meeting he would routinely ask, "You do know what you're doing, right?" We always assured him that we did, even though we were not always sure ourselves. We look back at Don's initial skepticism now with amusement, knowing how far we have all come and how committed the community is to the project. At the time, however, we took his skepticism very seriously. It made us painfully aware that our support was fragile, that there were risks involved, and that any mistake might very well have put an end to the project.

Given our neutral standing on the issues, what stake did we have in the community? In the beginning the PDC assumed an intermediary position between community residents and local government. The goal was to facilitate a series of activities that would bring city officials and citizens into a common decision-making process. Although we were neutral on the issues, we went out of our way to say that we were *not neutral on the form or pattern of communication used to define issues and make decisions*. Specifically, we said that our commitment was to foster a form of communication called *public dialogue*. Our position was that the community would be better served if members of the public could listen and speak to each other with curiosity and respect rather than confrontation and debate. If community members were to engage in a dialogic form of communication the quality of decision making would increase and the commitment to the choices made would be enhanced.

At the time, we conceptualized the public dialogue process as a sequence of turns in an on-going conversation between residents and city officials. Our plan called for us to begin with city residents so that they could take the first speaking turn in the conversation. While residents spoke, city officials would listen. At some point we would facilitate a conversational turn so that city officials could speak while residents listened. It was a simple model and it served us well during the first year or so of the project. Eventually, however, the project outgrew the model. Public dialogue turned out to be a far more complex process than we originally thought. Almost three years after the project began, we finally found ourselves in a position to articulate a community dialogue model that could adequately account for what we did in the Cupertino Project, and how we might go about designing other public dialogue projects in the future.

But I get ahead of myself. Let's begin at the beginning of Phase I and describe how we facilitated activities designed to give voice to community concerns, issues, and problems.

PHASE I: GIVING VOICE TO COMMUNITY CONCERNS

To begin the dialogue process, the PDC facilitated a series of focus-group interviews with a cross-section of community residents. The purpose was to create opportunities for participants to identify what they felt were the most important concerns, issues, and problems facing the city. The meetings were designed to be as open-ended and exploratory as possible. Among other things, this meant that we did not preselect topics and issues for discussion. Participants were simply encouraged to express their own views, in their own words, and from their own perspectives.

The relationship between the PDC and city residents during this phase mirrored the relationship between the PDC and city officials. Both in our initial phone calls and in the group interviews, residents repeatedly expressed a combination of curiosity, skepticism, and interest. The beginning of almost every meeting was marked by a flurry of probing questions: Who are you? How did you get my phone number? Are you working for the city? Are you affiliated with a political group or government agency? Do you work for a private organization? What will you do with the results of these discussions? Although we expected these sorts of questions and gave what we thought was sufficient background information at the outset, we were surprised by how many questions were asked and how intense the level of curiosity seemed to be.

We responded to the questions as best we could. This meant, first, acknowledging each question as a legitimate and valuable contribution to the conversation, and second, being as honest and nondefensive as possible. Answering the questions in this way, we believe, helped establish trust and confidence in the PDC and the focus group procedure. Our responses also served to model a nonconfrontational pattern of communication. Instead of responding to the questions as if they were intrusive interrogations, we treated them as genuine attempts to understand us and the focus-group procedure. Once it became clear to the participants that the PDC facilitators had no preconceived agenda or conflict of interest, suspicions seemed to fade. The discussions that followed were, in our estimation, open, candid, and revealing.

The PDC compiled summary descriptions, or data texts, from the focus-group interviews. The one issue that generated the most attention and interest centered on the rapid demographic changes in the ethnic composition of the city.[4] In every focus group, participants expressed concerns that the recent influx of new Asian and Chinese immigrants was creating tension, resentment, and fear among some segments of the community. Both the new immigrants and the established residents we talked with said that they were aware of the problem. Importantly, however, they also said that the issue was not being discussed openly in ways that might benefit the community as a whole. Those of us in the PDC were struck by the contrast between peoples' desire to deal with the issue and their perception that they did not know how to go about doing it. They feared the consequences of initiating conversations about it, and as a result defined it as an "undiscussible" topic, at least in public. Reflecting our commitment to working appreciatively, we called this issue "cultural richness."

PHASE II: ELICITING VISIONS AND ACTION PLANS

In keeping with the conversational metaphor, residents once again assumed the primary speaking position during Phase II of the project. Although the PDC did in fact brief the city manager and city council on the results of the focus-group interviews, we did not ask for nor did they offer to give a formal response. They assured us once again, however, that they would continue to listen to community residents.

The PDC sought to carry forward the concerns expressed by residents into the second phase of the project, melding the two in order to create a more focused discussion at a deeper level of engagement. Given the significance of the Asian immigration and cultural richness issue to city residents, and the perception among focus-group participants that it was not an appropriate topic for public discussion, we felt it necessary to include a second, less controversial topic in Phase II. Community safety was selected, in part, because it was not talked about as a particularly divisive issue, although it was seen as an important one.

Phase II progressed along two parallel tracks. The first track consisted of a series of dialogue-group meetings with a cross-section of Cupertino residents. The meetings were divided into two parts, corresponding to the two topics of interest: cultural richness and community safety. Participants first discussed their meanings for the term "cultural richness" and their visions for how Cupertino could best take advantage in the future of the recent demographic changes. Next, participants were asked to develop a series of action plans for how to turn their visions into reality. This same interview protocol was then used in the second half of the meeting in which discussion focused on community safety.

The PDC facilitators encouraged group participants to adopt dialogic forms of communication throughout the discussions. This was accomplished in several ways. First, the initial letter sent out to potential participants alerted them to the unique communication approach used in the Cupertino Project. Participants were told that the project avoids polarized debate in favor of a process that encourages people to explore both their differences and their shared concerns in a climate of trust and respect. Second, a short list of ground rules was established at the beginning of each dialogue-group meeting (respect differences of opinion, listen carefully, and one person speaks at a time). Additionally, the types of questions asked and the communication techniques employed by the facilitators encouraged participants to speak from personal experience and to link those experiences to others in the group and to larger community concerns. All of these actions were intended to invite participants into dialogic forms of communication and to enable them to move beyond their positions on the issues to underlying values and experiences.

The second track of Phase II consisted of training students from two of the local high schools to conduct intergenerational interviews with adult members of the community. The interviews, like the dialogue-group discussions, focused on visions and action plans associated with cultural richness and community safety. In terms of their contribution to the project, the interviews engaged hundreds of residents in situated conversations that demonstrated how the potentially volatile issue of ethnic diversity could be discussed in useful and creative ways.

The culmination of Phase II was a large Town Hall Meeting. Close to 150 community residents participated in the event. The meeting served several purposes. First, it functioned as an information-gathering session for all city residents to learn about the project and the work that had already been accomplished. Second, it demonstrated that it is possible to discuss issues, problems, and concerns in public in ways that affirm community values and do not lead to unproductive confrontations. Third, and perhaps most importantly, the meeting was designed as an invitation for other community members to join the conversation and help deliberate the future direction of the city. In this respect, it legitimated not only the discussion of these topics, but a focus on the patterns of communication in which these topics were discussed.

Given the widespread attention it received, the Town Hall Meeting was in some ways the first "real test" of the PDC and the public-dialogue process. It brought the results of the focus-group interviews, dialogue-group discussions, and intergenerational interviews to the attention of the larger community, and it created possibilities for future action. Although some people criticized these efforts for not getting at the "real" issues, there were many others who seemed to find some value in the process and were at least willing to join the conversation to see where it might lead. In the context of the unfolding public-dialogue process, the fact that the Town Hall Meeting led to other events (it kept the process going) is perhaps the most significant indicator of success.

PHASE III: WORKING THROUGH CITY LEADERS

Although there was a good deal of consensus following the Town Hall Meeting to continue the project, it was not entirely clear what the next steps should be. After talking with residents, city officials, and a group of outside consultants, the PDC decided that Phase III of the project needed to begin in close proximity to the Town Hall Meeting. We were also convinced, along with the city manager, that the council should use this phase as an opportunity to formally participate in the project. The time had come to facilitate the first significant conversational turn in the Cupertino Project, so the PDC set out in Phase III to help city officials craft a response to community residents.

Phase III also gave rise to a shift in process and a transformation in the relationships among the PDC, residents, and city officials. Although the PDC continued to design and facilitate events, it became evident that our team needed to take on new ideas and practices in order to assist community members in achieving their goals. For example, the council looked to us to assist them in building social capital by expanding communication networks and relationships among individuals and stakeholder groups in the community. In a related development, ownership of the project began to shift away from the PDC. By the end of Phase III, we had successfully dislodged ourselves as proprietors of the project and assumed more of a partnership role with city officials and community members.

Phase III consisted initially of hearing the council's views on cultural richness and community safety and inviting them to help define what the next steps of the project should be. To start this process, a senior member of the PDC team, Barnett Pearce, interviewed each of the five council members separately a few weeks after the Town Hall Meeting. A day-long City Council Team Building and Issue Formation meeting was then held after final copies of interviews were distributed to each of the council members. The purpose of the meeting was to assist the council in formulating a reply to the community and what they heard citizens saying in Phases I and II of the project. Among other things, the council decided that their contribution to the project should come in the form of a training and team-building program for community leaders.

The Training and Team Building Program was a two-day event. Over 100 community residents participated along with each of the five city council members. The meeting served a number of important purposes. First, it represented the first systematic attempt to train community members in the microskills of public dialogue and public deliberation. Second, the meeting was used to address the most difficult, contentious, and potentially volatile aspects of the Asian immigration and cultural change issue. The key point here is that participants did not simply discuss these concerns, but learned *how to* discuss them within the context of the training program. Finally, the meeting continued building on the ideas generated earlier in the project. Specifically, participants at the Training Program deliberated among the various action plans developed by community members and the city council and took steps to begin implementing them.

PHASE IV: SUSTAINING PUBLIC DIALOGUE

In Phase IV, those of us on the PDC team found ourselves having to rethink and revise our working model of public dialogue. Instead of an orderly and discrete set of conversational turns between residents and city officials, the project evolved into something that sounded more like a noisy cocktail party, with many different people all talking at once. New conversations emerged spontaneously in ways we could not have imagined or predicted. Many community residents, for example, stepped forward and began initiating interactions and activities on their own. City officials responded to these efforts and, in many cases, used them to suggest additional opportunities for citizen participation. With each new event and activity the circle of conversations grew wider, encompassing more and more community groups and organizations. It finally reached a point where there were so many conversations happening at once that it became physically impossible for those of us in the PDC to keep track of everything that was going on.

The goal of Phase IV was to build a communicative infrastructure capable of sustaining the public-dialogue process. This was accomplished in several ways. The PDC worked with different community groups to implement the action plans identified in earlier phases of the project. We also sought to institutionalize public dialogue by expanding communication-skills training throughout the community. These training programs were essential for building capacities that would allow community members to take control of the community-dialogue process. Finally, we sought to create opportunities in Phase IV for community members to critically reflect on public communication processes, especially those involving controversial topics.

One of the key developments for sustaining the public-dialogue process was the formation of a citizen's action group called the Citizens of Cupertino Cross Cultural Consortium (5Cs). Among other things, the 5Cs took the lead in implementing community-action plans and facilitating and designing large public events on diversity-related topics. As the group acquired capacities in public dialogue, a social structure for institutionalizing better communication in the city began to take shape. The PDC conducted additional training opportunities in the public schools and with other intact service organizations in order to reinforce and extend communication capacities within the community.

By the end of Phase IV, the Cupertino Project had achieved a level of success that exceeded our most optimistic expectations. We estimate that close to 2,500 people participated in one or more of the phases of the project. With the formation of on-going groups and initiatives like the 5Cs and the school training programs, we fully expect this number to increase in the future. The city itself took bold steps to ensure the success of the public-dialogue process. In one significant development, funding was allocated for a new community relations coordinator position to provide staff support for groups and organizations involved in the project. The city also worked with the Sheriff's Department to hire a community programs liaison to help create community policing programs and other outreach activities. A few months after Phase IV ended, the city manager, and by extension the city itself, was recognized for these and other efforts with a statewide advancement of diversity award from the League of California Cities.

It is fair to say that by the end of Phase IV the community was in a much better position to respond to concerns, issues, and problems than it was when the project started and cultural diversity was considered to be an "undiscussible" topic. This book provides a case study account of how that transformation came about.

COMMUNITY DIALOGUE PROCESS MODEL

The model depicted in Figure 1.1 was developed nearly three years after the project started (Pearce & Pearce, in press). It represents both a retrospective account of the Cupertino Project and a blueprint for how to design and implement other public dialogue projects. As indicated in the model, a community-dialogue process like the one developed in Cupertino consists of three levels. Level 1 ("Strategic Process Design") describes the overall structure of the dialogue process in terms of a series of interrelated phases. Level 2 ("Event Design") accounts for the fact that every phase in the dialogue process has specific events that are designed to achieve stated goals and purposes. Although many different types of events are possible, the ones listed in Figure 1.1 reflect those

Level 1: Strategic Process Design

Phase I:	Phase II:	Phase III:	Phase IV:
Voicing concerns, surfacing issues, identifying social problems	Eliciting community visions and and action plans	Responding to the community (from city government and city leaders)	Sustaining the public-dialogue process (implementing action plans; public dialogue training)

Level 2: Event Design

Phase I:	Phase II:	Phase III:	Phase IV:
Focus group interviews, community-wide meetings, concerns, visions, actions (CVA) model	Dialogue group discussions, inter-generational interviews, community-wide meetings, CVA model	Small group discussions, training & team building programs, community-wide meetings, CVA model	Project team meetings, training programs, community-wide meetings

Level 3: Communication Facilitation Skills

Event Structure:	Event Process:
Provide group organization, set ground rules, keep track of time, establish goals and objectives, keep detailed notes, and so on.	Create a safe and open environment, demonstrate neutrality and curiosity, listening, ask systemic and appreciative questions, and so on.

Figure 1.1. Community dialogue process model

that were used most often in the Cupertino Project. Level 3 ("Communication Facilitation Skills") highlights the notion that particular types of communication skills are needed to manage the structure and process of a given event. Some of the facilitation skills used in the Cupertino Project, although certainly not all of them, are included under "Event Structure" and "Event Process."

In conducting a community-dialogue process, it is essential to work simultaneously at all three levels. For example, developing and identifying specific facilitation microskills is always done within the context of a specific event, and the design of that event is always dependent on where it fits in the overall strategic process design.

COMMUNICATION FACILITATION SKILLS

When we first entered the Cupertino community most of our attention was focused on communication facilitation skills (Level 3 in Figure 1.1), particularly those listed under "Event Process." It was, and is, a standard operating principle of the PDC that public dialogue is made possible through the creative and effective application of various communication skills and techniques (demonstrating curiosity, listening, question asking, etc.). In developing a methodology, or social technology, that would enable us to facilitate dialogic forms of communication, we borrowed a variety of methods and techniques from other practitioner groups and organizations and adapted them to fit our purposes. Foremost among these are deliberation practices borrowed from the National Issues Forum (Gastil & Dillard, 1999; Osborn & Osborn, 1991), systemic intervention practices borrowed from the Kensington Consultation Centre (Cronen & Lang, 1994) and the Milan Group (Penn, 1982; Selvini, Boscolo, Cecchin, & Prata, 1980), pre-mediation and dialogue practices borrowed from the Public Conversations Project (Chasin et al., 1996), and organizational practices based in appreciative inquiry borrowed from David Cooperrider and his associates (Cooperrider, Barrett, & Srivastva, 1995; Hammond & Royal, 1998). The methodology that grew out of these various practices is grounded in a constellation of microskills. These skills and the methodological practices that frame them are discussed more fully in Chapter 2.

EVENT DESIGN

The microskills of public dialogue are always enacted within a particular context or event. When we began the Cupertino Project we were

unaware of the variety of event designs available to facilitators and practitioners interested in democratic participation and decision making
(Bunker & Alban, 1997). We have since become more familiar with some
of these methods, such as Future Search (Weisbord & Janoff, 1995) and
Open Space Technology (Owen, 1992), and have utilized aspects of them
in our work in Cupertino. Although enriched by these techniques, we
found that we could not simply pull them "off the shelf" and plug them
into the project. Inevitably we had to adapt, modify, and create new
designs to fit the unique circumstances and expectations of the moment.
As it turned out, every event associated with the Cupertino Project was
a customized event, coming as it did within an unfolding sequence of
other activities. The major events and activities of the project are listed in
chronological order in Table 1.1. In Chapters 3 through 6 I describe these
events in detail and try to account for the circumstances that shaped
them and the effects they produced.

STRATEGIC PROCESS DESIGN

Each of the events associated with the Cupertino Project was designed
as such because of where it fit within the overall structure of the community-dialogue process. At the beginning of the project we could not
have mapped out the phases of the Strategic Process Design (Level 1 in
Figure 1.1) because we were not sure where it was going or how it
would develop. Importantly, we did not seek to achieve some pre-estab-
lished outcome. Rather, we let the project emerge organically by designing each new phase based on previous phases and by having the participants themselves decide what the next steps in the process should be. As
each event unfolded, the larger shape and texture of the project came
into focus. Only now, with the advantage of hindsight, can we begin to
articulate the particular sequencing of the process and how each phase
set the context for the next. We do not pretend for a minute that other
public-dialogue projects can or should follow the same trajectory as
ours. What we do hope is that our experiences, and the theoretical and
practical work that it has inspired, will assist others in developing similar projects.

Table 1.1. Cupertino Project Timeline: A Selected List of Activities and Events.[5]

Phase I: March 1996 - June 1996

March 2	Focus group interview #1
March 2	Focus group interview #2
March 30	Focus group interview #3
March 30	Focus group interview #4
April 11	Focus group interview #5
April 11	Focus group interview #6
April 13	Focus group interview #7
April 13	Focus group interview #8
April 18	Focus group interview #9
April 20	Focus group interview #10
May 10	PDC briefs city manager on focus-group results
June 7	PDC briefs Cupertino city council on focus-group results

Phase II: September 1996 - November 1996

September 13	Training workshop for De Anza College students
September 14	Training workshop for San Jose State University students
September 16	Intergenerational interview training for Cupertino High School students
September 23	Intergenerational interview training for Monta Vista High School students
September 30	Joint intergenerational interview training for Cupertino and Monta Vista High School students
October 5	Dialogue group #1
October 9	Dialogue group #2
October 17	Dialogue group #3
October 19	Dialogue group #4
October 25	Dialogue group #5
October 26	Dialogue group #6
October - November	Intergenerational interviews conducted by high school students
November 8	Dialogue group #7
November 10	Town Hall planning meeting with Cupertino and Monta Vista High School students
November 16	Dialogue group #8
November 20	Cupertino Town Hall Meeting (150 participants)
November 20-21	Outside consultants evaluate Town Hall Meeting with PDC

Table 1.1. Cupertino Project Timeline: A Selected List of Activities and Events. (con't)

Phase III: December 1996 - March 1997

December 16-20	City council interviews
January 25	City Council Team Building and Issue Formation meeting
February 28- March 1	Training and Team Building Program for Cupertino Community Leaders (110 participants)

Phase IV: May 1997 - December 1998

May 13	First meeting of the Citizens of Cupertino Cross Cultural Consortium (5Cs)
June 17	5Cs meeting
June 26	First meeting of the 5Cs coordinating team
July 15	5Cs meeting
July - August	PDC conducts evaluation interviews with project participants
September 3	5Cs meeting
September 30	5Cs coordinating team meeting
October 8	Follow-up Training and Team Building meeting for Cupertino Community Leaders (100 participants)
October 22	5Cs meeting
November 4	5Cs coordinating team meeting
November 19	5Cs meeting
December 1	Training Workshop for Monta Vista High School students ("Helper" group)
December 8	Training Workshop for Monta Vista High School students ("Helper" group)
January 6	Focus group discussion with Cupertino Sheriffs
January 7	5Cs meeting
January 9-10	Training workshop for De Anza College and San Jose State University students for Cupertino High School Making Connections project
January 12	Training Workshop for Monta Vista High School students ("Helper" group)
January 12-13	Phase 1: Making Connections project. Cupertino High School students identify campus concerns
February 3, 10, 24	Training workshops for members of the Cupertino Emergency Preparedness program
February 5	Focus group discussion with Cupertino Sheriffs
February 19	5Cs meeting

Table 1.1. Cupertino Project Timeline: A Selected List of Activities and Events. (con't)

February 27	De Anza College and San Jose State University students train Cupertino High School students for Phase 2 of the Making Connections project
March 2	Training Workshop for Monta Vista High School students ("Peer Counselor" group)
March 3	Training Workshop for Monta Vista High School students ("Peer Counselor" group)
March 4	Training Workshop for Monta Vista High School students ("Link Crew" group)
March 5	5Cs coordinating team meeting
March 5	PDC briefing with Cupertino Community Relations Coordinator, Laura Domondon Lee
March 5	Student "fish bowl" discussion at Monta Vista High School (2,000 students in attendance)
March 6	Monta Vista High School students ("Helpers" and "Peer Counselor" groups) facilitate classroom discussions based on previous day's fish bowl
March 10	Phase 2: Making Connections project. Cupertino High School students identify visions and action plans
March 11	Monta Vista High School "Link Crew" students facilitate discussions at Kennedy Junior High School
March 17	Training workshop for De Anza College and San Jose State University students for Cupertino High School "Making Connections" project
March 18	De Anza College and San Jose State University students train Cupertino High School students for Phase 3 of the Making Connections project
March 24	5Cs meeting
April 9	Training workshop for members of Leadership Cupertino
April 21	5Cs coordinating committee meeting
April 22	Phase 3: Making Connections project. Cupertino High School students identify deliberate action plans
April 27	PDC briefs Cupertino High School administrators on results of April 22 deliberation
April 30	5Cs meeting
May 4	Cupertino High School site council meeting to decide next steps in the Making Connections project
May 27	5Cs meeting
May 28	5Cs coordinating team meeting
June 25	5Cs meeting
July 27	5Cs coordinating team meeting

Table 1.1. Cupertino Project Timeline: A Selected List of Activities and Events. (con't)

August 13	PDC briefing with Sheriff's Community Programs Liaison, Steve Angus
August 14	Outside consultants meet with PDC for reflections on Cupertino project
September 3	PDC facilitates first Collaborative meeting (Cupertino Multicultural Interagency Collaborative)
September 9	5Cs public dialogue training—session #1
September 16	5Cs public dialogue training—session #2
September 22	PDC facilitates second Collaborative meeting (Cupertino Multicultural Interagency Collaborative)
September 23	5Cs public dialogue training—session #3
September 30	5Cs public dialogue training—session #4
October 7	5Cs public dialogue training—session #5
October 15	Cultural Diversity Forum (100 participants)
November 4	5Cs meeting
November 6-7	Training workshop for Cupertino residents
November 17	5Cs Coordinating team meeting
November 23	Phase 4: Making Connections project. Cupertino High School students discuss implementation of action plans
December 1	Training workshop for Monta Vista High School students in group decision making
December 2	5Cs meeting
December 7	5Cs recognize *The Cupertino Courier* for responsible journalism based on their three-part series on race and immigration
December 17	Monta Vista High School students facilitate discussions with Kennedy Junior High School students on group decision making
February 17, 1999	The League of California Cities recognize Cupertino City Manager Don Brown with the 1999 Advancement of Diversity award

NOTES

1. The PDC is a nonprofit organization composed of communication researchers, teachers, and practitioners. Members of the group hold advanced degrees in communication, work as professors in departments of communication at universities and colleges, and do communication consulting, mediation, and organizational training. In addition to Kim Pearce and myself, the other members of the PDC who worked on the Cupertino Project are (in alphabetical order) Ralph Banks, Kevin Barge, Claire Calcagno, Victoria Chen, Michael Leitao, Stephen Littlejohn, W. Barnett Pearce, and Rita So.

2. The city of Cupertino (population 52,000) is located in the southern region of the San Francisco bay area, in the heart of Silicon Valley, approximately 10 miles east of San Jose. The area where Cupertino now sits was once a prime agriculture and farming region. Today, over 60% of adult Cupertino residents are employed in executive, administrative, or technical professions. High technology firms lead the way, constituting the single largest source of employment. Secondary and post-secondary education institutions, which include two school districts and De Anza College, account for the second largest source of employment (Cupertino Community Guide, 1998).

3. One of the reasons why the PDC entered Cupertino by way of the city manager, and not the city council, was because of the structure of the local government. Cupertino, like the majority of other cities in California, adopts a council-manager system of government (Burns, Peltason, & Cronin, 1987). In this system, the city manager serves in a nonelected position to supervise the administration of the government and advise the council on policies and programs. So although the council is the only entity with formal policymaking power, city managers nevertheless play a central role in running city government. Part of this is by design. In the council-manager system, for example, city managers are almost always full-time public professionals, whereas council members, at least in small- to medium-size cities like Cupertino, work primarily on a part-time basis and in a public-service capacity. And with the rise of term limits in recent years, city managers have become even more important in determining how city governments operate. It is also worth noting that Cupertino has enjoyed a stable local government and excellent management since officially becoming a city in 1955. Don Brown is only the third city manager in the city's history. Both of his predecessors served 17 years each. This is highly unusual given that the national average for city managers is less than five years (Berman, 1994). Both of these factors, the structure of Cupertino's local government and its history as a well-managed city, benefited the PDC and the development of the community-dialogue process. It would have been extremely difficult for us to gain the

broad access we did in a strong mayor system of government, with established coalitions and histories of partisan conflict. Instead, we were able to enter the community by way of a city manager who not only had the requisite influence and authority, but was also recognized by the community as a competent and fair public professional. We were also fortunate to work with city council members who either supported our efforts, or at least did not oppose them (which is itself a kind of support).

4. Statistical data clearly show that Cupertino's demography has changed significantly in the past two decades. According to the U.S. Census Bureau and the Association of Bay Area Governments, the Asian-American population in Cupertino surged from 6% in 1980, to 22% in 1990, to over 30% in 1999, an increase of over 20% in less than 20 years. Meanwhile, population among whites declined from 87% in 1980, to 70% in 1990, to 60% of the total population in 1999. Enrollment figures from the Cupertino Union School District reveal even greater racial and ethnic changes in the community. In the 1984-85 school year, for example, Asian Americans made up only 17% of total student enrollments. That figure almost doubled to 33% in 1993-94. Projections indicate a further increase in Asian enrollment to 45% by 2001. By comparison, whites made up 76% of the student population in 1984-85. That figure dropped to 61% in 1993-94, with projections indicating a further decline to 53% in 2001.

5. The timeline identifies only the *major events* of the Cupertino Project. A full and complete list would include hundreds of other smaller activities and meetings that either supported or grew out of the major events. Among those not cited are: (a) planning meetings with city officials, law enforcement personnel, school administrators, and university, college, and high school students; (b) follow-up meetings (conducted after every significant activity); (c) project team meetings with members of the 5Cs; and (d) meetings within the PDC team to plan activities and design events. Each of these smaller activities were, in turn, supported by hundreds of phone calls and e-mails, some of which dealt with substantive issues, others to simply schedule meetings. Also, as noted earlier in the chapter, there were numerous activities and meetings that took place "off line," without a PDC team member present. For obvious reasons, these too are not recorded in the Timeline. The point is that a great deal of preparation and follow-up was involved in each of major activities and events listed in Table 1.1.

2

FACILITATING
PARTICIPATORY DEMOCRACY

This chapter addresses the conceptual grounding of participatory democracy, identifies the distinctive features of public dialogue, and highlights a communication-based methodology for facilitating public dialogue and participatory democracy.

THE PROMISE OF PARTICIPATORY DEMOCRACY

In his well-known book on the subject, Benjamin Barber (1984) describes strong democracy "as a form of government in which all of the people govern themselves in at least some public matters at least some of the time" (p. xiv). The roots of this relatively simple idea are as old as democracy itself. The notion that citizens can and should govern themselves is a small thread that weaves its way through all democratic forms of government, dating back 2,500 years to ancient Greece and continuing through to the rise of modern democracy in the 18th and 19th centuries. Strong democracy, or participatory democracy, has never been a major social or political force, however, and its impact has actually diminished throughout most of the 20th century. So the question that concerns us here is, how can we draw from the traditions of strong democracy, take what is best and useful, discard that which no longer applies, and adapt what is left to meet the challenges of our complex and ever-changing social and political worlds?

There are many groups and organizations across the country and the world who are seeking innovative and creative ways to reinvigorate democratic participation. There are important differences among these groups, and well there should be, yet there are some common principles as well. First, citizens must seek out nontraditional forms of political participation that involve them directly in deciding how their communities are run. Second, disagreement and difference are dealt with in a nonadversarial manner, and conflict is resolved through pragmatic consensus and other methods that avoid win-lose outcomes. Third, all segments of society—government, citizens, and the private sector—must work together to solve the social problems that confront them. No single entity or institution can work alone to bring about the kind of political transformation that is necessary to revive participatory democracy.

Strong democracy is not antithetical to representative democracy, or what Barber (1984) calls "thin" democracy, but there are some clear distinctions. The way in which representative democracy is currently practiced in the United States, for example, places most of the responsibility for advancing the public good in the hands of elected leaders, public professionals, and the news media. This is where the political agenda is set, issues are framed, and policies for solving social problems are developed and decided. The best the public can do to engage the political process in a representative system of government is to *express their views and opinions* to the powers that be. So people go to the polls to vote for their preferred candidates, they respond to public opinion surveys that measure their attitudes on political issues, they contribute to their favorite political party or candidate, and they write letters or send e-mail messages to their elected representatives. This sort of political participation is limited and narrowly circumscribed. It not only establishes an asymmetrical relationship between the public and their elected leaders, it provides few opportunities for citizens to talk and reason together about what the public good is and how it can best be achieved.[1]

In participatory democracy citizens are actively engaged in public decision-making processes. This means that they are involved in shaping the issues that confront them, deciding among various policy options and developing concrete projects that allow them to achieve common goals. Participative politics does not displace the need for elected leaders; rather it brings government into a different kind of relationship with the public, and citizens into a different kind of relationship with each other. First, government officials and elected leaders assume more of an interdependent and collaborative relationship with citizens. Although we believe that this type of relationship should inform all government-citizen interactions, Mathews (1994) points out that it is indispensable when values and moral issues are at stake, when trade-offs have to be made, and when long-range planning is needed. Second, citizens must engage the political process in ways that extend beyond isolated acts of individual self-expression. Democratic participation depends on the reciprocal exchange of actions among an engaged citizenry, and the recognition among those involved that these mutual exchanges have social and political consequences.

PARTICIPATORY DEMOCRACY AND CIVIC RESPONSIBILITY

People become citizens in representative forms of democracy by virtue of their legal status, which among other things guarantees them a host of individual rights and protections. There is virtually nothing that people must do to exercise their citizenship once this legal status is established. People are encouraged to vote and express their opinions on the issues, of course, but failure to do so does not jeopardize one's citizenship status. Citizens in a representative system are also encouraged, although not required, to monitor the political process by keeping tabs on elected officials, especially those who directly represent them. As Barber (1984) points out, this notion of citizen as "watchdog" creates a climate of "passive distrust." Disengaged from public decision-making processes, citizens exert their democratic authority by checking in on elected officials and holding *them* accountable for *their* actions.

   In a strong democracy, citizenship is achieved through civic participation, or more specifically by joining with others in public decision-making processes. The emphasis is on cooperation and common action, and the voluntary commitment to pursue issues of common concern (Barber, 1984; Dryzeck, 1990). Citizenship, then, must be practiced to be realized. It is not something that can be bestowed on someone or attained by virtue of one's legal status, origin of birth, or national identity. The responsibilities of an active citizenry extend well beyond simply holding elected officials accountable, and then voting them in or out of office depending on the decisions they make. Citizenship at the participatory level is achieved when the people themselves, working together, make decisions about the issues that confront them. This suggests that in order to participate as citizens, people must not only be informed, they must also have abilities that allow them to engage in decision-making processes that unite them around a common set of activities.

Box 2.1. Differentiating Between Two Types of Democracy

Representative Democracy is characterized by:
- Voting and competitive elections among predetermined choices
- A procedural system of checks and balances designed to control private interests
- Solutions developed by government officials and technical experts
- The use of persuasion, debate, and advocacy to win consent
- Limited citizen involvement

Participatory Democracy is characterized by:
- Cooperative activities to determine what the choices are
- An inclusive system of opportunities for pursuing the public's interests and the common good
- Solutions developed by citizens in collaboration with government and technical experts
- The use of dialogue, deliberation, and discussion to achieve an action-oriented consensus
- Active citizen involvement

PLACES FOR PARTICIPATORY DEMOCRACY

Most established social and political institutions in the United States are not designed to support participatory forms of democracy. In the absence of real-world exemplars, what might these institutions look like? What are their essential features? According to Dryzek (1990), social institutions modeled on participatory forms of democracy should provide places for on-going communicative interaction:

> Individuals should participate as citizens, not as representatives of the state or any other corporate and hierarchical body. No concerned individuals should be excluded, and if necessary, some educative mechanism should promote the competent participation of persons with a material interest in the issues at hand who might otherwise be left out. The focus of deliberations should include but not be limited to, the individual or collective needs and interests of the indi-

viduals involved. Thus the institution is oriented to the generation
and coordination of actions situated within a particular problem
context. (p. 43)

Dryzek's (1990) approach to democratic participation draws
heavily on the notion of an "ideal speech situation." According to
Habermas (1970), an ideal speech situation is said to exist when competent, self-reflective citizens act together to make collective judgments
concerning the public good. The situation is free of strategic behavior,
deception, self-interest, and the coercive exercise of power (Habermas,
1984). Inspired by 18th-century salons and coffee houses, the public
sphere envisioned by Habermas (1984) is an ideal or hypothetical standard. The challenge for groups and organizations committed to reinvigorating democratic participation is to create the conditions that call forth
characteristics of the ideal speech situation in situated contexts, where
real people are engaged in common decision-making activities that have
physical, material, and social outcomes.

Fortunately, in creating the conditions for participatory democracy we do not have to invent entirely new social and political organizations from scratch. We can begin by locating the resources of democratic
participation in our local communities, in the places people occupy as
they go about their daily lives (Barber, 1998).[2] These include neighborhoods, schools, faith-based institutions, and the hundreds of thousands
of voluntary groups, associations, and organizations that exist in the
United States. Activities such as attending a community forum or town
hall meeting; joining a neighborhood crime watch program; going to a
parent-teacher meeting at the local school; participating in a city-wide
garage sale; volunteering to raise funds for a library, school, or charity;
or joining a citizens action group are all marked by free association
among the participants and a commitment to a common set of activities.

Local institutions and voluntary groups provide a fertile training ground for participatory democracy because they serve as mediating
structures between established government institutions and an active
and engaged citizenry. We know that government subverts strong
democracy when it does not actively seek citizen input in public decision-making processes. By tapping into the resources of existing community groups, government, especially local government, can begin to
create new opportunities for civic engagement. What is needed is
greater flexibility and more collaborative forms of leadership on the part
of public officials. It also means that citizens will need to be more persis-
tent and creative in seeking out new avenues for political participation.
The challenge is to utilize existing groups and networks to help shape
the public agenda in ways that extend beyond voting and other traditional forms of democratic representation.

There is no quick fix and there are no easy answers. Most government institutions and public professionals are in the business of solving problems and making decisions for the public. They are not equipped to foster direct and authentic forms of public participation. At the same time, not all community groups or concerned citizens are equally committed to democratic participation and the principles of an ideal speech situation. The challenge of participatory democracy, then, is to work across different levels of the community, with different groups and individuals, utilizing different types of civic activities, in order to forge new links between government and citizen volunteers.

Box 2.2. What the Politicians and Pundits Think About Participatory Democracy

Appearing on CNN's political talk show, "Crossfire," on June 17, 1998, New York Congressman Bill Paxon did something that few national politicians ever do. He suggested that the American public, not the Congress, take responsibility for developing a major piece of legislation, in this case, reforming the tax code. "I know this is going to be difficult to understand," Paxon said, "because debates in Washington always work this way: the public listens while we [politicians] talk. We're going to reverse it. . . . We want the American people to be at the heart of the dialogue on what should take place. . . . And I'm going to make a prediction. There's talk of a flat rate income tax or a national sales tax. The American people may design a system that nobody in Washington has thought of before, and that would be historic." Sound strange? A bit unusual? The other panelists on the show certainly thought so. Another New York Congressman, Charlie Rangel, responded to Paxon's suggestion with disbelief: "Do you really believe that? . . . Are you trying to have me believe that people understand the flat tax and understand the sales tax?" One of the shows moderators, Bill Press, simply dismissed the idea altogether, calling it a "political gimmick." Unfortunately, he might have been right. Shortly after appearing on the show, Paxon resigned from Congress and, as far as I know, never pursued his plan to involve the public in reforming the tax code. He now works as a partisan political consultant, helping fellow Republican candidates get elected to office.

PARTICIPATORY DEMOCRACY AND PUBLIC COMMUNICATION

The social and political practices that make participatory democracy possible are created and maintained through processes of human communication. This crucial point, implied throughout the discussion thus far, needs elaboration. Mathews (1994) provides a useful starting point:

> Democratic politics doesn't begin in voting to create governments; it begins in the choices about what kind of community or country people want. The most basic form of politics is conversation about these choices and about what is really in the public's interest. Serious public discourse is the seedbed, the wellspring, of democratic politics because the public is the only legitimate body that can define the public's interest. The quality of democracy depends on the quality of this kind of talk. Changing the quality of the public dialogue begins to change politics. (p. 40)

Participatory democracy, then, depends on the quality of communication in which choices are identified and decisions are made. And this quality requires that we treat public communication as more than just a decision-making tool—a means to an end. Public communication is the process through which decisions are legitimated and participation is made democratic.

There are many different varieties, forms, and patterns of public communication. It is our belief that participatory democracy works best when there is a complex array of communication patterns available, each intersecting with the others to create a robust and vibrant public sphere. Patterns of public communication, however, are not static or universal. Rather, they emerge over time within a given historical and social context. If it is indeed true that the future of participatory democracy depends on the development of new patterns of public communication, then the cultural and political traditions that inform public communication practices within a particular community will need to be part of that new pattern. But these traditions cannot be the only source. Communities built on democratic participation must draw from *all the communication resources* that currently exist in a particular community at any given time. They cannot be imposed a priori by a tradition, philosophy, or political theory (Strike, 1994). The development of a strong democratic community, then, is transformative in the sense that it discursively creates new avenues for collective judgment and action that transcend the boundaries of conventional communication channels.

It would seem that a common or "public" pattern of communication is central to reinvigorating the public sphere in ways that respond to the challenges of participatory democracy. The development of a shared pattern of communication is built up through the variety of local languages that reflect the many cultural frameworks and moral orders that exist within a community at any given time (Pearce & Littlejohn, 1997; Strike, 1994).[3] In this way, the pattern is temporary. It is always socially, historically, and materially situated, and thus exists only so long as democratic participation and interest can sustain it. The public sphere where all this is carried out predisposes an active citizenry who operate outside of the control of any external power that might jeopardize the legitimacy of their own collective form of self-governance. It is inclusive. All those who are effected by the decision are invited to participate.

Those of us in the PDC believe that we can revitalize the public sphere in ways that fulfill the promise of participatory democracy through a form of communication called public dialogue. Moreover, it is our contention that this form of communication has tremendous value for attaining social cohesion through processes that are most egalitarian and democratically productive.

THE POSSIBILITY OF PUBLIC DIALOGUE

Dialogue is typically thought of as a highly specialized form of interpersonal communication, one that involves a personal or "private" relationship among the participants. The expectation here is that people in dialogue converse about matters that are unique to their own circumstances, experiences, and histories. They are more interested in achieving mutual understanding than they are in making a good impression, gaining a tactical advantage, or advocating a particular course of action. According to philosopher Martin Buber (1958), there is a genuine openness and authenticity in dialogue that is simply not present in ordinary, everyday conversation.

The question here is whether it is possible to bring principles of dialogue into the public sphere and adapt them to public decision-making processes. What social conditions make public dialogue possible? What kinds of communication skills and abilities are needed to practice this "new" form of public communication? In recent years, a number of groups and organizations like the PDC (e.g., National Issues Forum, Study Circles Resource Center, Civic Practices Network, Center for Living Democracy, Search for Common Ground, the Public Conversations Project) have turned to dialogue and principles of interpersonal communication as a way to improve the quality of public communication.

PUBLIC DIALOGUE AND PARTICIPATORY DEMOCRACY

One of the ways that dialogue fulfills the promise of participatory democracy is by offering an alternative to the more conventional top-down method of decision making. In the public education model (Yankelovich, 1991), for example, political leaders, technical experts, public professionals, and others "at the top" initiate the process by first making decisions among themselves. Once a policy or course of action has been formulated, the leadership then sets out to persuade the public to go along with what they have already decided.[4] All large-scale representative democracies rely on some variation of the public education model to win public support.

Public dialogue operates out of an entirely different set of assumptions. As indicated in Figure 1.1, the public is engaged in the decision-making process at the very beginning of the process. They discuss what issues will be put on the table, how they will be framed, and the sorts of outcomes they hope to achieve. City government and elected officials help shape the process as well, certainly before any actual decision is reached. Yet, unlike the public education model, leadership is expected to engage with the public, not make decisions for them. In public dialogue the emphasis is on patterns of communication that occur "up-stream" in the process of policy formation, such as exploration, deliberation, discussion, and collaboration. Conversely, there is a concerted effort to de-emphasize persuasion, advocacy, information control, "spin," compromise, and other familiar forms of public communication. In a community-dialogue process, citizens and government officials collaborate together to both make decisions and plan for how decisions are to be made.

Box 2.3.

In public dialogue, the freedom to speak is joined by the responsibility to listen and the right to be heard.

CHARACTERISTICS OF PUBLIC DIALOGUE

The particular approach to public dialogue developed by the PDC, which is both similar and distinct from other groups (Pearce & Pearce, 2000), has several defining features. In what follows, I describe what we believe are the primary characteristics of public dialogue and give examples of how these features manifested themselves in the Cupertino Project.

FOREGROUNDING COMMUNICATION

To foreground communication means that we look at the actions people perform with each other while engaged in conversation. It draws our attention away from individual behaviors and internal traits to the "joint actions" (Shotter, 1993) that take place "between" people (Pearce & Cronen, 1980). Throughout the Cupertino Project the PDC attempted to bring the pattern or form of "interaction" (Pearce, 1989) to the forefront of each activity and event. We encouraged people to be mindful (or aware) that community issues and social problems are shaped through various patterns of communication, and that different patterns enable some types of responses while precluding others. One of the ways we accomplished this was to simply ask project participants to reflect on "how" issues in the community were being discussed, or in the case of the Cupertino Project, not discussed. In foregrounding communication, we also included an explicit value component. We wanted community members to recognize that some forms of communication are better than others for building community, managing conflict, and creating mutual understanding on sensitive and controversial topics.

Box 2.4

Public Dialogue Involves:
• An emphasis on listening as much as speaking.
• The free and honest expression of views and opinions.
• The ability to openly consider other peoples' views and opinions, no matter how different they might be from one's own.
• A focus on mutual understanding and coordination, not winning and losing.

The Practice of Public Dialogue Involves:
• Staying in the tension between standing one's own ground (or holding one's own position) and being open to the other.
• Using descriptions and nonverbal behaviors that express trust and respect.
• Showing the other that he or she has been understood.

But why dialogue? What are the advantages of this form of communication for public decision making? For many, dialogue is a welcome and useful antidote to the confrontational, adversarial, and war-like atmosphere that pervades public communication today (Chasin et al., 1996; Freeman, Littlejohn, & Pearce, 1992; Mathews, 1994; Pearce & Littlejohn, 1997; Spano & Calcagno, 1996; Tannen, 1998). By emphasizing the embodied, oral, face-to-face, and conversational nature of dialogue, these writers hold out the possibility that people, acting together as citizens in the public sphere, can achieve mutual understanding, empathy, immediacy, and other interpersonal qualities of communication. There is an expectation here that the quality of public communication will be enhanced when people treat each other with honesty and respect, and when they are able to share the experiences that lie behind their opinions and positions on the issues.

WORKING COLLABORATIVELY

Most people know that the primary meaning of the word "collaborate" is to work together. What some people might not know is the secondary meaning of the word: to "cooperate with the enemy." Webster's Dictionary, for example, defines a collaborationist as "a person who cooperates with an enemy invader of his [sic] country." This definition is a bit strong for our tastes, and certainly too narrow for our purposes, but it does draw attention to the notion that collaboration means cooperating with people who are in some way different from oneself. In public dialogue, attempts are made to establish communication links between and among stakeholder groups, individual citizens, and government officials. Special care must be taken to involve those who assume different positions in the community and/or have conflicting ideas on the issues. Because the PDC treats communities as complex systems of interconnected networks and conversations, it is critical that we go beyond simply identifying groups and individuals by carefully attending to the relationships and communication links between them.

In the Cupertino Project, concerted efforts were made to bring different groups and individuals into contact and conversation with one another. The linkages established between elected leaders and community residents is perhaps the most visible example of this. Other examples of collaboration include the intergenerational interviews involving high school students and adult residents; the two public school projects in which students facilitated small group discussions with parents, teachers, and administrators; and the 5Cs project teams in which citizens worked with city commissions, city staff personnel, and other community organizations to implement action plans.

FOSTERING DELIBERATION (WITHIN A DIALOGIC CONTEXT)

Many treatments of public communication, whether in mass media (Page, 1996) or face-to-face situations (Briand, 1999; Gastil, 1993; Guttman & Thompson, 1996; Mathews, 1994), locate deliberation at or near the center of political talk. Deliberation itself is a communication process in which participants weigh the advantages and disadvantages of a given issue or policy and make choices about the kinds of actions that should be taken. In the Cupertino Project we began with public dialogue as the overarching framework, and from there we built in opportunities for deliberation (see Figure 2.1). The decision-making power embedded in a community-dialogue process comes about primarily from the "choice work" that is involved in deliberation.

Rendering decisions through deliberation is not a uniform process. It can and often does involve elements of argumentation, debate, and persuasion.[5] A slightly different view of deliberation emerges, however, when it is framed within a dialogic context. As Cissna and Anderson (1994) point out, dialogue is characterized by emergent unanticipated consequences, so that what ultimately transpires cannot be predicted in advance. To deliberate within this "zone of uncertainty" is to recognize that the contours of a given issue are malleable and that new and unforeseen choices can emerge through discussion. The focus on dialogue, then, distinguishes deliberation from related processes like argumentation, debate, and persuasion, in which participants work toward fixed outcomes.

Deliberative processes were used extensively throughout the Cupertino Project as a way of helping participants narrow choices that would eventually move them toward particular decisions and outcomes. At the first Town Hall Meeting, for example, participants were organized into small groups and asked to deliberate among various action plans. The purpose was to select the one plan that would benefit the

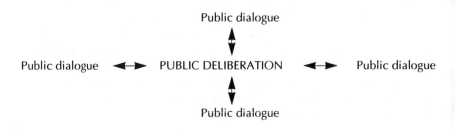

Figure 2.1. A model of dialogic deliberation

community the most. The results of these deliberations were carried forward into subsequent phases of the project and used in other small-group contexts. Eventually community members selected a core set of action plans and organized project teams to implement them.

ATTENDING TO DIFFERENCE, DISAGREEMENT, AND CONFLICT

We assume at the outset that to engage in public communication today is to encounter difference, disagreement, and conflict. Now, perhaps more so than ever, those who participate in democratic processes come to the table with different backgrounds, ideologies, experiences, histories, and ways of communicating. It is the inevitable consequence of living in an increasingly diverse and sophisticated society and world culture. Public dialogue responds to this challenge by creating spaces for people to explore their differences at the same time that they seek out their commonalties. "Conflict is just as important in dialogical encounters," writes Bernstein (1992), "because understanding does not entail agreement. On the contrary, it is the way to clarify our disagreements" (pp. 337-338). In public dialogue people cannot simply agree to disagree. They must try instead to find ways *to agree on how they are going to disagree*. We believe that if people are willing and able to stay in the dialogue, they will come to a deeper understanding of their differences and similarities and will ultimately be in a better position to make decisions that move them forward.

Throughout the Cupertino Project we encouraged people to talk about their differences and to identify their disagreements. In fact, one of the ways we judged the success of a particular event or activity was in terms of how many different perspectives it elicited and whether people felt comfortable voicing disagreement. The critical factor for us, however, was not simply that people were able to disagree, but rather *how they did it*. The ultimate indicator of success was whether the differences and disagreements expressed by the participants enriched the discussion by creating new possibilities, perspectives, and actions. We attempted to facilitate this type of transformative conflict (Pearce & Littlejohn, 1997) in several ways, such as establishing ground rules, negotiating a shared set of expectations and skills, and carefully planning and moderating the communication structure and process for each event and activity.

ACHIEVING PRODUCT <-> PROCESS

The symbol "<->" is intended to denote a reflexive relationship between product and process. Put differently, it assumes a reciprocal influence between the two so that the product (or outcome) of public dialogue affects the process and vice versa. The way that this reflexive relationship played itself out during the course of the Cupertino Project turned out to be one of the many delightful surprises we encountered. Here is how it worked. The commitment of the PDC to the process of public dialogue led many in the community to criticize our efforts in the early phases of the project as "all talk, no action." Without a tangible product to point to, some people felt that their efforts would not produce meaningful change. As the project unfolded, however, and community members began selecting and implementing action plans, what emerged was a series of products that provided opportunities to further engage the process. Thus, the reflexive relationship between product and process.

One concrete example clearly illustrates this point. From the very beginning of the project participants consistently identified neighborhood social events as a way to bridge cultural differences between whites, Asians, and other cultural groups in the city. This idea was eventually selected as an action plan and taken up by one of the 5Cs project teams who developed a neighborhood block party program, complete with a packet of directions, forms, and information for how to organize such an event. The packet and the actual neighborhood block parties that were held in the city are all "real" outcomes, products of public dialogue and deliberation. At the same time, these block parties provided opportunities for community residents to meet, talk, and get to know one another on a more personal basis. So in the process of engaging in public dialogue, participants created a *product* that had the effect of enhancing and extending the dialogue *process* in new and creative ways.

Box 2.5. Excuses to Talk

If you think about it, a lot of the action plans that have come out of the project are really just excuses for people to get together and talk.
—Don Allen, Cupertino resident and 5Cs member

PROMOTING TEACHING AND LEARNING

In order to create and sustain a public dialogue project, on-going capacity-building activities must be built into the process. One of the reasons for this is that public dialogue is a rare form of communication. There are few models and exemplars for people to follow. Moreover, citizenship education, at least as it is practiced in most public school systems throughout the United States, emphasizes a knowledge base that either

perpetuates a representative form of democracy or an advocacy model
of citizen participation (Parker, 1996).[6] In the former, students typically
learn about the mechanics of government (e.g., executive, legislative,
and judicial branches), the importance of voting, and the historical contexts that gave rise to various constitutional rights and protections. In
the latter, students learn the importance of developing political opinions
and how to argue, debate, and persuade others to go along with their
views. In neither case are students expected to acquire the knowledge,
skills, and abilities that would enable them to participate competently in
a community dialogue process.

> Box 2.6. The Confidence to Speak
>
> I have been very impressed with the training workshops con-
> ducted by the PDC. I think its a wonderful way for regular cit-
> izens to feel welcome in the public dialogue process.
> Everyone begins having certain reservations about speaking
> out, but with enough training one begins to feel a part of the
> process and therefore less intimidated to participate . . . And
> with more trained people, the more likely it is that we can be
> responsive to the needs of the community.
> —Zahra Pavlovic, Cupertino resident and 5Cs member

    Throughout the Cupertino Project, we worked against the grain
of conventional citizenship education models by training adult residents
and public school students in dialogue and communication facilitation
skills. In Phase II, for example, we trained high school students to conduct intergenerational interviews, and in the third phase we executed
the first formal public dialogue training for adult members of the community. In Phase IV alone we conducted over 16 separate training programs and workshops with at least nine different community groups
and public school organizations. Most of these trainings focused exclusively on communication facilitation microskills. As we learned more
about designing public dialogue events, and how these fit within a larger strategic-process design (see Figure 1.1), we began incorporating these
skills into our training programs. The capacities of the PDC thus developed in coordination with community residents and within the context
of the unfolding community dialogue process. This leads us to believe
that public dialogue involves mutual learning among all those who participate in the process.

SEEKING TRANSFORMATION AND CHANGE

Public dialogue seeks to transform public decision-making structures and processes within a given community. When political officials and technical experts develop solutions to social problems, no matter how effective or ineffective, they perpetuate the dominant top-down model of public communication. Public dialogue, on the other hand, seeks a fundamental shift in the way that decision making is normally practiced.[7] First, it engages community members in a process that requires them to coordinate differences and negotiate disagreements among themselves and with government officials. Public decision making is thus seen as a collaborative activity. Second, the process is ongoing from the point of initial exploration to final decision and then back again. Public dialogue is both a means and an end, both a product and a process. Third, public dialogue is sustained by the collective interests of the community and by the abilities of those who participate in it. Community members must have capacities to practice public dialogue if this form of communication is to become an institutionalized practice. Finally, all this helps to create a *learning community* where people collectively reflect on how issues and problems are defined, how decisions are made, and how solutions are ultimately implemented.

One clear example of the transformative nature of public dialogue was the Cultural Diversity Forum, held in October 1998 (see Table 1.1). The purpose of this event, which was designed and facilitated by members of the 5Cs, was to foster critical reflection on public communication processes in the city. The specific agenda called for participants to take both a retrospective view on how groups and individuals communicated about diversity issues in the past, and a proactive view about how public communication about such issues might be improved in the future. One of the more tangible results of the forum was a series of proposals, subtitled "A Blueprint for Public Communication," that outlined how the community can better position itself to respond to controversial public issues. We believe that the Diversity Forum stands as an example of how a community-dialogue process can create the conditions for transforming public communication processes (see Chapter 6 for a detailed description of the forum).

WAYS OF WORKING: A METHODOLOGY FOR PUBLIC DIALOGUE

The methodology developed by the PDC depends on the skillful application of various communication techniques in order to call forth the characteristics of public dialogue described earlier. A note of caution is in order here. When those of us in the PDC use terms like "techniques," "methods," and "skills" to describe our methodology we are immediately confronted with a semantic difficulty. On the one hand, these terms imply a mechanistic or instrumental type of action (Barrett, 1978), and yet we also know that public dialogue cannot be enacted by following a standard formula or rigid set of procedures. "We can be prepared for dialogue," write Cissna and Anderson (1994). "We can have certain abilities and attitudes that will predispose us in its direction (or away from it), but dialogue cannot be willed. No standard method . . . can ensure dialogue" (p. 22).

The practice of public dialogue is more art than science. It involves a particular kind of sensibility, a "knack" or social competence that some have referred to as "practical wisdom" (Bernstein, 1983; also see Stewart's contribution in Chapter 9). To facilitate a community-dialogue process, practitioners and researchers need to have a repertoire of basic methods, techniques, and skills, yet also have abilities to improvise, extend, and elaborate on them in creative ways. This is one reason why the PDC avoids "off the shelf" methods and other techniques that assume "one size fits all." Our ways of working are always customized to fit the unique circumstances of each community and each public dialogue event. This does not mean, as some have suggested (Hickson, 1996, 1998), that we have to create new techniques from scratch with every situation we encounter. What it requires instead is an open and fluid methodology that develops organically and is refined through on-going practice, trial and error, and reflexive assessment (Spano, 1996, 1998).

THE ROLE OF THE FACILITATOR/TRAINER

Public dialogue is not likely to happen on its own without some type of intervention. In the Cupertino Project, the PDC, operating as a neutral third party, initiated the community-dialogue process by engaging in actions designed to disrupt "normal" patterns of public discourse. We believe that the methods, techniques, and skills used by facilitators to bring about public dialogue need to be distinct enough so that they create the conditions for alternative forms of communication, yet they cannot be so distinct that they preclude community members from learning them and ultimately using them. Public dialogue itself must be democratic. If only those with specialized knowledge and expertise can practice it, it will fail as a vehicle for promoting participatory democracy.

The facilitator/trainer in a community-dialogue project assumes a unique position of being both inside and outside of the process. In the Cupertino Project, for example, the PDC team was clearly "in" the process to the extent that our actions influenced what happened. At the same time, we were also "outside" the process in that we were not members of the community and thus not directly influenced by the decisions that were made. We were also inside and outside of the process in another way. When the project began we saw ourselves as the "skilled performers," as the group responsible for enacting dialogue techniques and methods. As the project unfolded, we sought to help others in the community become skilled performers as well so that they could also facilitate events and design activities. The PDC thus enacted the techniques of public dialogue in our role as outside facilitators, and also joined in the process with community members in order to teach them how to engage in and facilitate the community-dialogue process.

Many of the techniques used in the Cupertino Project were adapted from other programs, groups, and organizations. Our approach was to tailor these techniques to fit the unique demands of the Cupertino community and to combine methods to produce new communication practices. In what follows, I provide an outline of the PDC methodology by describing some of our basic skills and advanced practices. This should not be taken as a complete account or "the final word." Our methodology cannot be codified into a set of formal statements or propositions without adequate attention as to how the techniques and skills are performed in situated contexts and at all three levels of the community-dialogue process: strategic process design, event design, and facilitation skills. What follows, then, is simply a taste or sample of our methodology and ways of working.

BASIC COMMUNICATION SKILLS

NEUTRALITY AND A NOT-KNOWING POSITION

A basic technique common to most facilitators is the notion of *neutrality*. Throughout the Cupertino Project we carefully attended to communication processes, and just as carefully assumed a neutral stance in regard to the content of what was said. Neutrality implies an attitude of openness and curiosity. The goal is to suspend prior expectations and assumptions in order to remain as fully open to unanticipated outcomes as possible. In order to accomplish this, we have found it useful to take on a *not-knowing position*. Instead of interjecting our views and experiences on what others said ("That idea sounds familiar"), we tried instead to approach each situation with the expectation that it offered some unique perspective or some new nugget of information ("What an interesting idea, can you tell us more about it?").

DIALOGIC LISTENING

To adopt an attitude of openness and curiosity is to engage in what Stewart and Logan (1998) call "dialogic listening." The goal here is not to analyze or evaluate what is said, but to actively attend to the messages of others in order to cultivate a shared understanding of meaning. In the Cupertino Project we tried to achieve this by suspending assumptions and expectations, "being present" by letting others know we were fully engaged in what they were saying, and attending not only to what people said but how they said it. We taught dialogic listening in all of our training programs, often telling participants that in public dialogue listening is as important as speaking.

ELICITING EXPERIENCES AND STORIES

The use of open-ended questions and follow-up probes are techniques that encourage participants to speak from personal experience. We have found that public communication can be enhanced when participants move beyond their positions on the issues by sharing stories about the circumstances that brought them to their particular point of view. These experiences can be found in the rich "human" detail that lies behind statements of opinion. One simple technique we used in the Cupertino Project to encourage storytelling was to connect an initial open-ended question ("What does the term 'cultural richness' mean to you?") with a follow-up probe designed to elicit a personal experience ("What in your background might have led you to this view?").

ADVANCED COMMUNICATION PRACTICES

Facilitators need to achieve some level of mastery of the basic facilitation skills described above in order to enact the advanced communication practices described below.

APPRECIATIVE INQUIRY

To work appreciatively is to act in ways that call forth what is positive and what is productive within an organization, group, or community (Cooperrider, Barrett, & Srivastva, 1995; Hammond & Royal, 1998). It involves helping participants to clarify and uncover what has worked in the past, and how they can draw on these resources to chart a future

course of action. Appreciative inquiry is often contrasted with traditional problem-solving approaches typically used in organizational and
community-development programs (see Table 2.1). By focusing on
"what works best," appreciative inquiry moves discussion away from
the kind of deficit language that we normally hear when people identify
problems and talk about "what is wrong" with their community.

As will be discussed in Chapter 4, one of the complaints lodged
against the PDC during the early stages of the Cupertino Project was
that our use of appreciative inquiry submerged conflict and prohibited
people from talking about controversial issues. We disagree with this
interpretation and offer a different assessment of the technique. For the
PDC, the primary value of appreciative inquiry is that it creates a positive frame or context from which to address difficult concerns and
issues. As facilitators, it is critical that we listen for the serious problems
and deeply held differences that divide community members. But as our
PDC colleague Stephen Littlejohn (personal communication) reminds
us, we must also "listen for the wisdom in the whining." By this, he
means that every negative story, every disagreement, has an underlying
positive shadow, a vision for what the community can and should be.
Instead of getting bogged down in the problem and its potential causes,
facilitators can inquire into the underlying vision and bring it to the forefront of the dialogue. The goal of appreciative inquiry, then, is not to circumvent difficult issues, but rather to reframe them in a constructive
manner.

The CVA Model

Our application of appreciative inquiry, and our insistence that we listen
for the wisdom in the whining, led to the development of what we call
the CVA Model (concerns, visions, action plans).

The model is relatively simple and straightforward. It says that
the *concerns* people have about public issues, like cultural diversity, are
related to the *visions* people have about the future of their community.

Table 2.1. Comparing Problem-Solving and Appreciative Inquiry.

- Problem-solving begins with a problem—what is wrong with the community—and then feeds these results back into the system in order to
  identify causes and arrive at a solution.
- Appreciative inquiry begins by identifying positive resources—what
  works best in the community—and then feeds these results forward as
  a frame for creating some future course of action.

Action plans are the concrete steps people can take to realize their visions and turn them into reality. In light of appreciative inquiry, it is important to recognize that the model situates concerns or problems within a context that also includes positive visions of the future and potential sources of action.

As the arrows in Figure 2.2 indicate, the model is reflexive and transactional, not linear or causal. This means that we can start at any point and move to any other point—there is no prescribed pattern that must be followed. For example, we can begin with a specific action plan and work to uncover the underlying concern the plan addresses or the future possibility the plan envisions. Each point in the model both shapes and is shaped by the configuration of the other points. Moreover, the model is dynamic, consisting of multiple causes and effects. A single concern might lead to several action plans, or a single action plan might address several different concerns.

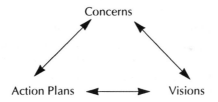

Figure 2.2. The CVA model

Box 2.7. Look for What's Right in the Community

I was surprised and impressed that the position taken in the project was to look for what was right about the city of Cupertino. Over the years I have been involved in numerous projects identifying problems in the community. Outside groups would discuss the issue in a negative format to determine who was at fault. This project clearly focused on what was right in the community, what we could do to make it better, and how we as a community could interact to make things work. I found this to be refreshing and much easier to sell to the Sheriff's Department personnel. This was unique. This was different, and absolutely a challenge.

—Bob Wilson, Captain, Santa Clara County Sheriff's
     Department

The CVA Model was used throughout the Cupertino Project. During the Training and Team Building Program in Phase III, for example, we used the model to structure some of the small-group discussions. In one group, participants expressed *concern* that the city was becoming fragmented into separate ethnic enclaves, each with their own values, customs, and traditions. Aided by the facilitator, additional discussion revealed a *vision* that Cupertino ought to be a harmonious and unified community where residents are able to achieve common ground, perhaps not in all areas but at least in some. The group then suggested that the local newspaper might run a series of articles on the experiences of recent Asian immigrants to the city. The purpose of this *action plan* was to show that many of the values that motivated immigrants to move to the city and the United States are similar to those of established residents. The group then deliberated among a number of action plans in order to make decision about which ones to pursue.

SYSTEMIC QUESTIONING

Like appreciative inquiry, systemic questioning is not a problem-solving technique. The purpose is to elicit responses that demonstrate connections and reveal the relationships that operate within a community, group, or organization. This is achieved by targeting perceptions of "difference" and by inviting comparisons among various patterns of communication (Penn, 1982; Selvini et al., 1980). In the focus-group interviews in Phase I, for example, participants were asked to make a number of comparisons between those issues that were being discussed in public and those that were not. The PDC facilitators asked participants to consider who was involved in the discussions, who was excluded, and how discussion might be improved in the future. This line of systemic questioning was clearly focused on specific issues, yet it also drew attention to the differences that existed between various patterns or forms of communication. Instead of solving the "problem," the goal was to focus attention on the ways in which communication does and does not make discussion of particular issues possible.

The abilities needed to engage in systemic questioning are not easily identified, yet like other public dialogue techniques they can be learned through training and reflective practice. First, good systemic questioners are flexible. As facilitators cannot know in advance where the discussion is going, they must be able to generate questions that respond to the contingencies embedded in a situation at any particular moment. Second, good systemic questioners recognize that their questions impact the direction of the discussion and the outcomes that are achieved. Facilitators ask questions that they think will have a positive influence on the participants, the community, and the public-dialogue process. Finally, good systemic questioners do more than draw links between patterns of communication. They also provide opportunities to develop alternative patterns that will enable participants to move forward in productive ways. For example, facilitators might invite participants to consider how a particular community issue can be discussed differently in the future in order to bring about results that are more equitable, satisfying, and the like.

REFLECTING

Like appreciative inquiry and systemic questioning, reflecting is a technique used to help community members come to a deeper understanding of the problems and issues that confront them. Facilitators use this technique when they listen carefully to what others say, interpret what they hear, and then reflect their understanding of the situation back to participants. The purpose is not to arrive at the "correct" interpretation or solution, but to offer possible connections that allow community members to view their situation from a new or different perspective. Reflections are offerings; they are given in the spirit of helping. Examples of reflecting can be as simple as paraphrasing the comments of a group participant or summarizing the results of a group deliberation. A more complicated example from the Cupertino Project occurred when members of the PDC team analyzed data from the focus-group interviews using qualitative research methods, and then reported the results to the city manager and city council in order to determine the next steps in the process.

Reflecting can be a very sophisticated process when it involves reframing what is said and done (Andersen, 1992). In these cases, facilitators extend and elaborate on what they hear so that it is placed in a different frame or context for the participants. This is often done through creative techniques and counter-intuitive questions. One of the ways the PDC accomplishes this is through a facilitation technique that consists of three interrelated types of reflections. The first category *reveals the grammar of the participants*, suggesting new ways of understanding what the participants are saying ("I'm struck by how many different definitions of 'cultural diversity' the group was able to generate here today"). The second category *questions the grammar*, suggesting possible constraints or limitations on what is said ("It seems to me that some of the definitions of cultural diversity expressed here today are compatible, but others seem to contradict one another"). The third category *imagines possible futures*, suggesting directions for future actions ("I wonder what would have to happen for this group to achieve some common understanding about cultural diversity?").

The PDC methodology for facilitating a community-dialogue process includes a variety of basic skills and advanced practices. The application of these techniques depends on the abilities and sensibilities of the facilitator. They must be enacted "in the moment," in response to what is happening in the situation and in the larger community at any given point in time. The skills and practices are also teachable. As trainers, our role is to share our methodology, techniques, and skills with community members so that they have abilities to facilitate and thus perpetuate the community-dialogue process. Finally, the PDC methodology operates at all levels of the community-dialogue process: strategic process design, event design, and communication facilitation skills. This requires that facilitators carefully attend to the ways in which the communicative actions performed at any given moment fit within the context of the unfolding public dialogue event, and how each event fits within the context of the unfolding community-dialogue process.

SOCIAL CONSTRUCTIONISM: CONNECTING THEORY AND PRACTICE

The methodology and communication practices used by the PDC to facilitate public dialogue are grounded in a social constructionist theoretical perspective (Pearce, 1994; Shotter & Gergen, 1994). A key point about social constructionism is that it treats communication as a primary process, the process through which humans construct their social realities. This idea has a rich intellectual tradition, but it is not a commonly accepted view. In this section I present a broad sketch of what social constructionism is, what it is not, and what it has to offer those of us interested in public dialogue and communication practice. While an in-depth discussion of communication theory is beyond the scope of this chapter,[8] those of us in the PDC have found that people have a better appreciation and understanding of public dialogue and the PDC methodology when they are familiar with the theory that informs the practice.

FROM TRANSMISSION TO SOCIAL CONSTRUCTION

Traditionally, communication has been viewed as a process of transmitting information from one place to another; or similarly, a process of transmitting meaning from one mind to another (see Figure 2.3).

For most people, the transmission model provides a complete and accurate picture of what communication is and what communication does. This is not particularly surprising given that *Webster's*

Source ➤ Encoding ➤ Message ➤ Channel ➤ Decoding ➤ Receiver

Figure 2.3. Transmission model of communication

Dictionary defines communication as "the act of transmitting" or "the giving or exchanging of information." A critical examination of the model (see Figure 2.3), however, reveals a number of limitations with the transmission approach. First, the model relies on a linear view of communication. Information is transmitted from a source and travels through a channel to a receiver—its a one-way process. The goal is to be accurate and efficient so that the message intended is the message received. The model also sets up a mechanical view of communication. In fact, it can be applied to electronic mediated communication (television, e-mail, etc.) as easily as it can be used to describe face-to-face conversation. Finally, the model relies heavily on internal, psychological concepts to explain communication.[9] Encoding, for example, involves converting internal thoughts and attitudes into message form, and decoding involves interpreting the message in light of speaker's thoughts and attitudes.

Although social constructionists do not necessarily disagree with the transmission model—who could argue, after all, that communication is a vehicle for sending and receiving information?—they strongly believe that it distorts and limits our understandings of communication. The social constructionist position is that communication is much more than transmission; it is also the process through which humans *construct and (re)construct their social worlds.* It assumes that what people do together through social interaction will shape what it is that they produce together. Communication is thus a process of making and doing. As the model in Figure 2.4 indicates, our social worlds are expressed in conversations and these conversations, in turn, construct—or reconstruct as the case may be—our social worlds.

One significant aspect of social constructionism is that it focuses attention on the verbal and nonverbal actions that people perform together in conversation. Instead of viewing communication as a psychological product of internal thoughts and attitudes, as the transmission model does, the emphasis is on what people say and what people do while engaged in *interaction.* Each individual action or utterance performed by a person in conversation is both a response to the acts that

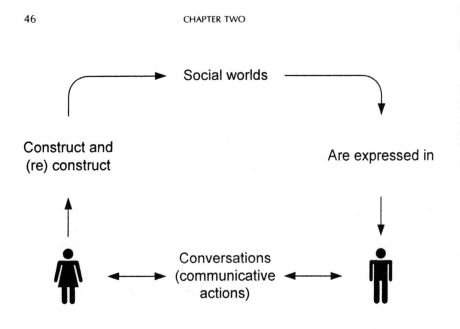

Figure 2.4. Social constructionist model (Adapted from Pearce, 1989)

preceded it and a condition for the acts that will follow it. When the people engaged in conversation begin to string together multiple actions, a pattern of interaction emerges that follows a kind of logic or grammar that guides the communicators in determining what to do and how to act (Pearce & Littlejohn, 1997; Spano & Calcagno, 1996). People act into patterns of interaction that have been created for them, and sometimes by them, and yet they can also change the pattern of communication depending on the specific actions they take together.

Adopting a social constructionist orientation allows us to see how our social worlds are fluid, ever-changing, and always open to negotiation and change. The kind of social world that people express and (re)construct at this moment depends on the actions they took a moment ago, the many other actions performed many moments before that, and the pattern of communication they are acting into and out of at any given time. The actions people take at this moment will also shape future actions, and thus will shape the future of what it is that they create together. And there is nothing set in stone to suggest that it has to be made one way or another. In fact, there is always an element of unpredictability because neither one of the participants, acting alone, can control the process. Because each act both shapes and is shaped by other acts, a change in any one will lead to different responses, which in turn will shape the formation of a different outcome. Although people cannot control the process, they are not at the mercy of it either. As participants, they can act on the knowledge that what they do in communication will inevitably affect the process in some way, shape, or form.

FROM THEORETICAL REPRESENTATION TO SOCIAL INTERVENTION

One of the implications of social constructionism is that it calls into question the nature of theory itself. Traditionally, social theory has been treated as a kind of representation of some phenomenon. From this account, the value or validity of a theory rests on its ability to provide an accurate picture of the reality it seeks to represent. Social constructionism, on the other hand, claims that theories do more than represent the world. Theory, or more specifically the "act of theory-building," helps to construct the social worlds it seeks to describe. "A theory is simply a language resource that permits particular forms of action and suppresses others," write McNamee and Gergen (1999). "Perhaps the central issue, then, is what kinds of social worlds do different theories make possible" (p. 5).

By drawing on Cronen's (1995b) notion of practical theory, the PDC has extended the social constructionist perspective into the realm of intervention and practical action. If theories make social worlds possible, as McNamee and Gergen (1999) suggest, then the next step is to consider how theorists can join with participants in order to improve the quality of human life. Cronen (1995b) describes it this way:

> Practical theories are assessed by their consequences. They are developed in order to make human life better. They provide ways of joining in social action so as to promote (a) socially useful description, explanation, critique, and change in situated human action; and (b) the emergence of new abilities for all parties involved. . . . A practical theory coevolves with both the abilities of its practitioners and the consequences of its use, thus forming a tradition of practice. (pp. 231-232)

Practical theory, then, is a type of communication practice, and practical theorists are, by definition, communication practitioners (Spano, 1998).

The focus on applied social constructionism and practical theory, or what is sometimes referred to as "praxis" (see Stewart's contribution in Chapter 9), is one of the most distinctive aspects of the PDC and our work on the Cupertino Project. We are not content to simply describe or criticize patterns of public communication, although we see tremendous value in these activities for the way we work. We have chosen instead to go the road of intervention, to join with citizens, government officials, and stakeholder groups to improve the quality of public

decision making in communities. As a result, we find ourselves travers-
ing the worlds of theory and practice, believing that both can be
enriched by the other.

SOCIAL CONSTRUCTIONISM AND PUBLIC DIALOGUE

The PDC obviously believes that there are benefits for public communication if people begin to think in accordance with the social constructionist model and act in light of a practical theory orientation. First, this
approach makes us aware that every pattern or form of communication
allows us to do some things but not others. For example, a pattern of
communication that consists of yelling, shouting, and name-calling is
very effective in producing polarized conflict, but not for promoting
mutual understanding, trust, and respect. Public dialogue does a much
better job of that.

Second, the patterns of communication normally used to discuss
sensitive and controversial issues are not particularly effective in promoting mutual understanding and public decision making. Sometimes
these patterns create the aforementioned polarization, other times they
lead to avoidance. All too often, discussing these differences is thought
to be so fraught with danger and so personally threatening that people
simply avoid talking about them at all. This can certainly be the case
when the issues involved deal with cultural, ethnic, and racial differences as they did in the Cupertino Project. To participate in a common
decision-making process, regardless of the topic, people must be willing
and able to engage each other, not avoid each other.

Third, the good news is that people can participate in patterns of
communication that will allow them to develop healthy, positive, and
affirming public relationships with each other. Those of us in the PDC
believe that these relationships can be created when community members actively engage each other around issues of common concern in
dialogic patterns of communication. Although these patterns are not
particularly common or readily available, they can be facilitated by
adopting a practical theory orientation and by incorporating some of the
qualities of interpersonal communication into the public sphere. It is difficult and challenging work, to be sure, but our experiences working in
Cupertino have convinced us that it is indeed possible.

Finally, adopting a social constructionist approach to public
communication can empower citizens to become more engaged in the
civic life of their communities. It enables people to see social problems
and issues as made in patterns of interaction, as fluid and evolving, not
fixed or static. If it is true that what a community will be is determined
by the communicative acts that "the public" performs or does not per-

form, should citizens not feel empowered to take the kinds of actions that will create the best of all possible futures? Yes, it is difficult on an individual level to know what actions to take because people must always respond to the unfolding actions of others—communication is a co-constructed activity. What all of us can do, however, is acquire competencies and skills that enable us to manage and guide the communication process toward the attainment of what we, "the public," decide is in our "own" best interest.

COMMUNITY-BASED ACTION RESEARCH

In the Cupertino Project, we exercised our various theoretical commitments within the context of a community-based action research approach (Stringer, 1996). Most of us in the PDC have extensive training in traditional quantitative and qualitative social science research methods, particularly as they are used by academics in the study of human communication. None of these traditional research methods, however, are sufficiently responsive to practical theory or the type of interventionist work that is necessary to facilitate a community-dialogue process. Our interest in conducting scholarly inquiry, and our commitment to practical theory and the practice of public dialogue, led us to adopt an action research framework for our work in Cupertino.

Action research is used in a variety of fields for different purposes, and thus does not represent a single or unified approach to inquiry. Stinger's (1996) focus on *community-based* action research, for example, carves out some distinctions with other approaches used in nonpublic situations. In spite of the many differences, there are number of common themes that link most action research approaches together (Reason, 1994). In what follows, I identify three core principles of action research and describe how they apply to the practice of public dialogue and our work with the Cupertino Project.

ACTION RESEARCH AS DEMOCRATIC PARTICIPATION

Action research requires that *all participants*—community residents, public officials, and outside facilitators—be involved in developing the research agenda. In traditional social research methods, by contrast, the individual researcher or research team assumes this responsibility. This is certainly the case with experiments, surveys, and other more scientific methods, yet even ethnography and other highly qualitative approaches place the researcher in the position of making observations about other people. As Heron (1996) notes, however, action research is research *with* and *for* other people, not *about* them. This means that the knowledge produced through an action research project is co-constructed through the joint interactions of the research facilitators and community participants. It also explains why participants in an action research project are often referred to as co-researchers, and not subjects.

One of the reasons why action researchers engage with community members is because the research process is being conducted, first and foremost, for their benefit. The goal of action research, writes Stringer (1996), "is to assist people in extending their understanding of their situation and thus resolve problems that confront them" (p. 9). It is a "practical tool for solving problems" that "make a difference" in the lives of those who participate in the research (p. 11). Because the purpose is to introduce positive social change, an action research project must involve those who are most familiar with the situation and those who will ultimately be responsible for defining social problems and developing action-oriented solutions to them. What is needed, in short, is a democratic approach to social research. Action research certainly satisfies this criteria, as Greenwood and Levin (1998) note:

> AR [action research] embodies democratic ideals in its core practices. This democracy is involved in both the research process and the outcomes of the research. In AR, the research process must be democratic in the sense that it is open, participatory, and fair to participants. In addition, the outcomes of AR should support the participants' interests so that the knowledge produced increases their ability to control their own situation. (p. 113)

From the beginning of the Cupertino Project those of us in the PDC worked with community members to help them identify concerns and develop actions for resolving problems. This does not mean, however, that we always practiced "good" action research. As described in Part II of this book, when the project started we assumed most of the responsibility for designing events, interpreting results, and deciding next steps. As the project unfolded, however, we were able to involve more and more community members in the process. Consistent with action research principles and practices, the more we shared responsibility for the public dialogue process the more successful it became.

THE ACTION RESEARCHER AS SKILLED FACILITATOR

Most accounts of action research emphasize the skills needed by researchers to join with community members in order to develop and enact the research agenda. We believe that the methodology described earlier in the chapter to facilitate public dialogue is ideally suited to an action research approach. In fact, we were delighted to find that some of the facilitation skills and techniques that we adapted from other practitioner groups are also referenced in the action research literature (Greenwood & Levin, 1998; Stringer, 1996). In any case, both action research and public dialogue require that researchers be more than technical experts who are called in to solve problems for others. Instead of "expert," action researchers are better described as facilitators, teachers, consultants, resource people, or conversational partners. Action researchers must always adapt whatever specialized knowledge they might possess to the needs of community members in ways that will make sense to them.

A Method for Action Research

The PDC developed an informal research procedure that combined action research principles with traditional social science research methods. The procedure consisted of four interrelated steps. Step one involved listening to community members, asking systemic and appreciative questions, and collecting information based on what participants said and did. We utilized a number of standard data-gathering techniques to collect information, such as interviews, participant observation, field notes (or data texts), and survey questionnaires. We also videotaped and transcribed all large public events. The second step involved analyzing and interpreting the data. As indicated in Chapter 3, we relied primarily on qualitative discourse analysis and other techniques that allowed us to interpret underlying themes, categories, and meanings.

In step three we summarized our findings and reflected them back to community members. Although these reflections were given in a variety of different ways, they were always conducted in interaction with participants. The purpose was not to accurately represent what was said, but to draw out connections in the data in order to clarify points and facilitate a deeper understanding of the issues, problems, and concerns. In the final stage, we helped participants to consider what the next set of actions should be given their understanding of the situation. At every major event and activity, for example, previous phases of the project were summarized and participants were encouraged to participate in determining subsequent phases in the process. This action research procedure was enacted repeatedly throughout the Cupertino Project, yet never exactly in the same way twice.

ACTION RESEARCH AND PRACTICAL OUTCOMES

A cornerstone of action research is that it produces outcomes that benefit the participants and the community in some material way. The research procedure described earlier, for example, was designed to help participants develop institutionalized action plans that would ultimately transform public decision-making processes in the city. Even though much of the information we collected and analyzed was interesting in its own right, the data would have been incomplete had we not reflected it back to participants so they could use it to improve their community in some tangible way. Action research can, of course, also lead to more "academic" outcomes, such as a book, scholarly paper, research report, or conference presentation. These sorts of products are not the primary goal of an action research project, however. They are more like a bonus, a reward derived after the fact. Nevertheless, it is possible for action researchers to use their academic outcomes to benefit the community as well. I certainly hope that Cupertino residents and project participants read this book, for example, and find some value in it for continuing to improve their community.

Action research also produces another outcome that on the surface, at least, looks to be less altruistic, although it is certainly practical in its own way. Namely, it has tremendous potential to enhance the understandings and abilities of the research facilitators, and thus increases the sophistication of the communication practices used in an action research project. So while action researchers work to improve social conditions in a community, they are simultaneously learning to improve their own abilities and practices. Ideally, this should create a win-win situation: as action researchers help others they reflexively help themselves, which in turn puts them in better position to subsequently help others. And on it goes.

The abilities and practices that community-based action researchers bring to a project develop over time, thus forming a tradition of practice. Once started, these practices will continue to grow, evolve, and develop as they are put to use in new situations, in response to different social problems, and in collaboration with different project participants. But what happens when a tradition of practice does not readily exist at the outset, as in the case of public dialogue? There is no other option here except to roll up one's sleeves, join together with others, and go out and create one. This is essentially what the PDC did in the Cupertino Project. Fortunately, we did not have to embark on this journey completely by ourselves. We were aided by the experiences of other practitioner groups and organizations, and by the principles of applied social constructionism, practical theory, and action research. By sharing our experiences working in Cupertino, we hope to contribute to what we believe is an emerging tradition of practice around the concept of public dialogue.

In the following section of the book, I describe how the community dialogue process in Cupertino developed over four interrelated phases: (1) giving voice to community concerns, (2) eliciting visions and action plans, (3) working through city leaders, and (4) and sustaining the public dialogue process. A separate chapter is devoted to each of the phases. We begin in the next chapter with Phase I.

NOTES

1. Participatory democracy is often criticized on the grounds that the public cannot engage in effective decision making because they are too apathetic, selfish, ignorant, and/or lazy. As a result, participatory democracy is considered to be dangerous. It threatens the public's interest because average citizens are not willing or able to make informed, intelligent decisions. Yankelovich (1991) refers to this as the "Culture of Technical Control." It assumes that public decisions are best left to experts, political professionals, and other elites who, unlike the public, have specialized knowledge and skills that allow them, and them alone, to formulate effective policy. This view, of course, is antithetical to public dialogue and participatory democracy.

2. There are a number of advantages to implementing public dialogue and participatory democracy at the local, community level. First, it helps to offset the problem of scale. Opportunities for large-scale, face-to-face public participation are obviously restricted in heavily populated urban areas and in smaller rural communities that are spread across geographic regions. Working in relatively small communities like those the size of Cupertino (52,000 people) creates opportunities for participation that do not exist in larger cities or rural areas. Second, working at the local level also responds to the problem of technology. Mass-mediated forms of communications have clearly become the primary mode of public discourse. They are dominant precisely because they reach large segments of the population instantaneously while compensating for geographic distance. Decentralized forms of media, like the World Wide Web, might yet provide new and fruitful avenues to participatory democracy. Internet technologies notwithstanding, however, the vast majority of mediated channels of communication today (i.e., television and radio) are so beholden to commercial, economic, and private interests (and not the public's interest!) that it moves us far away from the principles of strong democracy and the ideal speech situation envisioned by Habermas (1984). In relatively

small cities like Cupertino it is possible to bypass mediated forms of communication in favor of face-to-face communication, or conversely, to use mediated channels of communication to complement face-to-face conversation. This does not mean that everyone can or will participate, of course. By working at the local community level, however, it is possible to involve enough people in face-to-face conversation to produce a "trickle-up" effect that will have some sort of lasting impact on the community as a whole.

3. The need to develop a common framework for public communication can also be taken as a response to pluralism, diversity, and the challenges these pose for participatory democracy. The question is, how is it possible to create the conditions for a common form of public communication in a society consisting of many different cultural groups, each with their own unique languages and forms of expression? People who live in societies that are more or less homogeneous may disagree about a given public issue, but they are likely to share implicit assumptions about how to discuss the issue; whether it is even worth talking about and, if so, who can talk about it, when, where, and to whom. Participatory democracy requires forms of public communication that lead to coordinated actions and mutual understanding among participants who do not always share common cultural experiences. As Strike (1994) suggests, the solution is to build a common communication framework from the different cultural groups, languages, and modes of expression that exist in a community at any given time. The challenge is to develop a process that maintains the integrity of each cultural group, yet at the same time also transcends each of the groups in the accomplishment of a common or public form of communication. We believe that public dialogue is well suited to meet this challenge.

4. Political leaders are often split between two or more policies or courses of action, which, in turn, requires them to debate and defend their positions. This leads to what might be called the *public debate model* of decision making. It works like this. There are differences among the leadership concerning which policies or courses of action to pursue. The leadership frames these choices, and then they engage in debate with each other in an attempt to persuade the public to go along with their preferred policy recommendation. So although public debate might appear as though the public is being given a choice, it is actually a false choice, or at least a severely limited one, in that the options have already been determined in advance. In this way, public debate is actually an extension of the public education model. Another dynamic that comes into play with public debate is that it is often marked by confrontation and polarization. When debate is conducted ethically and honestly it is indispensable tool for a fully functioning representative system of government. But public debate can also be degenerative,

polarizing, and dysfunctional. The heated rhetoric, personal insults, and general lack of civility that we see in "bad" debate might make for entertaining political theater, but it erodes our representative system of government, alienates people, and contributes to political cynicism and apathy.

5. To deliberate among choices that have been established in advance by government officials, technical experts, and others who act for the public is consistent with representative democracy and top-down decision-making models. It is thus contrary to public dialogue and democratic participation. For example, if city leaders were to ask the public to choose among three different types of cultural celebrations that they themselves had developed, they would be failing to acknowledge the full range of options that might exist, including the concerns of some community members who believe that these types of celebrations should not be conducted at all. When the public is asked to choose between a set of prepackaged options it is already too late in the process for them to shape the agenda. In public dialogue, the public is involved early, often, and deeply in framing the choices. This means the citizens select among an array of options *that they themselves have developed and defined through ongoing conversation and discussion.*

6. Many of the newer community members who participated in the Cupertino Project did not attend American public schools. Having immigrated to the United States from Hong Kong, Taiwan, and mainland China, these citizens came out of an educational system that offered few opportunities to learn about either representative or participatory forms of democracy.

7. The focus on transformation also explains why bargaining and other zero-sum techniques are not consistent with public dialogue and participatory democracy. Barber (1984) writes:

The basic difference between the politics of bargaining and exchange and the politics of transformation is that in the former, choice is a matter of selecting among options and giving the winner the legitimacy of consent, whereas in the latter, choice is superseded by judgment and leads men and women to modify and enlarge options as a consequence of seeing them in new, public ways. For this reason, decision without common talk always falls short of judgment and cannot be the basis of strong democratic politics. The test of legitimacy is whether an individual value has been changed in some significant way to accommodate larger—that is, more common or public—concerns. If a value emerges from the political process entirely unchanged by that process, then either it remains a private value masquerading as a public norm or it denotes a prior consensus that has been revealed by the political process. In neither case has participatory politics accomplished its task of legitimation. (p. 136)

8. A more complete discussion of our communication theory would reference at least three additional sources. The first is Wittgenstein's (1953) meaning as use philosophy of language, an approach that has become central in most accounts of social constructionism. The second is Bateson's (1972) ecological perspective and systemic orientation to co-evolutionary processes. The third, and the one that comes closest to the discussion of social constructionism offered here, is the Coordinated Management of Meaning (CMM) theory developed by Pearce and Cronen (1980; see also Cronen, 1995a; Pearce, 1989). CMM is one of several theoretical strands emanating from the social constructionist orientation and is a major influence in the work of the PDC.

9. There is a fairly large and still-influential group of communication theorists who continue to adhere to a psychological perspective. One of the principles of this approach is to look behind or through communication to the underlying mechanisms that cause individuals to behave as they do. Put differently, communicative behaviors and actions are considered to be a function of cognitive structures and mental processes (Green, 1984). From this perspective, the internal operations of the mind are primary, making communication a secondary process. Like the transmission model itself, we find this approach to be limited, misguided, and counterproductive to the development of practical communication theory and the practice of public dialogue (Spano, 1995).

II

THE CUPERTINO
COMMUNITY PROJECT

3

GIVING VOICE TO
COMMUNITY CONCERNS

This chapter focuses on the work completed in Phase I of the Cupertino Project. The chapter begins with an overview of the focus-group discussions, the primary activity of this phase. The chapter then describes some of the details involved in organizing and facilitating the focus groups, including how the PDC went about contacting participants, and the interview guide used to generate discussion about community issues. Results of the focus groups are covered next. Using qualitative analysis, summary themes are examined, and excerpts from participants are included to illustrate how the two primary topics, cultural richness and community safety issues, were discussed. The fundamental organizing theme of this chapter is how the PDC assisted Cupertino residents in identifying community concerns, issues, and problems.

THE FOCUS-GROUP PROCESS

Focus-group interviews were used in Phase I of the Cupertino Project to give residents the opportunity to identify and discuss issues facing the community. Although focus groups can be used to answer specific research questions established prior to the group interviews (Morgan, 1997), we adopted a more fluid and open-ended approach. In fact, we deliberately went into the interviews without knowing what particular topics would emerge or how they would be discussed. As Stewart and Shamdasani (1990) state, focus groups "are particularly useful for exploratory research where rather little is known about the phenomenon of interest" (p. 15). The open-ended nature of the focus groups also provided an opportunity for participants to share their concerns about the community in their own words and from their own perspectives. The overall objective of the focus group interviews at this stage of the Cupertino Project was to maximize citizen participation in the formation of public issues and to assist stakeholders in defining community problems.

THE CO-CONSTRUCTION OF SOCIAL REALITY

The decision to use focus-group interviews, as opposed to individual interviews, was predicated on the assumption that public issues and community concerns would emerge through group interaction and the co-construction of social reality. According to Stewart and Shamdasani (1990), "focus groups allow respondents to react to and build upon the responses of other group members. This synergistic effect of the group setting may result in the production of data or ideas that might not have been uncovered in individual interviews" (p. 16). Emphasizing the interactive qualities of focus-group interviews is consistent with the goals of community-based action research, which, as Stringer (1996) notes, "includes the careful management of research activities so that stakeholders can formulate jointly constructed definitions of the situation" (p. 40). According to this perspective, the concerns and issues that emerged during the interviews were socially constructed through the interaction that took place in the groups.

GROUP INTERACTION AND PUBLIC DIALOGUE

Facilitating group interaction also demonstrates how the focus-group process established the conditions for participatory democracy and public dialogue. Consistent with the principles of participatory democracy, group participants were asked to adopt a broad, public perspective when defining community problems. Consistent with the principles of public dialogue, participants were encouraged to relate these problems to their own personal experiences and those of others in the community. "Problems do not exist in isolation," writes Stringer (1996), "but are part of a complex network of events, activities, perceptions, beliefs, values, routines, and rules, a cultural system maintained through the ongoing life of the . . . community" (p. 60). In the focus-group interviews we invited participants to share their personal experiences and stories and to reflect on how their experiences were linked to larger community problems. We believe that these kinds of discussions, created and sustained through social interaction, are central to the practice of public dialogue and participatory democracy.

ESTABLISHING A DEMOCRATIC GROUP CONTEXT

Using focus groups as a vehicle for participatory democracy and public dialogue naturally requires that the groups themselves be democratic. Consistent with our design of the focus-group procedure, Gastil (1993) states that:

> A small group is democratic if it has equally distributed decision-making power, an inclusive membership committed to democracy, healthy relationships among its members, and a democratic method of deliberation. Group deliberation is democratic if group members have equal and adequate opportunities to speak, neither withhold information nor verbally manipulate one another, and are able and willing to listen. (p. 6)

The characteristics of democratic small groups identified by Gastil (1993) are best achieved through the situated performance of the group, and can be nurtured through facilitation and careful attention to small-group communication processes.

FEEDING RESULTS FORWARD

It is important to recognize that the focus-group interviews were not designed as an isolated activity or self-contained study. They were developed instead as part of an *on-going process* to involve Cupertino residents in public conversations about their community. The working plan at the time called for the PDC to summarize results of the focus-group interviews by developing descriptive accounts of the concerns, issues, and problems facing the community (Stringer, 1996). These accounts would then be fed forward into the next phase of the project and submitted to further discussion, interpretation, and negotiation by community members. In this way, we sought to use the results of the focus-group interviews as "conversation starters," as a way of initiating a long-term public dialogue process.

RECRUITING PARTICIPANTS

The PDC recruited 72 volunteer Cupertino residents to participate in 1 of 10 focus-group discussions. Participants were selected using a combination of purposive and convenience sampling, an approach that is consistent with the qualitative nature of focus-group research (Morgan, 1997; Stewart & Shamdasani, 1990). Our primary goal in recruiting participants was to ensure that a variety of different stakeholders be included in the discussions. We also included a variety of different types of groups. As Stewart and Shamdasani (1990) note, the quality of discussion is determined by the composition of the focus group and how a particular collection of people interact with one another. The reason for creating multiple groups of varying composition was to ensure a range of different contexts for group interaction.

Participants in the first five focus groups were selected from a list of Cupertino residents provided by the City and the official Santa Clara County Registrar of Voters. Because we did not know that cultural diversity was going to emerge as a major community issue, we made no special effort to control the ethnic composition of these groups—we simply wanted to ensure that a range of participants be included. As it turned out, three of the groups included both Asian and white participants; the other two groups consisted of white participants only. We labeled these two types of group "mixed" and "all white," respectively.

After the first four focus-group interviews were completed it became clear that cultural diversity was emerging as a serious community concern. Based on this finding, we felt it necessary to create two additional focus groups composed solely of non-white participants (labeled "diversity" groups). The purpose here was to create a safe context for non-white residents to speak openly and freely about their concerns— the two "all white" groups served the same function, albeit from a different side of the issue. Participants for these groups were selected from the sampling frame described earlier, as well as from informal, personal contacts. One of the diversity groups consisted of all Asian participants; the other included Asian and black members.

Three other focus groups were created to represent other stakeholder interests in the city. Two of these groups were composed of students from Monta Vista and Cupertino High Schools (labeled "student" groups). The final group was composed of patrol officers from the County Sheriff's department (labeled "law enforcement" group). Participants for the student and law enforcement groups were selected through personal contacts established with school administrators and the Captain of the Sheriff's department. It is also worth noting that these groups were "mixed" to the extent that they included participants from different cultural and ethnic backgrounds. Table 3.1 includes a breakdown of the different focus groups.

All of the focus groups included a combination of strangers and acquaintances, which is an important consideration when considering the quality of the group discussion. In those cases in which participants knew one another, there was an opportunity for the discussion to be more open as a prior relationship had already been established. However, there was value to including strangers as well. Morgan (1997), for example, states that the "rule of thumb favors strangers because, although acquaintances can converse more readily, this is often due to their ability to rely on the kind of taken-for-granted assumptions that is exactly what the researcher is trying to investigate" (p. 37). Given the exploratory nature of the focus-group interviews and the emphasis on public dialogue and participatory democracy, it was essential to include participants with a wide range of perspectives, backgrounds, and histories. Including strangers, as well as acquaintances, was one way to ensure this variability. Including both homogeneous and heterogeneous ethnic groups was another.

The PDC contacted focus-group participants by telephone. A script was developed in order to ensure some level of consistency in the information provided. Although there was some variability in the way the individuals presented the information, Figure 3.1 includes a script that those of us making phone calls agreed to use as a guideline.

A follow-up letter was sent to each person who agreed to participate, confirming his or her participation along with the date, time, and place of the focus-group meeting. We also included a copy of an article published in the *Cupertino Courier* (Mehta, 1996) with the follow-up letter. The article, "Can the public influence what the city should be?," was useful in our recruiting efforts because it helped establish the legitimacy of the focus-group process and the work of the PDC.

As difficult as it was to make "cold phone calls," we were pleasantly surprised with the responses we received. The phone calls netted a success rate of approximately 20%. That is, we were able to recruit one focus-group participant for every five phone calls we made.

Table 3.1. Focus Group Composition.

* Three ethnically mixed groups—21 participants
* Two all white focus groups—13 participants
* Two diversity focus groups—12 participants
* Two student groups—18 participants
* One law enforcement group—8 participants

Hello, my name is [PDC member]. I work with a group called the Public Dialogue Consortium. The purpose of our group is to improve the quality of public communication between community members and local city government. We are in the process of meeting with Cupertino residents to hear their views about the city—what they like about it, what their concerns are, and what their hopes are for the future. These meetings, we call them focus groups, are a grass roots effort to give the citizens of Cupertino a voice in their community and how it is run. On Saturday, March 2, we are holding two focus-group meetings, one in the morning and one in the afternoon. The meetings will consist of approximately eight people who, like you, are residents of Cupertino. The meetings are informal and designed explicitly to give you a chance to express your views. We are eager to hear what you have to say about the community and invite you to join us for one of the meetings. Are you interested in attending?

Figure 3.1. Telephone script

FACILITATING FOCUS-GROUP DISCUSSIONS: WORKING APPRECIATIVELY

Each of the focus-group discussions was co-facilitated by members of the PDC team. To assist the facilitators and participants, a third PDC team member recorded the discussion on a flip chart. At various points in the discussion the facilitators checked with the participants to be sure that their comments were being accurately recorded. A fourth member of the PDC team sat unobtrusively in a corner of the room and took detailed notes of the discussions. These notes served as the primary vehicle for collecting data as no audio- or video-recording was made.[1]

One of the challenges in facilitating the focus-group interviews was to marshal the highest hopes and aspirations of the group while also encouraging participants to talk about concerns and problems. This can be a difficult task because open-ended discussions that touch on social problems can quickly degenerate into a complaining sessions in which participants simply take turns identifying what is wrong. Worse yet, these discussions can unintentionally lead participants to create new problems or exacerbate existing ones. In addition to other facilitation techniques, the PDC worked to avoid these pitfalls by utilizing appreciative inquiry in the group interviews (Cooperrider, Barrett, & Srivastva, 1995). For example, we encouraged participants to talk about the possibilities for the future of their community based on the positive resources that currently existed in the city. This positive framing helped to establish a context for people to later voice their concerns in productive and useful ways.

As facilitators, we recognized the importance of creating an inclusive and nonthreatening communication environment. We thus made a conscious effort, both in our initial telephone calls and in the focus-group interviews, to carve out time to talk with people about general events and activities. For example, as participants arrived for the interviews we offered them refreshments and spent some time talking informally with them about the weather, current events, and other such topics that typically surface in non-task oriented conversations. We purposefully avoided any pretense of scientific objectivity and worked instead to develop empathic understandings that would allow us to connect with participants on an interpersonal level. Here in the focus-group interviews, and throughout the Cupertino Project, we sought to develop healthy and positive relationships with community members.

The facilitators opened the working session of each meeting by introducing the PDC team and by providing background information about the group. We also discussed our application of focus-group methodology by stressing the open-ended and exploratory nature of the interviews. We then suggested three ground rules (respect differences, one person speaks at a time, and all participants are ensured confidentiality), checked to ensure that these were acceptable, and asked participants if they would like to add any of their own. We concluded these introductory remarks by asking participants if they had any questions. They did. In every focus-group meeting, participants asked for additional information about the PDC and our purposes for conducting the interviews. As indicated earlier in Chapter 1, we tried to use these questions as an opportunity to model the kinds of communicative actions that we were trying to promote and facilitate among the participants.

THE INTERVIEW GUIDE

The interview guide, or protocol, consisted of a series of nine open-ended questions. Table 3.2 provides the list of focus-group questions and the order in which they were asked.

Although the content of the focus-group interviews was open, the kinds of questions we asked and the sequence in which they were asked were designed with particular outcomes in mind. First, we sought to create a safe and appreciative context at the very beginning of the focus-group interviews. In the opening question, for example, we asked participants to identify positive resources in the community. Participants were then encouraged in the next three questions to take a long-term view of the city by relating their past experiences in the community to what they hoped the community would be in the future. Second, we asked participants to talk about concerns and issues only

Table 3.2. Focus Group Interview Guide.

1. Please tell us your name, how long have you lived in Cupertino, and what you most like about Cupertino. (round robin question)
2. What changes have you seen living in Cupertino? (question open to the group)
3. What changes would you like to see in Cupertino?
4. What kind of community would you like Cupertino to be?
5. What are your chief concerns?
6. What issues divide the community that are currently being discussed?
   a. How and when are these issues being discussed?
   b. Who is included and excluded in these discussions?
   c. How could the discussion of these issues be improved?
7. What issues divide the community that are not being discussed?
   a. Who would agree and disagree with that?
   b. What would have to change for these issues to be discussed?
   c. What is preventing these issues from being discussed?
8. Given the concerns that you've identified, how can we move forward as a community to become the kind of community you want Cupertino to be?
9. Is there anything that has not been covered that you would like to address today?

after a positive and safe context had been created. As indicated in Table 3.2, difficult and potentially controversial topics in the focus-group interviews were not addressed until questions five, six, and seven in the interview guide. Third, focus-group participants were encouraged to consider *how* divisive issues in the community are discussed and *how* they can be discussed differently in the future. The follow-up probes under questions six and seven, for example, were designed specifically to address the communicative form of public issues. Among other things, these questions serve to illustrate one of the ways that we *foregrounded communication* in our work with Cupertino residents.

It is worth noting that rarely, if ever, did the PDC facilitators work sequentially through each of questions in the interview guide. Once the groups moved into the second question the discussion opened up considerably, which was not only expected but encouraged given the exploratory nature of the focus-group interviews. The primary goal of facilitators in asking questions was to enable participants to elaborate and reflect on issues and concerns in their own words and from their own perspectives.

MAKING SENSE OF FOCUS-GROUP DATA

As noted earlier, detailed notes were made of each focus-group discussion. These notes, along with the summary points from the flip charts, were used to generate a written account, or text, of the focus-group discussions. According to Lindlof (1995), "the creation of data-texts is the first arena in which analytic decisions are made. These texts . . . convert field experiences into running records that can be consulted, broken down, and reorganized" (p. 199). Once the focus group-data texts were compiled, we then engaged in a process of qualitative data analysis (Creswell, 1998) in order to reduce the data from the text into a small number of coherent themes or categories.

The data-analysis process involved three interrelated activities. First, we carefully examined all of the data-texts from the group discussions to get an overall sense of what the participants said. This involved a holistic reading of the texts in order "to identify major organizing ideas" (Creswell, 1998, p. 144). Next, we looked for recurring patterns within the data (Owen, 1984) and broke the text down according to what we perceived to be common themes or categories. Creswell (1998) describes this as "winnowing the data, reducing them down to a small, manageable set of themes" (p. 144). Once the categories were identified we then made an explicit move to a higher level of interpretation. Interpretation involves making sense of the data in light of the social context from which the text was derived. "At this point in their analyses," writes Creswell (1998), "researchers step back and form larger meanings of what is going on in the situations or sites" (p. 145).

Even though this description might suggest that the data-analysis process proceeds in a linear fashion, Figure 3.2 indicates that it actually follows more of a cyclical pattern (Lindlof, 1995). The implication here is that we were constantly moving back and forth among each of the various data-analysis activities. For example, as we were creating the data texts we were simultaneously interpreting the larger meanings associated with the discourse. As part of an on-going cycle, however, those interpretations were tentative and open to revision based on our examination of the full text and our attempts to locate specific themes and categories. This process of moving through the data-analysis cycle continued until we felt confident in our understandings of the data and secure in our interpretations.

IDENTIFYING COMMUNITY RESOURCES

When asked what they liked most about living in Cupertino, focus-group participants had very little difficulty describing positive features

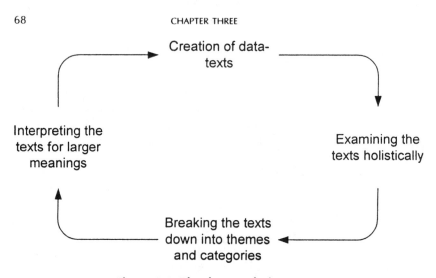

Figure 3.2. The data-analysis process

of their community. Based on our analyses, we classified participants' responses to this question into seven categories. We then broke these categories down into three primary categories and four secondary categories. Primary categories are those that were identified in all 10 focus groups. Secondary categories are those identified in less than 10 but more than two focus groups.

PRIMARY CATEGORIES

According to participants, the quality of the *public school system* is one of Cupertino's strongest assets. To support this point, five of the participants we talked with said they moved to Cupertino principally because of the public schools. "We came to Cupertino," one of these participants said, "so that our daughter could go to the kind of public school that would enable her to go to a good college." The fact that the public schools were singled out for special praise is not surprising given that the two school districts which serve Cupertino (the Cupertino Union and Fremont Union School Districts) consistently rank among the top school districts in California (Cupertino Community Guide, 1998).

Another primary category revolved around Cupertino being a *safe, low crime community*. As one participant said, "if my wife and I want to take a walk at night we can without worrying about getting mugged or hassled in some way." A high school student echoed this sentiment: "You can go out at night alone." Many of the participants said that community safety was Cupertino's most important asset. "The strongest thing I like about Cupertino is that I feel safe and comfortable here." Community safety in Cupertino was often discussed relative to other nearby cities, particularly San Jose. When making this comparison, Cupertino was always viewed as a more desirable place to live. According to one long-time resident, "it is more secure here than in other cities."

Active participation among city residents was the third primary category. This feature was discussed mainly in terms of the willingness of residents to get involved in civic affairs and community events. One participant said that she appreciated "the sense of involvement" she feels with the community and the way that residents exercise their "civic muscle." "I have a voice," she said, "and I can participate in what the city is doing." Participants also talked about participation in terms of the city creating opportunities for civic engagement. "If you live in Cupertino," one participant said, "you can affect change. I have always been able to do the things that I feel strongly about." Another participant expressed it this way: "Things get done here; people believe you can make a change."

The final primary category was labeled *small town atmosphere*. All of the participants who discussed this feature did so in one of two ways. First, participants talked about Cupertino as a "friendly community," with "friendly people" and a "small town feeling." "I like the people who live in my neighborhood," one participant said, "there's a real feeling of community there." Some participants talked about Cupertino's small town appeal in terms of the size of the city. With an incorporated area of just over 10 square miles, most of the businesses and residences in the city are centrally located. Participants talked about the "convenience" that comes from living in a city this size, and the "ease of access" it permits. As one participant said, "I like Cupertino because it's smaller and more manageable than other cities like San Jose."

SECONDARY CATEGORIES

One secondary category, *cultural and ethnic diversity*, was identified in four focus groups. Participants said they appreciated "the exposure to different cultures" and the way that the influx of recent Asian immigrants had "transformed the community." Another secondary category, identified in three focus groups, centered on Cupertino's *natural environment*. In discussing this feature, participants said that they appreciated the views of the local foothills, the open spaces and city parks, and the mild weather. The final category, called *intellectual capacity*, was identified in three focus groups. Typical of this view was the participant who said that she appreciated the "intellectual stimulation" in the city and that people are "open to new ideas." Table 3.3 provides a summary of the primary and secondary categories identified in this phase of the focus-group discussions.

Table 3.3. What Residents Like Most About Cupertino.

Primary Features:
- The quality of the public schools
- The lack of crime and feelings of safety in the city
- The active participation among city residents
- The small town atmosphere of the city

Secondary Features:
- The cultural and ethnic diversity of the residents
- The natural environment
- The intellectual capacity of the city and people

Based on these findings, it was apparent that the people we interviewed genuinely enjoyed living in Cupertino. Those of us on the PDC team were struck by both the number of positive features identified, as well as the enthusiasm participants demonstrated when talking about the city. We interpreted this as a strong demonstration of civic pride. Moreover, the features identified by participants suggest that there is a tradition of community cooperation and collaboration, or what Putnam (1995) calls "social capital." As the Cupertino Project unfolded, we sought to draw on existing networks of community organizations to help promote the practice of public dialogue.

CONCERNS WITH CULTURAL DIVERSITY

About midway through the focus-group interviews we asked the participants to talk about their concerns and what they perceived to be the major issues facing the city. This discussion was far ranging and covered an array of different topics, but the most compelling issue to surface concerned the influx of Asian immigrants into the city. There was a clear sense that this issue, discussed in all 10 focus groups, elicited more interest, passion, and energy from the participants than any other topic covered during the focus-group interviews. It was also clear from our analyses of the data-texts that diversity in Cupertino is a multifaceted issue. It evokes a range of positive and negative responses and is situated in a variety of different community contexts, including neighborhoods, business establishments, and the public schools. We detected three core themes in the way focus-group participants discussed their concerns with the issue.

DIVERSITY CREATES COMMUNITY PROBLEMS

Talking about diversity as a community problem was a dominant theme in the two all white focus groups and the three mixed groups. In fact, most of the participants who considered diversity to be a problem were white, long-time residents of Cupertino (20 years or more). In terms of numbers, approximately 20% of the focus-group participants expressed views consistent with this theme. This parallels results of an independent community survey, which found that 15% of the 400 Cupertino residents sampled agreed that the city's increased racial diversity made them more resentful ("Survey Shows," 1998).[2]

Participants expressed a number of problems associated with the influx of Asian immigrants moving to the city. Many of their concerns centered on the notion that diversity creates *separation, division, and fragmentation* in the city. There was considerable discussion about the lack of assimilation between whites and Asians, which created, in one participant's words, "visible communities within a community." Another participant put it this way: "There's some real concern among people who've lived here for a long time not wanting to lose the identity of Cupertino. There's resentment that it's becoming the Chinatown of Silicon Valley."

Fragmentation was, more often than not, attributed to a perceived unwillingness on the part of Asians to participate in community and civic events. "I have neighbors who are Asian," one participant said, "and they don't get involved or accept our invitations." Although a number of other examples of community fragmentation were discussed, the two identified most often included a private Chinese language school conducted on the weekends and a Chinese Little League Baseball program which was run separately from the Cupertino Little League Association. Participants voiced concern that such programs, designed specifically for children, excluded non-Chinese city residents and thus created divisions in the community.

Another way that diversity creates problems in the community is through the *language barriers* it erects between Asians and whites. A number of participants voiced concern that recent Asian immigrants to the city were not learning to speak English. "Speaking English is hard," said one participant, "and I'm concerned that they [Asians] are not taking the time to learn it." Another participant said that "it makes a lot of people feel resentful that they [Asians] don't care to use English." In addition to creating divisions in the community, the language issue is significant because of the attribution among white participants that Asians are intentionally not learning English in order to retain a separate identity in the community.

Box 3.1. "We are Dividing this Community"

It seems that it is no longer fashionable to assimilate, rather it appears that staying separate and having one's cultural differ- ence recognized is now what is important. . . . By continually focusing on cultural diversity we are dividing this community. Mr. Mcloskey [in a previous letter to the editor] suggests that we "recommit ourselves to the time-honored ideals of toler- ance and mutual respect." I wholeheartedly agree, but I sug- gest that this tolerance and respect is a "two-way street." The newcomers to Cupertino need to show some 'tolerance and respect' for those whose families were also immigrants but chose to assimilate and by doing so became part of the fabric that makes this country great.

—C. A. Lafrancoini, Letter to the Editor, *Cupertino Courier* (July 22, 1998)

Fragmentation was also seen in local business establishments that, as one participant said, "cater to Asians only." A number of partici- pants shared similar experiences about shopping at an Asian owned grocery store and feeling that they "didn't belong." A related issue that came up repeatedly in the focus-group interviews concerned monolin- gual, Chinese signs on local businesses. The signs were viewed as an overt attempt by Asian business owners to exclude non-Chinese cus- tomers, again fueling the perception that the city was becoming frag- mented into distinct and separate ethnic communities. Perhaps because of the visibility of the signs, this issue received more public attention than any of the other concerns identified. Several months after the focus- group discussions, the local newspaper, the *Cupertino Courier*, reported that city officials received a numerous letters and phone calls criticizing the monolingual signs (Collins, 1996a, 1996b). Although the city chose not to pursue a policy prohibiting non-English signs, due in part to First Amendment considerations, they did encourage business owners to include bilingual or multilingual signs, with English as one of the lan- guages.

Participants also expressed concern that the influx of Asian immigrants created *problems in the public schools*. An overriding concern among participants was that the increase in the Asian student popula- tion was creating uncomfortably high levels of competition and stress among non-Asian students. As one participant said, "students are being academically overwhelmed." Another participant from the law enforcement focus group talked about "kids being stressed out" and "suicide rates going up" as a result of the "super competitive environment" in the schools. Even among the students in the two high school focus groups, who for the most part spoke favorably about the city's diversity, there was recognition that diversity "has added to academic competition." (It is not entirely clear from the data texts if the students viewed this competition as positive or negative.)

Another concern related to the public schools was the perception that Asian immigrants were moving into Cupertino for the sole purpose of enrolling their children in the public schools. This was not framed as a problem in and of itself, but it did become problematic when coupled with the perception that the immigrants do not participate in civic events and choose to remain separated from the community at large. Several participants claimed that Asian parents living abroad were sending their children to live in Cupertino "just so they could attend the public schools." One participant said, "they [Asian parents] do this in order to take advantage of the public schools, but its not fair because they aren't paying taxes like we [Cupertino residents] are." Underlying these concerns was the perception that both Asian residents and Asian parents living abroad take advantage of Cupertino's highly touted school system without adequately compensating or giving back to the community.

> Box 3.2. "Think and Act Like Us"
>
> We all talk about "valuing diversity," but from comments, attitudes, and behaviors I've seen throughout the community, I'm convinced the majority of the dominant white population still expects the newcomers to ultimately "think and act like us." There is a lack of awareness of the differences between celebrating cultural heritage and respecting different values and communication behaviors. If we really want everyone coming here from other backgrounds to think and act like us, then we are narrow minded and ethnocentric, unrealistic, and losing a valuable opportunity.
> —Piper McNulty, 5Cs member

Economic concerns related to the Asian newcomers also threaded their way through the focus-group interviews. One interesting facet related to economics is the difference between new immigrants in Cupertino compared to immigrants in other parts in the country. According to Goode and Schneider (1994), "research on the economic incorporation of immigrants into the United States almost universally confirms that newcomers generally start near the bottom of the economic hierarchy" (p. 12). Although an ethnic underclass is generally considered to be an economic liability, the same cannot be said about the Asian newcomers to Cupertino, who tend to be affluent, educated professionals. One concern over economic disparity is that it creates resentment toward upper income Asians. As one Chinese participant said, "I think there's been resentment that the Asian population is able to buy real estate so easily compared to people who've lived here for a long time."

Box 3.3. The Attraction of High Tech Jobs and High
Performance Schools

Whereas immigrants in the past came to Cupertino to work in agriculture, the newcomers today are attracted to the city's high-tech, high-income jobs, and the Cupertino public schools. As Don Brown notes in the Foreword, the profile of the new Chinese residents is "high education/high income with a preeminent value on education for the children." Ku and Marino (1998) write in the *Cupertino Courier* that the city "has become a magnet for immigrants from all over Asia" because of "its location in the middle of Silicon Valley and its worldwide reputation for an excellent school system" (p. 13). Writing for the *San Jose Mercury News*, Stocking (1999) describes the Chinese newcomers in Cupertino as "highly educated, affluent, high-tech-workers" who "have been drawn by jobs in Silicon Valley and by the excellent reputation of the Cupertino Union School District" (p. 14A).

The economic power wielded by the newcomers, combined with rather dramatic changes in the city's ethnic population, led some established residents to the conclusion that the City is "being taken over" or "invaded" by Asian immigrants. A white woman who grew up in Cupertino typified this concern. "The prices of houses have gone up so high," she said, "that the only people that are able to afford to buy into them are the Asians. And it seems like a lot of the businesses in the area are now owned by either Vietnamese or Chinese." When asked to describe how she felt about these changes, the woman replied, "its kind of disheartening for me to see. I mean, I'm not prejudiced in any way . . . but the other cultures are, you know, they're grabbing everything up. They're buying the businesses and moving into the neighborhoods. Its kind of . . . I don't know . . . its just weird because it wasn't like this before. . . . I honestly feel like I'm becoming a minority in my own country here." These concerns, of course, are tied to demographic changes in the city's ethnic population, yet they are also the product of the economic status of the new Asian immigrants.

DIVERSITY CREATES CULTURAL MISUNDERSTANDINGS

This theme was dominant in the two diversity groups and was also evident, although to a lesser extent, in the three mixed groups. Although most of the Asian and black participants voiced concern over cultural misunderstandings, a number of white participants also expressed concerns that reflected this theme.

The theme revolves around the notion that cultural diversity in Cupertino creates misunderstandings between Asian and white members of the community. According to participants, these misunderstandings arise because *the two groups lack sufficient knowledge of each other*, which in turn leads them to *perceive each other in erroneous ways*. What is perhaps most striking about this concern in the context of the focus-group interviews was that it was talked about primarily in terms of whites misunderstanding the actions of Asians. Asian participants consistently called into question the claims made by white participants that the new immigrants are responsible for creating fragmentation and discord in the community. The concern is not that Asian newcomers are actually creating divisions in the community, the concern is that non-Asian members of the community misunderstand Asian newcomers.

One clear example of cultural misunderstanding centered on a local shopping center, which at the time of the focus-group interviews had been purchased by a group of Chinese business interests. Several group participants, all white, were concerned that the new owner was going to ask the current tenants to leave and then rent the businesses exclusively to Chinese retailers. This development was seen as yet another attempt by Asians to separate themselves from the rest of the community. Asian participants, however, told a different version of the story. They believed that the concerns about the shopping center were based on what one participant said was a "false perception." Another participant said, "we are concerned that this misconception [about the shopping center] will lead to discord in the community." Note that the concern here is with the "misconception," not with the situation that lies behind the misconception.

A number of other examples illustrate the concerns people have with cultural misunderstandings. In response to the criticism that Asian-owned businesses create fragmentation in the community, one participant said that there is an "economic advantage" to having these businesses because "they tend to be more successful and are less of a financial risk." In response to the criticism that Asian members of the community do not participate in civic and neighborhood events, an Asian woman said that "behind the scenes work is being done," but that it is "not being recognized." Another Asian woman said that when she does participate in community events she is often accused of "coming in and

wanting to take over." For her this created what communication theorists call a "double bind" (Watzlawick, Beavin, & Jackson, 1967). If she
chooses to get involved she is criticized, yet if she chooses not to get
involved she is criticized as well.

In another example, an Asian male strongly disagreed with the
claim that monolingual signs are purposeful attempts to exclude non-
Asian members of the community. "We don't want to stand out," he
said, "we want people to live here in harmony." In response to the concern that Asian parents were sending their children to Cupertino to
attend the public schools, one participant said, "Its more the other group
[Asians living abroad] that makes people resentful, not the Asians who
live here." Finally, in response to the concern that the academic focus of
Asian students in the public schools was creating undue stress and competition, a number of participants, both Asian and non-Asian, said that
the concern was rooted in different cultural attitudes about education.
One Asian male suggested that the "change is to accept this competitive
attitude and to view it as a positive thing."

It is important to note that the concerns over cultural misunderstandings were not always directed toward non-Asian members of the
community. There was also recognition, by both Asian and non-Asian
participants alike, that all members of the community were susceptible
to cultural misunderstandings, misperceptions, stereotypes, and the like.
Indeed, the notion that cultural misunderstandings were widespread
and pervasive throughout the community was itself a reason for concern. As a result, focus-group participants talked extensively about the
need for both established residents and newcomers to learn about each
other's cultures. "We can't just expect one group to adapt to the other,"
said one Asian participant. "The new immigrants also need to learn
about American customs." The focus, he said, should be on "mutual
understanding."

DIVERSITY CREATES AN UNCERTAIN FUTURE

The comments that fell into this category acknowledged the difficulties
that came with living with diversity in Cupertino, yet they also recognized the potential benefits of diversity. Typical of this kind of response
was a weighing back and forth of the positive and negative implications
of diversity. We labeled this category "diversity creates uncertainty"
because there was a recognition that Cupertino was in the process of
struggling with diversity and that the outcome had not yet been decided—it could go in any number of directions. Evidence for the uncertainty theme was found to be evenly distributed across each of the focus
groups, with comments attributed to both white and Asian participants.

> **Box 3.4. Local Issues are Connected to National Concerns**
>
> I think it would be very interesting for this group [the 5Cs] to listen to President Clinton's speech that he just presented in Michigan on celebrating unity in diversity in America. He spoke about the unfortunate human weakness, despite our progress, to fear people who are different, and to dehumanize them. He then spoke about the richness of being able to celebrate our diversity in religion, culture, ethnicity, etc. and yet be bonded together by our COMMON HUMANITY . . . very touching indeed, and highlights the very strength of American society.
>
> —Laina Raveendran Greene, Cupertino resident and 5Cs member (in an e-mail message sent to 50 members of 5Cs April 17, 1999)

One set of concerns centered on what some participants perceived as a *potential for backlash* by some white residents against Asian members of the community. Consistent with the uncertainty theme, there was some question whether the backlash would actually happen. The influx of Asian immigrants "has caused a lot of resentment among some people in the community," said one participant, "and it could lead to some real problems unless the city does something about it." Another participant warned that "the potential is there for a possible backlash . . . if people don't talk about their perceptions of the community." Still another participant described the issue as a "potential powder keg," evoking the image that it might blow up at some point in the future. These rather ominous warnings that diversity in Cupertino might backfire and detract from the community were usually tempered by the possibility that solutions to the problem could be found and implemented.

Another set of concerns evoked a more positive reading on diversity. While acknowledging that the city was still struggling to adapt to the influx of Asian newcomers, there was a sense that the change could ultimately *strengthen the community.* "This is almost an experiment in multiculturalism that is unparalleled," said one participant. "As far as I know it's working." A number of participants talked about the possibility that Cupertino could become a "model for other cities" that are experiencing rapid cultural and ethnic changes. These comments reflected a cautious optimism about diversity in Cupertino by emphasizing the potentially positive results while downplaying negative consequences. By contrast, the concerns over backlash described earlier are weighted in the opposite direction.

> Box 3.5. Better is Not Easy
>
> Our community is better for the richness we get from different peoples. But it's not always easy.
> —Barbara Rogers, Cupertino resident (*San Jose Mercury News*, April 15, 1999)

Another set of concerns related to the uncertainty theme focused on the challenges of diversity in terms of peoples' abilities and capacities. The participants who expressed this concern wanted diversity to work, yet they were unsure whether they possessed the *social skills* necessary to make it happen. One participant, for example, noted that he had encouraged Asians to attend city events in the past, but said "its hard because I don't know how to get them involved." Another participant said, "I want to get to know my [Asian] neighbors, but I don't know how to bridge the gap." Asian participants, who said that new immigrants to the city often lacked the cultural knowledge and communication abilities necessary to adapt to living in a new country, expressed similar views. We interpreted these comments to reflect a tacit acknowledgment among participants that new resources and skills would be needed in order for the community to effectively adapt to cultural and ethnic changes. (For a summary of the concerns expressed about cultural diversity see Table 3.4.)

Table 3.4. Concerns With Cultural Diversity.

Diversity creates community problems
- The city is fragmented into different cultural and ethnic groups
- Language barriers exclude cultural and ethnic groups from interacting
- Competition in the public schools leads to stress and anxiety
- Economic advantages of new immigrants create resentment and fear

Diversity creates misunderstandings
- Established residents and new immigrants lack sufficient knowledge of each other's culture
- Negative attitudes and stereotypes lead to misperceptions
- New immigrants are faced with incompatible demands and expectations

Diversity creates uncertainty
- New immigrants might experience a backlash by established residents
- Diversity has the potential to strengthen the community in the future
- Residents are not sure how to bridge cultural differences

THE COMMUNICATION FORM OF
CULTURAL DIVERSITY

How community members talk about public issues determines, in part, how the issues are defined and constructed. In this section we step back from the content of the focus-group discussions and examine the form of communication in which the concerns were expressed. Three interpretations follow from this analysis.

The first is that the focus-group discussions were framed exclusively in terms of a bifurcation between established white residents and new Asian, or more specifically, Chinese residents. It is clear from the data texts that concerns related to community problems, cultural misunderstandings, and uncertainty were all situated along a fault line separating whites from Chinese. This proclivity to talk in terms of two mutually exclusive ethnic groups was altered somewhat as the Cupertino Project unfolded and community members from other cultural groups joined the conversation. Nevertheless, the Chinese-white distinction continued to be the dominant categorical system for discussing diversity in Cupertino.

A second interpretation centers on the way in which diversity emerged as a discussion topic in the focus-group interviews. Specifically, group participants were reluctant to talk about the issue, at least initially. In no case was diversity the first issue to surface, even though it was talked about in every focus-group meeting and generated more interest than any other topic. Typically, one of the participants would mention a concern related to cultural diversity after other issues had already been identified. If no one else followed up on the comment, it was dropped and the group moved on to another topic. Inevitably, however, the issue would come up again later in the discussion. It was as if the participants were carefully assessing whether it was appropriate to mention the topic before directly acknowledging it.

We characterized this pattern in terms of three developmental stages. The first stage was *skepticism*. Here participants were initially suspicious of the PDC and the focus-group process. As a result, they asked several background questions. In most cases, group participants were strangers, so there was also a level of curiosity and skepticism about the other members as well. At this stage, participants were reluctant to talk openly and candidly about the issue. Once the discussion was underway and the group had covered several different topics, someone would eventually comment on the influx of Asian immigrants in the community. This was indicative of the second stage, *testing*. It was our sense that these innocuous statements were made in order to determine whether the topic was appropriate for group discussion. Apparently, the responses to these "testing" statements were favorable because in the final stage, *acceptance*, most of the participants readily joined in and expressed their views on the issue. The initial hesitation among group participants implied to us that they were reluctant to discuss the issue, at least in public with strangers.

The third interpretation concerning the communication form of cultural diversity focused on how the issue was being discussed in the community at large. This interpretation comes primarily in response to question #6 ("What issues divide the community that *are* being discussed?") and question #7 ("What issues divide the community that *are not* being discussed?") of the interview guide (see Table 3.2 for follow-up probes to these questions). There was strong consensus in all of the focus groups that the issue was not being discussed in public. According to participants, the issue was being discussed privately among "like-minded" people but not formally in public settings. "Even though these are things that we should talk about," said one white participant, "we don't because its not politically correct, you could get into trouble." Another participant suggested that "fear" and "hypersensitivity" prevents it from being discussed. Still another participant said that when people talk about the issue, "things tend to get heated—feelings override logic." In short, people avoided talking about the issue because they perceived it to be too sensitive, controversial, and threatening.

Avoidance was indicative of both Asian and non-white participants. One Asian participant bluntly stated that, "Asians are scared to say anything in public about this issue." Another Asian participant in the same group noted that although the issue was being discussed privately among residents of the city, it was not discussed in intercultural encounters involving Asians and whites. These encounters might "look friendly on the surface," she said, but they mask "a sense of underlying resentment by whites toward Asians."

The overall sense among all of the focus-group participants was that community members were afraid to discuss the cultural diversity issue in public. White residents were reluctant to discuss the issue for fear of being labeled racists. The new Asian immigrants felt threatened by the issue because they were the targets of the criticisms. As a result, both groups and the community as a whole simply avoided talking about the issue in public. This created a sense of frustration among many of the focus-group participants. For some, the lack of public communication meant that the issue would continue to divide the community, perhaps leading to larger and more serious problems. For others, the lack of public communication was a lost opportunity because the potential benefits of cultural diversity were not being realized. People in the community thus recognized a potential problem lurking below the surface, yet they were unsure how to bring it to the forefront so that it could be dealt with productively.

CONCERNS WITH COMMUNITY SAFETY

As noted earlier, the participants we talked with recognized Cupertino's safety as a major community asset. It also emerged in the focus-group interviews as a potential concern. Specifically, we noted three sets of concerns with the safety and crime issue. First, participants expressed concern that crime, although not a serious issue in the community yet, could spread from nearby cities into Cupertino.[3] Participants felt strongly that proactive steps were needed to guard against this happening. A large part of this concern was fueled by a recent increase in graffiti, which several participants said was evidence of gang activity. "Where are the gangs coming from," asked one participant, "from inside the city or from outside?"

A second set of concerns with safety and crime centered on the threat to children, teenagers, and young adults. Several participants noted that the city needs to build safe and healthy places for young people. "There really aren't very many places for these kids to go and be with their friends," said one participant. "Without some kind of teen center they're just going to end up getting into trouble." Another participant suggested building more neighborhood parks and "safe" wild, open spaces for "exploring and playing." Several participants in the Sheriff's focus group talked about safety and crime issues in the public schools. "Kids are bringing alcohol to school at a younger age," according to one participant, "and drugs are being handled in a reactionary way." The Sheriff also talked about gang problems in the schools and said that many in the community were ignoring the problem. One of the participants said, "People are not willing to admit that there are gangs; they pretend it doesn't exist."

A final set of concerns focused on traffic and the threat this poses to community safety. There is little doubt that traffic is a major concern for the residents of Cupertino (the same could be said for the majority of the 6 million people living in the greater San Francisco Bay Area). Participants in the focus groups shared a number of examples of how traffic in Cupertino threatens peoples' safety. Some of these included confusion with navigating around one-way streets, the lack of synchronization of signal lights, and people running red lights. Several participants noted that the traffic issue is related to larger issues of growth and development. As more people moved into the city the need for new housing developments increased, which in turn contributed to traffic problems. All of these factors were seen as jeopardizing peoples' ability to move freely and safely around the city.

Box 3.6. Gathering Input from Citizens and Sheriffs

Once public safety was identified as a topic of concern, it was important to collect input from citizens and members of the Sheriff's Office in order to focus on the problem and possible solutions. This empowered not only the people who felt a problem existed (the public), but allowed those who might have an effect on the problem (Sheriff's deputies) to give input on their proposed solution.
—Steve Angus, Sergeant, Santa Clara County Sheriff's Department & Cupertino Community Program Liaison

In summary, concerns related to safety and crime were not considered to be nearly as controversial or sensitive when compared with concerns about cultural diversity. Participants readily talked about the issue, and for the most part were in agreement about their concerns. In fact, we detected few if any differences among participants and across focus groups in the way the issue was framed. Importantly, participants did not view the issue as creating divisions in the community. Yes, there is concern that Cupertino remain and safe and secure community, but this is a concern shared by the community as a whole.

LOOKING BACK-LOOKING FORWARD

According to focus-group participants, cultural differences between whites and Asians was the most divisive issue facing the Cupertino community. Concerns over the issue were expressed in terms of two mutually exclusive categories, with whites on one side and Asians on the other. Some participants expressed concern that the influx of Chinese newcomers divided the city, leading to a loss of community identity and a threat to traditional American values. Other participants said they were concerned that the changing demographics in the city created cultural misunderstandings between white and Asian residents. Still other participants voiced concern that the community was in a transition period and would continue to face an uncertain future unless appropriate ways of managing cultural differences between whites and Asians could be found.

The communicative form of cultural diversity in Cupertino fits neatly into a pattern of avoidance. Almost all of the focus-group participants were aware of the issue as an underlying source of tension in the community, yet they were reluctant to talk about it in public. The consensus was that this pattern was characteristic of the community at large. The focus-group interviews themselves provided some indication of how reluctant people were to confront the issue. At the same time, the interviews also demonstrated that it was possible to create contexts that enabled people to talk openly about their concerns and problems. As the PDC moved into the second phase of the project we sought to recreate some of the conditions that made discussion of the issue possible. At the same time, we sought to develop additional contexts for public communication beyond focus-group interviews and to expand opportunities for other community members to participate.

As the Cupertino project unfolded over the following three years a number of new concerns and problems related to cultural diversity came into public focus. Some of these concerns surfaced in the public discussions and research interviews conducted by the PDC. Others were played out in contexts that were not officially part of the Cupertino Project, including city council meetings, school board meetings, and the local media. The letters to editor section of the *Cupertino Courier*, for example, was one of the more prominent public outlets for residents to express their concerns. That the diversity issue became fodder for extensive public communication illustrates that it was eventually transformed from an undiscussible to a discussible issue.[4] It also indicates the deep-seeded and long-term significance of the issue to the community. Consistent with the communicative approach of the PDC, we were less concerned with the content of these "new" issues and more focused on providing opportunities for residents to discuss problems within the framework of a public dialogue process.

NOTES

1. We brought a tape-recorder to the first two focus-group interviews and asked participants for permission to tape the discussions. Because several people in each group said they were reluctant to have their comments recorded, we dispensed with the idea of tape-recording the interviews and arranged instead to have a note taker present at each meeting.

2. The survey of 400 Cupertino residents was conducted January 7-11, 1998, by the independent public opinion agency Godbe Research and Analysis. It was a telephone survey using a random digit dial sample. Results indicated that "79% of those sampled rated race relations in Cupertino as either 'excellent' or 'good;' 14% rated race relations as 'poor' or 'very poor.' Nearly half said the city's increased racial diversity has made them more sympathetic and open toward people of

other races; 15% said it made them more resentful" ("Survey of residents," 1998, p. 2).

3. In the same community survey described in footnote 2, results indicated that half of those sampled said that crime in Cupertino "had stayed about the same" over the past five years; 20% said that it had increased; 8% said that it had decreased ("Survey of residents," 1998, p. 3).

4. There is substantial evidence indicating that this transformation was widespread, extending well beyond the specific activities of the Cupertino Project. For example, during the 1997 Cupertino city council campaign, all five candidates identified cultural diversity as one of leading issues in the election (Cronk, 1997b; Marino, 1997). In an article recapping the major stories of 1998, the *Cupertino Courier* dubbed it the "year of diversity." There was an "emotional outpouring over diversity issues in the community," the article said, as "residents expressed their opinions at city-hosted forums, at school board meetings and on the letters page of the *Courier*" ("1998: A look back," 1999, p. 1).

4

ELICITING VISIONS AND ACTION PLANS

This chapter describes the three interrelated activities that comprised Phase II of the Cupertino Project. In the first activity, community residents participated in a series of dialogue-group discussions. The format and results of these discussions are examined using a format similar to the one used in the previous chapter to describe the focus-group discussions. The second activity consisted of intergenerational interviews involving high school students and adult residents. In addition to covering the content of the interviews, the chapter also describes how the PDC trained students to conduct the interviews. The Town Hall Meeting, the third activity of Phase II, is described in terms of its episodic structure and includes an analysis of significant turning points that impacted the results of the meeting. The primary organizing theme of this chapter is how the PDC assisted Cupertino residents in developing visions and action plans relating to cultural diversity and community safety.

GOALS AND PURPOSES OF PHASE II

DISCUSSING UNDISCUSSIBLE ISSUES

Consistent with what we learned from the focus-group interviews, we developed Phase II with the goal of transforming the cultural diversity issue from an undiscussible topic to a discussible one. If the communication form of the issue was avoidance, then our goal in Phase II was to foster a communicative engagement of the issue. Given the circumstances, we proceeded very carefully in bringing the issue to the forefront. On the one hand, we understood the issue to be volatile—people were threatened by the situation and afraid of what might happen if they spoke about it in public. On the other hand, we heard people saying that the issue needed to be addressed publicly, and that a failure to do so would only exacerbate the problem and damage the community.

This tension points to a dilemma in public communication today. Although people value talk and communicative engagement of issues, most people are not comfortable with the kind of polarized conflict, negative debate, and incivility that often attends discussion of ethnic and cultural differences. Unfortunately, adversarial conflict is pervasive throughout the media and is deeply embedded in our legal and political institutions (Tannen, 1998). The question is, how can ordinary citizens and city officials engage issues of diversity in ways that cut against the grain of what Tannen (1998) calls the "argument culture"? We set out to address this question in Phase II by developing communication activities and intervention techniques that invited participants into patterns of public dialogue and deliberation rather than public debate and polarized conflict.

CREATING A SAFE CONTEXT

Developing trust is essential for the practice of public dialogue. As Ellinor and Gerard (1998) write

> typical conversational patterns in organizations are built on competition, fear of authority, and survival of the most politically astute. There is no magic formula for building trust. But an unswerving dedication to listening, curiosity, suspension of judgment, and nondefensiveness will see you a long way down the road. (p. 180)

Given the sensitivities surrounding Asian immigration and ethnic change in Cupertino, it was critical that steps be taken to ensure that people were able to speak honestly and candidly about the issue, without threat of recrimination or attack.

MODELING APPRECIATIVE LANGUAGE

The PDC named the issue "cultural richness" rather than cultural diversity, multiculturalism, or some other commonly used term. This reframing reflected our methodological commitments to appreciative inquiry and our theoretical commitments to social constructionism. The act of naming or labeling a social issue, or any other aspect of our social environment, is never neutral or objective because words and language prefigure how people will respond to that which is named. Because "cultural diversity" and "multiculturalism" have been used extensively in popular discourse they have an established set of meanings that prefigure a range of potential responses. The deliberate use of the term "cultural richness" was designed to elicit responses that spoke to the potential benefits that diversity might have for the Cupertino community. As indicated later in the chapter, this attempt to reframe the issue was criticized by some members of the community who felt that the term revealed a "politically correct" ideology, and unfairly tilted the conversation toward the positive implications of diversity while downplaying negative consequences.

TAKING A SYSTEMIC PERSPECTIVE ON COMMUNITY ISSUES

In addition to cultural richness, we also chose to include "community safety" as a secondary issue in Phase II. Although focus-group participants expressed a number of concerns with this issue, it was not framed as the kind of problematic topic that divided the community. In fact, there was a good deal of consensus that safety is a common goal of all community residents, regardless of ethnic origin. The discussion surrounding community safety offset and complemented the problems and concerns that emerged over cultural diversity. Another attractive feature of the issue is that, like cultural richness, it is systemic in that it cuts across all segments of the community. As Bunker and Alban (1997), note, "the issue must be important enough so that a critical mass of people has information to share on the subject as well as a strong desire to influence it" (p. 218). Both cultural richness and community safety met these criteria.

FOCUSING ON VISIONS AND ACTION PLANS

The overall purpose of Phase II was to facilitate action-oriented consensus (Dryzek, 1990) concerning cultural richness and community safety. This was accomplished by, first, facilitating discussions around peoples' *visions* for the future of the community in terms of cultural richness and community safety, and then asking residents to generate *action plans* for realizing those visions. Note that the product of these discussions consisted of specific action items, whereas the product of the focus-group interviews in Phase I consisted of the identification of *concerns* and community problems. The evolution of the project from Phase I to Phase II was thus based on the CVA model of public communication described in Chapter 2.

DIALOGUE-GROUP DISCUSSIONS

The first activity in Phase II consisted of eight dialogue-group discussions involving 38 Cupertino residents. The procedure for recruiting and contacting participants was similar to the one used in the focus-group interviews, with a few modifications. First, the PDC initiated the process by mailing hundreds of letters to potential participants asking them to participate in the dialogue-group discussions. A week or so later we contacted the people by phone to ask for their participation. The letters served not only as a recruitment tool, they also alerted people in the community about the Cupertino Project and informed them about the process (Figure 4.1 includes a copy of the letter). Second, the discussions were advertised as public events, which among other things meant that participants were not assured of anonymity as they were in the focus-group interviews. To reinforce the public nature of the events, both the *Cupertino Courier* and *The Scene* published articles about the dialogue groups and invited the public to attend. Third, given that the discussions were open to the public, there was no attempt made to control the ethnic composition of the groups. Our goal was simply to create a public forum that would attract a variety of different stakeholders in the community. As it turned out, six of the eight groups were heterogeneous, involving a mixture of Asian and white participants. The other two groups were composed of white participants only.

In order to foster an in-depth discussion of cultural richness and community safety, the dialogue-group discussions lasted anywhere from 3 to 4 hours. The rather lengthy time frame apparently had a negative effect on recruitment because the response rate was less than 10%. In addition, a number of people who agreed to participate simply did

Dear Cupertino Resident:

I am writing to introduce you to the Cupertino Community Project: Voices and Visions, sponsored by the Public Dialogue Consortium, De Anza College, and the City of Cupertino. This project involves citizens discussions designed to create a vision of the future of the city. This is an exciting and new form of grassroots democracy. You were selected from a citywide resident list to be contacted.

The project is entirely citizen-based and is not affiliated with any political party or interest group. Neither the sponsors nor the city council will determine the outcome of the discussions. With the exception of a little staff assistance and use of city facilities, no City tax dollars are used to support this project.

Earlier this year, my colleagues and I met with over 70 citizens of Cupertino to listen to their concerns about the community. We are now expanding these conversations. I would like to call you in a few days to discuss the project and invite you to participate.

The topics for this phase of the project will be cultural richness and community safety, two concerns that emerged in our earlier groups. This fall we will host a number of dialogue groups, work with students from the public schools, and organize a town meeting. I will tell you more about the different aspects of the project when we talk on the phone.

The Cupertino Community Project is very different from the customary polarized debate that is so familiar to us. Our group helps citizens explore their differences honestly and respectfully, discover their shared concerns, frame their issues, build a common vision, and move forward together. We use a variety of ground rules and techniques to help establish this kind of communication, and we ask our participants to contribute in the spirit of this undertaking.

The Public Dialogue Consortium is a small, informal, non-profit group dedicated to advancing the quality of communication on public issues. Several of our members live and work in the South Bay, but we have active members in several other parts of the country. We maintain a neutral position on all community issues and are not stakeholders in the community. I would be pleased to tell you more about the PDC when we talk.

I am looking forward to meeting you in the near future.

Figure 4.1. Dialogue group recruitment letter

not attend. By comparison, we had a 20% response rate with focus-group interviews, which lasted 2 hours, and had very few no-shows. Grappling with issues of time and recruitment became an on-going tension throughout the remainder of the project. We certainly wanted to attract as many people as possible to the project, yet we also recognized that many people were not able to volunteer large amounts of time. As we planned activities it became necessary for us to balance the rather extensive time requirements necessary for public dialogue with the time constraints of citizen volunteers.

FACILITATING DIALOGUE-GROUP DISCUSSIONS

Similar to the focus-group interviews, each of the dialogue-group discussions was co-facilitated by members of the PDC team. Additionally, we had at least one person record comments on a flip chart and, when possible, a second person taking notes. We opened each meeting by introducing the PDC team and then briefly reviewing Phase I of the project and what we hoped to accomplish in Phase II. The following is a typical context-setting statement: "Our goal in this discussion is to create a vision for the Cupertino community in terms of cultural richness and community safety, and to turn that vision into specific action plans by outlining the steps both residents and city officials can take to make cultural richness and community safety happen in the future." We then suggested two ground rules for the meeting (respect differences, one person speaks at a time) and asked the participants if they would like to add any of their own.

The dialogue-group protocol consisted of questions designed to elicit in-depth discussion of visions and action plans. Importantly, the two issues were not defined in advance for participants. The idea here was to encourage an open discussion in which participants were free to interject their own meanings and perspectives. As indicated in Table 4.1, dialogue-group participants were asked eight questions during the 3- to 4-hour discussions. Obviously, the questions served as prompts for initiating deeper levels of discussion. Using follow-up probes and other small-group facilitation techniques, the PDC facilitators encouraged participants to move beyond surface-level positions on the issues. The facilitators also encouraged participants to listen and respond to one another as a way of moving the conversation away from an interview format and toward a more fully distributed small-group discussion.

Table 4.1. Dialogue Group Questions.

Question #1: What does the term cultural richness mean to you and how does it apply to the city of Cupertino? (asked round-robin style)

Question #2: Can you tell me about a positive experience you have had with cultural richness?

Question #3: How can we make these positive experiences with cultural richness happen in the Cupertino community in the future?

Questions #4: What does the term community safety mean to you and how does it apply to the city of Cupertino? (asked round-robin style)

Question #5: Can you tell me about a positive experience you have had with community safety?

Question #6: How can we make these positive experiences with community safety happen in the Cupertino community in the future?

Question #7: Do you see any connections between cultural richness and community safety. Can you tell me how the two areas might be related to one another?

Question #8: Is there anything else you would like to add that we have not covered during our discussion?

CULTURAL RICHNESS: THEMES AND CATEGORIES

Results from the dialogue-group discussions were examined using qualitative data analysis (Creswell, 1998; Lindlof, 1995). As indicated in Figure 3.2, this involved developing data-texts from our written accounts of the discussions, examining the texts holistically, breaking the texts down into themes and categories, and interpreting the texts in light of larger social forces and situational constraints.

Visions of Cultural Richness Rooted in Pluralism

The major theme of the dialogue-group discussions centered on a pluralistic conception of cultural richness. Participants envisioned Cupertino as a community composed of a variety of different cultures, each with their own unique histories, customs, and practices. In this vision, all members of the community would promote pluralism by supporting different ethnic groups in their attempts to retain their own cultural practices. At the same time, the vision also entails the corollary aspect of pluralism, which is the exploration of cultural differences as a way of uncovering common ground and common values. So while the community would recognize and celebrate the variety of different ethnic groups and cultural traditions existing in the city, it would also seek to integrate these differences into a common set of understandings that tie members of the community together. The key is to promote unity and common ground without sacrificing cultural differences. This pluralistic vision of cultural richness replaces the old metaphor of the United States as a "melting pot" with new metaphors such as a salad, quilt, tapestry, or stew.

The following summary statements from each of the eight dialogue groups demonstrate how visions of cultural richness were rooted in a pluralistic conception of the community.

Group one talked about cultural richness in terms of finding the right balance between a group's cultural identity and developing appropriate sensitivity to other cultures. The group talked about the need for shared values that create a sense of community and commonality. They also talked about how to accomplish this without denying a person's cultural heritage. As one group participant put it, "we want diversity and common ground, and both can be achieved." Group two discussed the tension that exists between maintaining one's own personal and cultural identity and developing/expressing appropriate sensitivity to other cultures within a multicultural society. Members of the group felt that it was not good to lose one's own identity, and that this can happen in the attempt to be sensitive to other cultures.

Group three envisioned Cupertino as a community where people from different ethnic groups and cultures come together and cooperate as neighbors. There is a demonstration of shared values. The group felt strongly that particular groups should not isolate themselves or be isolated from the community. Group four agreed that cultural richness involves blending the experiences people bring from their own culture with the historical culture of the United States. Members of the group agreed that this could be accomplished in ways that do not detract from any one culture.

Group five said that cultural richness should promote the inclusion of all groups of people in the city. For example, white members of the community should be encouraged and allowed to attend Chinese school, learn the Chinese language, or be included in a Chinese New Year's celebration. The group felt that cultural richness should encompass the entire community so that particular groups are not isolated. All cultural groups are made to feel a part of the community and all groups choose to participate in defining the larger community. Group six felt that cultural richness should involve a good balance between preservation of culture and integration of cultures. If this balance is right, the group said, community members could learn more about their roots, develop rich identities of both separate and common cultures, have a peaceful community without strife, and learn new perspectives. One of the participants said that, "cultural richness should involve tolerance of difference without shame."

Group seven envisioned a culturally rich community as one where the contributions of all cultural groups are valued and celebrated. As an example, one member of the group talked about his Tai Chi class, which he said has 50% Asian and 50% white participants. Group eight said that there is a sense of unity, blending, and inclusiveness in their vision of cultural richness, but not at the expense of having to give up one's cultural identity. One group member put it this way, "coexistence does not equal assimilation."

Overall, there was a clear consensus among dialogue-group participants that cultural richness in Cupertino is best achieved by balancing the demands for the integration of cultural groups with the preservation of cultural identities. Achieving this balance was thought to be possible within existing social, political, and economic arrangements in the city. Although issues related to institutional racism or structural inequality were briefly mentioned in some of the groups, they never emerged as a dominant theme or vision. The closest example of this was in the case of two dialogue groups whose vision included more affordable housing for lower income residents. Institutional racism presupposes an economic and social hierarchy in which whites control the distribution of wealth while immigrants and people of color assume positions at the bottom of the ladder (Goode & Schneider, 1994). Given the affluent status and high-economic standing of the new Asian immigrants in Cupertino, visions related to institutional racism or structural inequality were not evident, nor were they particularly relevant.

Action Plans: Focus on Education

As the dialogue groups discussed action plans for bringing about cultural richness, it became clear once again that cultural pluralism, and not institutional racism, was the overriding framework for dealing with new Asian immigrants in Cupertino. As Goode and Schneider (1994) note, the "the solution to institutional racism is to change the structure of society" (p. 18), whereas "the cultural-pluralist strategy focuses on informing both newcomers and established residents about their own cultures and those of others" (p. 19). The action plans generated by dialogue-group participants focused almost exclusively on activities that promote intercultural understanding and information exchange among the ethnic groups living in Cupertino. As such, they are best viewed as an extension of cultural pluralism, not institutional racism.

Consistent with cultural pluralism, education was the dominant theme underlying the action plans generated by dialogue-group participants. All of the groups talked about the need for residents to learn about different cultural traditions, including both the native cultures of recent immigrants as well as the American culture of established residents. Although the public schools were singled out as leading the way in promoting educational opportunities, group participants felt that adults needed to learn about other cultures as well. Each of the following categories of action plans, identified in all eight dialogue groups, includes an explicit educational component and is inclusive of adult members of the community.

The first category, community celebrations, calls for cultural events that allow various groups to demonstrate and share their cultural practices with the rest of the community. Some of these celebrations would simply continue existing events, such as the Japanese Cherry Blossom Festival and Octoberfest. Others would expand existing events, such as the Fourth of July celebration, to include a more explicit multicultural focus. Participants also suggested a number of new celebrations, such as a performing arts event highlighting music and dance from different cultural groups. The groups felt that these celebratory events should be framed as educational opportunities for learning about the various cultural groups living in Cupertino.

The second category centered on neighborhood activities as a way of promoting cultural richness and learning about different cultures. A number of participants felt that everyday conversations involving residents from different cultures is the best way to achieve intercultural understanding and respect. One specific suggestion for promoting social interaction was to develop a neighborhood block party program that would provide opportunities for residents from different cultures to interact in a nonthreatening, social situation. Another suggestion was to develop a "welcoming committee" that would be available to greet new city residents. In addition to providing new residents with information packets, the committee would also begin to establish a context for the development of interpersonal relationships.

The final set of action plans focused on cultural information dissemination. Participants talked about the need to make information about cultural events accessible to the community through either existing media or the development of new media, such as a city web page. Other suggestions included the development of a fact sheet, pamphlet, or multicultural calendar containing relevant cultural and demographic information. Similar to the fact sheet, it was suggested that a welcome booklet be created to help people who move to Cupertino acquire information about the community. Regardless of how it was packaged, the groups viewed the welcome booklet as an educational resource for the community and an opportunity for both newcomers and established residents to learn about each other's cultures.

COMMUNITY SAFETY: THEMES AND CATEGORIES

In general, dialogue-group participants spoke favorably about the current status of community safety in Cupertino. Similar to the focus-group findings, participants noted the relative safety of the community, especially when compared with other neighboring cities. The facilitators did not specifically ask for concerns, however, a number of participants nevertheless volunteered what they perceived as "early warning signs" that the safety of the community might be threatened in the near future. These concerns were similar if not identical to those that surfaced in the focus-group interviews. Consistent with the purpose of the dialogue groups, the facilitators guided the discussion away from concerns and encouraged participants to talk about their visions of community safety and how to maintain and enhance Cupertino as a safe and desirable place to live.

Three Visions of Community Safety

Dialogue-group participants discussed community safety in terms of three interrelated visions. The first and perhaps most obvious is *physical safety*, which refers to Cupertino as a community free of crime and violence. Participants talked about a safe community as one in which citizens can walk and move around the city without fear or threat of violence, and in which families experience a sense of security at home and in their neighborhoods. One participant, for example, talked about growing up in England and being able to play outdoors without having to worry about crime and violence. The sense of freedom revealed in this story captures the vision of physical safety expressed throughout the dialogue-group discussions.

Community safety was also envisioned as having an emotional and relational component in which residents work together to prevent crime and help make Cupertino a safe place to live. Labeled *emotional safety*, this vision calls forth mutual support among residents and comes about when people who live close together demonstrate concern for each other's welfare. The prototypical example of this type of safety is watching a neighbor's home when they are away. In addition, several participants told stories about neighbors helping each other in times of crisis and need, such as an earthquake or garbage strike. Another participant talked about a group of people in her neighborhood who joined together to persuade Cupertino officials to install barricades to prevent traffic accidents on their street. Each of these examples demonstrates how a vision of emotional safety comes about through community solidarity at the neighborhood level.

The third vision, called *transportation safety*, was discussed primarily in terms of traffic. Specifically, participants envisioned a community where automobile traffic is monitored and controlled in such a way as to minimize accidents. A number of participants felt that pedestrians and bicyclists should also be included in their vision, especially when children are concerned. For these participants, a safe community is one in which children can walk or bike to school safely, and in which the traffic is diffused in the areas surrounding the schools so that children do not have to cross busy streets. Like the other visions of community safety, the impetus behind transportation safety came out of peoples' experiences dealing with traffic in the city. Participants in every dialogue group told stories of witnessing traffic accidents, or near accidents, involving motorists, pedestrians, or bicyclists.

Action Plans: Focus on Community Policing

Although participants identified a number of specific plans for bringing about community safety, the one that generated the most interest and consensus was *community policing*. Participants felt strongly that their visions of community safety would be enhanced if members of the Sheriff's Department interacted more with community residents at the neighborhood level. By increasing the amount of personal contact, participants felt that Sheriff's deputies would be in a position to develop positive and productive relationships with community residents, which in turn would create what one participant called "a city culture of mutual support and care."

It is worth noting that the discussion of community policing in the dialogue groups was consistent with the principles and goals of community policing practiced in hundreds of cities throughout the United States (Lappé & Du Bois, 1994). The San Antonio Police Department, for example, developed a special community policing unit in 1995 called SAFFE (San Antonio Fear Free Environment). As described on their web site,

> community policing is a collaborative effort between a police department and community that identifies problems and involves all elements of the community in the search for solutions to these problems. It is founded on close, mutually beneficial ties between police and community members. At the center of community policing are three essential and complementary core components: (1) Partnership

between the police and the community, (2) Problem solving as a method to identify and solve problems of concern to the community, (3) Change management within the police organization to accommodate increased community involvement. (www.ci.sat.tx.us/sapd)

The discussion of community policing in the dialogue groups was not only consistent with community policing projects in other cities, it was also consistent with suggestions made by members of the local Sheriff's Department. In the law enforcement focus-group interviews from Phase I, participants advocated community policing as a useful way for patrol officers and citizens to develop trustful relationships with one another. One of the deputies in the focus groups said that "citizens other than law enforcement have to get involved" in order for Cupertino to become as safe as possible. "We [Sheriff's personnel] can't do it alone." Another deputy said that, "we [Sheriff's personnel] need to get away from dependence on the patrol car and have more direct involvement with the community."

In comparison to the dialogue-group participants, the participants in the Sheriff's focus group put greater emphasis on the reciprocal nature of community policing. That is, community residents need to become actively involved with law enforcement at the same time that law enforcement needs to reach out to residents. One deputy said that, "citizens don't understand the laws we [Sheriff's personnel] have to work under and they are frustrated because they don't understand." For the Sheriffs, community policing works best when residents are aware of their own involvement in law enforcement and the limitations of law enforcement officials.

Box 4.1. Sheriff's Officers are Part of the Community

I think the most significant contribution of the project is the way it has opened up communication between Sheriff's officers and community residents. My officers now feel as though they are a part of the community. They can actually sit down, discuss issues, and talk to people in the neighborhoods. People are aware of who they are and what they represent. My officers are involved, they are present, and their voices are heard.
—Bob Wilson, Captain, Santa Clara County Sheriff's Department (June 3, 1999)

The other action plans that emerged from the dialogue-group discussions were actually extensions of the community policing theme. For example, participants encouraged the continuation and expansion of the Emergency Preparedness Program and the various Neighborhood Watch Programs that were currently in place throughout the city. Although these programs were seen as useful in and of themselves, participants also saw them as opportunities for developing on-going relationships between law enforcement and community residents. The actions suggested here called for Sheriff's deputies to attend neighborhood meetings and consult with residents, or give presentations on topics such as burglar proofing homes and business establishments and developing a Neighborhood Watch Program.

Another action plan suggested in the dialogue groups was to form a Citizens Advisory Group that would help law enforcement meet the unique needs of community residents. The advisory group would be multiethnic and include people who could translate both language and cultural knowledge between residents and law enforcement. In this way, the advisory group would serve as an intermediary in helping to create positive relationships between law enforcement and nontraditional residents. Participants suggested that the advisory group could serve both an educational function in terms of crime prevention and a conflict resolution function for dealing with linguistic and cultural misunderstandings.

In hindsight, it made good sense to include the community safety issue along with cultural richness. It not only gave dialogue-group participants a less divisive topic to discuss, it also provided opportunities for connecting cultural richness to other community concerns. The Citizens Advisory Group action plan just described, for example, clearly demonstrates how community safety intersects with cultural richness. Developing positive relationships between the Sheriff's Department and the various ethnic groups who live in the city enhances both intercultural understanding and community safety. Similarly, peoples' visions of emotional safety and cultural richness both called for relationship-building activities that lead to trust, respect, and understanding. These attempts to explore the links between cultural richness and community safety helped encourage participants to adopt a systemic perspective on the community.

INTERGENERATIONAL INTERVIEWS: WORKING WITH STUDENTS

In addition to dialogue-group discussions, the PDC trained over 100 high school students to conduct interviews on cultural richness and community safety with adults in the city. Gaining initial access to the students involved meeting several times with administrators and faculty at the two local high schools, Monta Vista and Cupertino High, and educating them about the value of the project to the students, the schools, and the community at large. Going through this process turned out to be a useful exercise for the PDC because it required us to reflect on how the project and our methodology could be adapted to fit the needs of the public schools. What role should the public schools play in advancing participatory democracy and public dialogue in the larger community? Can the skills of public dialogue be taught to students, and if so what is the best way to teach them? Can the larger community provide opportunities for students to practice public dialogue? Like other questions that surfaced during the course of the project, the answers were worked out in response to the specific situational demands we encountered while working in Cupertino.

Our approach was to train students to conduct open-ended interviews using appreciative inquiry (Cooperrider, Barrett, & Srivastva, 1995) and qualitative interviewing techniques (Lindlof, 1995). Each of the 100 students then conducted an average of four interviews with adult residents on their experiences dealing with cultural richness and community safety. In the case of cultural richness, the students assisted the larger community by promoting conversations about an issue that was widely considered to be undiscussible. And the community in turn helped the students by providing a "real-world" situation in which to apply their interviewing and appreciative inquiry skills. This mutual collaboration between the community and the schools and between adult residents and students stands as an example of community service learning in which the community itself becomes a learning lab for students to practice the communication skills that make participatory democracy possible (Barber, 1997; Battistoni, 1997; Lappé & Du Bois, 1994).

The PDC also used the intergenerational interviews to begin developing a model for training young adults in the microskills of public dialogue. One unique feature of the model involves using students to train other students. In the case of the intergenerational interviews, we trained 17 students from De Anza College and San Jose State University to assist the PDC in training the 100 Monta Vista and Cupertino High School students. To accomplish this, we first conducted two separate trainings for the college and university students, each of which were followed by separate training sessions at the two high schools and one large training for all of the high school students. All of the trainings began with an overview of appreciative inquiry and qualitative interviewing skills. The interviewing skills were relatively straightforward to teach, however, appreciative inquiry presented more of a challenge. In the end, we decided to simplify the technique and not teach it as an advanced communication practice. A copy of the appreciative inquiry handout is included in Table 4.2.

Table 4.2. Appreciative Inquiry Student Handout.

Appreciative inquiry (AI) is a communication technique that celebrates positive stories and experiences and explores how those positive stories and experiences can be extended into the future. AI is sometimes contrasted with traditional problem-solving forms of discussion. We can identify two differences between the two:

1. Problem solving normally begins by identifying the problem. By contrast, AI begins by valuing what is best about people, communities, and organizations.
2. Problem solving naturally includes an analysis of the causes of the problem. By contrast, AI involves envisioning the positive outcomes that can and should happen in the future.

Characteristics of Appreciative Inquiry

•   AI expresses an attitude of curiosity and wonder. When using the AI interviewing technique it is important that you communicate genuine enthusiasm and interest in what is being said. Be an active listener and ask plenty of questions to show your interest.
•   AI focuses on that which works rather than that which does not work. When using the AI interviewing technique the goal is to focus the conversation on positive stories and positive experiences rather than problems and complaints.
•   AI allows the expression of passion, interests, and vision. When using the AI interviewing technique encourage people to talk about what is important to them—their hopes, their dreams, and their fears. AI pro vides an opportunity for people to express what they really think and feel in a positive way.

Students were given an interview guide that was identical to the one used in the dialogue-group discussions (see Table 4.1) except that it included follow-up questions and prompts. Although the additional information might have inadvertently led the students to expect certain types of responses, we nevertheless included it to help the students in case they got "stuck" during the interviews. Table 4.3 presents the interview questions with the additional information and prompts. A series of role-play interviews were then staged so that students could practice their skills. PDC members worked with the college and university students during the practice sessions providing support, feedback, and critical reflections. The college and university students assumed this role during the practice sessions with the high school students.

Box 4.2. Bringing Generations Together

I think the most interesting thing about the project is the way it brings different generations together. When all the generations are involved, it gives everyone in the community an opportunity to learn more about each other.
—Fariba Nejat, Cupertino resident and 5Cs member

Table 4.3. Intergenerational Interview Guide.

Question 1: What does cultural richness mean to you? (*If necessary, explain to the interviewee how we are using the term. Cultural richness refers to the different cultural traditions and people who live in Cupertino and the possibilities that this mix can have for the community in the future. We are interested in exploring how the Cupertino community might be enriched as a result of its diverse people and traditions.*)

Question 2: Could you tell me about a positive experience you have had with cultural richness? (*Follow-up questions if they do not have a personal story to tell: Imagine if you were to have a positive experience with cultural richness, what would that experience be like? Could you tell me about someone you know who has had a positive experience with cultural richness?*)

Question 3: What can the Cupertino community do to help make positive experiences happen in the future? (*Follow-up questions if interviewee needs help getting started: What can average citizens do to help make positive cultural richness experiences happen in the future? What can the Cupertino schools do? What can local businesses do? What can city officials do? What can you do? What educational opportunities can help make positive cultural richness experiences happen in the future? What city events can help make positive cultural richness experiences happen in the future?*)

Questions 4-6: Identical to questions 1-3, except that "community safety" is substituted for "cultural richness."

Question 7: Now that we have covered the two areas of our interview, I am interested if you see any connections between cultural richness and community safety. Can you tell me how the two areas might be related to one another?

The high school students conducted approximately 400 intergenerational interviews over a three-week period following the training sessions. The interviews provided students an opportunity to put their communication interviewing skills into practice, and it provided adults in the community an opportunity to share their views, experiences, and ideas for advancing cultural richness and community safety. Consistent with the goals of Phase II of the project, the interviews demonstrated how potentially divisive topics can be talked about openly and in ways that are affirming rather than polarizing.

TOWN HALL MEETING: THE FIRST LARGE PUBLIC EVENT

The culmination of Phases I and II of the Cupertino project was a Town Hall Meeting held on November 20, 1996, at a local community center. Approximately 150 residents participated in the 2-1/2-hour event, which was open to the public and advertised through the local media. Billed as a "public dialogue on cultural richness and community safety," the meeting was described in the program and in various press releases as follows:

> Tonight's meeting is the culmination of over six months of work in which citizens have thought about the things they value most about this community. In this Town Meeting, we have the opportunity to learn about their visions for the future and their suggestions for how these visions might be realized. We will have a public discussion of these proposals and we will decide what next steps we should take.

As this description indicates, the meeting was designed to inform the larger community about the work completed in the focus groups, dialogue groups, and intergenerational interviews, and to enable those attending to participate in the project by joining and extending the on-going discussion. A subtler but no-less important purpose of the meeting was to provide additional opportunities for community residents to publicly discuss cultural and demographic changes in the city. Our hope was to use the forum to demonstrate how this potentially contentious issue could be discussed in a large public venue without it degenerating into acrimonious debate and conflict.

WORKING WITH LARGE GROUPS

Bunker and Alban (1997) state that facilitating transformation and change in organizations, communities, or any other complex social system requires that the whole system participate together in defining and solving the problems that confront them. When dealing with a community-wide project in a city the size of Cupertino, however, it is impossible to get the "whole system in the room" at the same time, as Bunker and Alban (1997) recommend.[1] What is possible is to bring a critical mass of people together who represent a variety of constituencies and major stakeholders in the community. When assembled together these large groups act as a microcosm of the larger community. This suggests that the communication resources mobilized within the context of a large-group meeting can potentially impact the greater community, much in the same way that a subsystem influences the larger systems it is connected to.

The Town Hall Meeting was the first opportunity for a significant number of Cupertino residents to gather together in public to address cultural richness and community safety issues in ways that encouraged collaboration, dialogue, and deliberation. Although this was obviously intended to marshal the resources of those who attended the forum, it also extended to other stakeholders who became aware of the event through media coverage and by talking with those who did attend. Ideally, the networks and relationships established at the Town Hall Meeting would expand opportunities for dialogic forms of public communication beyond the large group setting, thus creating the conditions for large-scale systemic change.

In large-group events designed to foster public dialogue it is critical that all those in attendance actively participate in developing concerns, visions, and/or action plans. The number of participants and the inevitable time constraints of large-group events, however, make it difficult for participants to engage in the kind of face-to-face interaction and shared decision-making activities that are necessary for public dialogue. The solution is to design large-group events so that the participants spend a significant amount of time working in small groups on specific activities. Similar to large-group interventions used in organizational settings (Bunker & Alban, 1997), the Town Hall Meeting included a combination of small-group interactions and large-group plenary discussions.

Box 4.3. The Value of Small Groups in Large Forums

The most intimate and productive times in the community forums I've attended are the small table discussions. This is where inhibition gives way to honesty and the free expression of opinions.
—Zahra Pavlovic, Cupertino resident and 5Cs member

EPISODES AND TURNING POINTS IN THE TOWN HALL MEETING

In what follows, the Town Hall Meeting is described in terms of seven episodes and a number of related turning points.[2] The episodes are punctuated around the development of the meeting and how it evolved. The turning points represent fluctuations in the meeting and indicate how particular communication acts performed at particular points in the meeting altered the direction and scope of the discussion. The turning points that are examined here are significant precisely because they created contextual forces that moved the discussion along a new trajectory. As the discussion was tracked onto the new trajectory, participants developed a set of expectations about what should happen next. These normative expectations continued to shape subsequent discussion until the next turning point occurred and new contextual forces were called into being.

Episode One: Creating the Context (20 Minutes)

A great deal of planning went into the Town Hall Meeting, not the least of which was the physical arrangement of the meeting space. The room was equipped with five overhead projectors at the front, a podium in one corner, and a raised stage in the center. Participants sat at one of 20 round tables, each with eight chairs. Colorful posters depicting the results of the intergenerational interviews were developed by the high school students and displayed around the room and in the hallway leading into the room. The purpose was to provide visual variety and sight lines that would draw attention to the range of activities planned for the meeting. Figure 4.2 provides a diagram of the layout of the Town Hall Meeting.

　　　Two members of the PDC team served as co-masters of ceremonies. They introduced the meeting as "both a celebration and a working session" and provided a brief background summary of the work previously completed in Phases I and II of the project. The PDC member who gave the summary concluded by saying:

> What we are doing tonight is the official presentation of the Cupertino Community Project. In all our previous discussions, we encouraged citizens to speak of their hopes and passions in a constructive manner and listen to each other attentively with patience, respect and curiosity. We hope this kind of sincere and passionate involvement continues tonight.

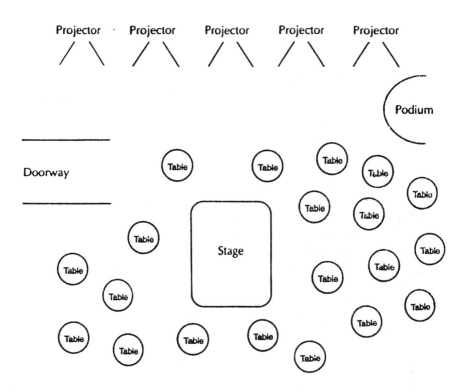

Figure 4.2. Diagram of town hall meeting

The other PDC member then gave an overview of the Town Hall Meeting and instructions for the group activities. The critical point emphasized here was that the meeting was not simply informational but involved direct participation by those in attendance. The tables were defined as the "work unit" for the forum, and participants were asked to utilize the small-group format to select visions and action plans for future implementation. "The first thing we are going to do is get to know the people in your work group, that is, the other people at the table, so that you can begin to work together on the project." This led into the first activity, which involved table introductions and assigning the roles of discussion leader, reporter, and timekeeper to group members.

Episode Two: Hearing From the Students (15 Minutes)

After the table introductions and role assignments, the meeting moved into the second episode in which six high school students described their experiences with the intergenerational interviews. The students, who were seated in a circle on the stage, were led by a member of the

PDC team who asked the following questions: What did you learn about cultural richness from the interviews you conducted? What did you learn about community safety from the interviews you conducted? What did you find most interesting or unusual about your interviews? What did you learn about the Cupertino community as a result of doing the interviews?

Turning Point

The student discussion represented the first turning point in the Town Hall Meeting. All of the discussion leading up to this point was focused on introductions and context-setting remarks; cultural richness and community safety had not yet been discussed in any substantive way. What was significant about the students' discussion was that they framed the issues within an appreciative context that set a decidedly positive tone for the forum. This, of course, was to be expected given the nature of the intergenerational interviews and explicit training students received in appreciative inquiry. It is difficult to overestimate, however, just how affirming and enthusiastic the students were about the issues, both in their content and in their manner of presentation. It is our interpretation that the report by the students created a context and set of expectations that led others to accentuate the positive features of cultural richness and community safety in their discussions.

A number of features in the student presentation illustrate the qualities of appreciative inquiry. First, the students demonstrated a sense of wonder and surprise about the interviews. One student said, "I was just amazed at the fact that the people of Cupertino are so open." Another said, "I was surprised because we have so many different cultures presented here and basically everyone has the same goals of having a safe community and learning about other cultures rather than focusing on one." Students also demonstrated openness and an ability to deal with multiple points of view. For example, one student said it was "fun to talk to all these different people and hear what they had to say . . . because before I had my own opinion . . . and I just assumed that everybody is going to have the same general idea and they didn't. It was neat to hear all these different experiences."

In terms of specific content, the students emphasized themes related to cultural pluralism and the need for cross-cultural learning. Again, these were framed appreciatively. One student reported that a person she interviewed "said that they should really encourage kids to share their ideas about their own culture, especially in school because that's where a lot of this begins. Instead of having kids mold into one culture, they should all share their ideas and help to hopefully improve the community as a whole." "I think Cupertino should be lucky to have such a diverse group of people," another student said, "rather than having different races secluded from each other. . . . In fact, they want to interact with one another not only to teach others about their culture but to learn from different types of other cultures that surround them."

The enthusiasm displayed by the students and the content of what they said was infectious. It spilled over into subsequent episodes and impacted the direction and tone of the meeting. Two people who spoke in the plenary session immediately following, for example, commented on the students and validated their presentation. One speaker said that "after listening to those young people talk, I think the future of our community is in very good hands." The other said that "the young people who talked tonight were a good example of . . . how we can involve student groups in the city. . . . Perhaps there is a way they can work with us who are a little bit older." Later in the meeting, the city council member who at the time was serving as mayor also referred back to the students: "Some of the best ideas I heard tonight came from the six kids that were sitting up here and who went out into the field and talked to people."

Episode Three: Hearing From the Dialogue Groups (15 Minutes)

Participants from three of the dialogue groups reported on the results of their discussions during this episode.[3] A member of the PDC team first described the dialogue-group process for the Town Hall participants and then introduced each of the speakers in turn. The report given by the first speaker was clearly grounded in a pluralistic vision of culture and community. Speaking for the group, he said:

> We [the dialogue group] were concerned with cultural groups that tend to isolate themselves. . . . We think that there should be a balance . . . we should accept and appreciate other cultures, learn from those cultures, develop ways of improving ourselves based on those cultures, but not to isolate ourselves. Perhaps what we need are individual cultures and also a community culture that evolves from the diversity of the various different cultures.

Throughout his report, the speaker reflected the pluralistic themes addressed in his own dialogue group, and most of the other groups as well. The remarks were also consistent with those expressed by the students in Episode Two.

Turning Point

A turning point in the meeting occurred when the second speaker summarized the results of her dialogue-group discussion. Instead of advancing a pluralistic vision of cultural richness, the speaker introduced a critical discourse that evoked themes more closely associated with structural inequality and institutional racism. She said that her group talked about the need to help "members of the dominant culture change their ethnocentric attitudes," and that actions should focus on "redefining notions of dominance, power, and class." Interestingly, these points were not readily evident in the data-text from the dialogue-group discussion, yet they were the ones she chose to emphasize in her presentation. In any case, the discourse challenged some of the conventions that had been established at the meeting. It certainly provided a more radical vision of cultural richness than the pluralistic themes advanced by the students and the first dialogue-group speaker.

The third speaker spoke extensively about the need for affordable housing and thus continued some of the structural inequality themes of the second speaker, at least as they related to economic inequality. When introducing the topic she made reference to the second speaker and said, "not everybody in this community is making a hundred-thousand dollars a year. . . . There are lots of students here. There are lots of single people who aren't making that. There are lots of jobs here that are not the highest paying jobs in the world and people have to travel an hour and half . . . to work in our community because they can't afford to live here." Although these comments were clearly focused on class distinctions and economic considerations, the speaker did not identify race or ethnicity as a factor in producing the inequalities, nor did she suggest that structural changes were needed to solve the problem. As a result, the speaker's comments did not challenge the conventions of the Town Hall Meeting to the extent that those of the second speaker did.

The critical discourse and structural inequality themes that were forcefully presented by the second speaker, and to a lesser extent by the third speaker, did not surface in any of the subsequent plenary sessions of the Town Hall Meeting. This turning point, then, created a brief disruption in the pluralistic pattern of discourse. The effect of the disruption dissipated quickly and pluralism reemerged later in the meeting as the dominant vision, as we will later see. It is interesting to note that structural inequality themes were periodically introduced throughout the entire Cupertino Project, but like the Town Hall Meeting they never seemed to gain any traction or sustained attention. To underscore this point, one of the consultants hired by the PDC to attend the meeting reported that during the small-group discussion one participant at his table identified affordable housing as a serious concern. When it came time to report to the larger group, however, the spokesperson did not mention the topic, and no one else at the table made an effort to bring it into the larger discussion.

Episode Four: Working Session (35 Minutes)

This was perhaps the most significant episode of the meeting in terms of advancing public dialogue and institutionalizing the principles, goals, and practices of the Cupertino Project. Each table was assigned one of the two topics. A member of the PDC team instructed each group to, first, discuss their vision of cultural richness or community safety, and then to collectively come to a decision about the one action plan that "most excites your imagination" and "would benefit the community the most." The results of these deliberations were written on note cards by the reporters at each table, collected and sorted by members of the PDC, and organized into a summary chart that was used later in the meeting.

Box 4.4. "The Participants are the Panelists"

Compared to other events I've covered over the past few years, the Cupertino Project is probably the most unique I've ever been involved with. I think that the sheer openness of it is the thing that stands out the most, and the enthusiasm of most of those who were there participating. It is very rare for any type of community forum. Normally, these forums are led by a moderator or moderators, who allow audience members to ask a panel or panelist various questions. Never have I seen anything where participants all get an equal chance to speak face to face, without a panel of "experts" running the show. In the PDC's forums, the participants are the panelists, all opinions are respected, and the floor is open to whoever wishes to speak.
—Steve Enders, Reporter for the *Cupertino Courier*

Turning Point

The purpose of the working session was to join the voices of the participants at the meeting with the voices of residents who had previously participated in the project. The episode was significant because it enabled all the participants at the meeting to directly engage the issues with others at their table, and thus it shifted the focus of the meeting from informational presentations during the plenary session to small-

group discussions. As such, it also shifted the responsibility for the outcome of the meeting away from the organizers of the event to the participants. A related purpose of the working session was to encourage participants at the tables to engage in a deliberative form of communication.
As indicated in the instructions, each group was asked to go through a
process of selecting one action plan for future implementation. The
results of these deliberations served as the basis for a large-group discussion later in the meeting.

Episode Five: The City Council Responds (15 Minutes)

Four of the five city council members attended the Town Hall Meeting
and participated in the table discussions along with community residents. After the working session, the council members gathered on the
stage in the center of the room and offered their responses to the visions
and action plans that had previously been discussed at the meeting.

Turning Point

This was the first time that the council formally participated in the project. By design and agreement, the council agreed to give up some of the
responsibility and control normally afforded elected officials during the
first two phases of the project while residents took the initiative in identifying issues and engaging in long-term community planning. This
rather unconventional arrangement continued at the Town Hall Meeting
in that the council first listened to the views expressed by community
members and then responded by offering their perspectives on what
was said. The episode was significant if for no other reason than it put
residents and council members into a different type of public relationship with each other. From the perspective of public dialogue, the discussion was significant because it signaled a willingness on the part of
the city leaders to shift away from a top-down decision-making
approach to one that encouraged broader participation and collaboration with community residents.

Two members of the PDC team facilitated the council discussion,
which revolved around the following two questions: What surprised you
most from what you heard? What would you want citizens to know
about the challenges you face as a city council member? In response to
the first question, the council expressed surprise that many of the participants at the meeting were unaware of basic city services and programs.
To their credit, the council expressed this "concern" in a nonjudgmental
way. For example, one council member responded by saying, "the message to me is that we have to work even harder at making people aware

of what we do." Another member simply pointed out that it was not necessary to form a public safety commission, as suggested by one of the dialogue-group presenters, because the city already had one.

In response to the second question, council members agreed that their biggest challenge was, as one member put it, doing what "is best for the community as a whole." The council went on to call for greater public participation in the decision-making process. "To expect change very rapidly is a quick fix or a band aid on a situation," one council member said. "To really solve problems and really improve the community takes the effort of the entire community." Another member said, "I think we have a council that's willing to take leadership . . . to have a process . . . but we can only introduce it. We need help. And that's the challenge . . . that we need to go to the community." By listening to the community and by encouraging citizen involvement in the decision-making process, the councils' response admirably demonstrated a collaborative approach to leadership.

Episode Six: Closing and Opening Possibilities (25 Minutes)

While the city council was engaged in their round table discussion, members of the PDC team collected the action plans from each of the table groups and gathered in a separate room to categorize and thematize the results. After the council concluded their discussion, a member of the PDC team briefly reviewed the results for the large group, which were displayed on the overhead projectors at the front of the room. The action plans generated for both cultural richness and community safety were similar, if not identical, to those generated by the dialogue groups and discussed earlier in this chapter. For example, the action plans for cultural richness focused on education and included community activities and cultural celebrations. Action plans for community safety centered on neighborhood activities, including references to Neighborhood Watch Programs and the Emergency Preparedness Program. Community policing was not specifically mentioned, but it was later added to the list at the request of one of the audience participants.

In terms of generating action plans and making decisions about them, the Town Hall Meeting included episodes that oscillated between opening up possibilities and narrowing choices. Having summarized the actions from the table discussions to a few key categories, the next turn in this episode involved opening the discussion to new perspectives and ideas. To accomplish this, a member of the PDC team asked participants to comment on the action plans posted on the overhead projectors and to make any additions they felt were necessary. Participants volunteered to speak using a microphone. The first response came from a participant who said that his group wanted community policing to be added to the list of action plans for community safety. From that point on, the discussion deviated considerably from the original question, and in one case moved into a topic area that extended well beyond the agenda for the meeting.

Turning Point

No one at the meeting up to this point had made any specific reference to the issue of Asian newcomers living in the city, or the cultural differences that were thought to exist between Chinese and white members of the community. That changed when the microphone was handed to a participant who proceeded to speak at some length about his experiences moving from Taiwan to Cupertino. The monologue was significant not only because the speaker directly acknowledged the problem, but because he did so in a way that was substantive, informative, and nonconfrontational.

He started by responding to the concern that Asian residents do not participate in the community and are taking over the city. "I heard a lot of comments that the Asian community or Asian owners don't participate," he said. "They're takers, not the givers." And yet when he was elected to the Cupertino School Board along with another Chinese male, he recalled that a local newspaper reported the event with a headline saying that a "dynasty" was "taking over Cupertino." The participants, hearing the contradiction in the story and the playful way in which the speaker presented it, laughed at the incident along with the speaker. In a more serious tone, he went on to say, "I mean we are accused of not coming out to serve, or to help, to participate. And then when we come out they say you are taking over Cupertino, which . . . doesn't feel quite well." From the perspective of the speaker, the double-bind situation (Watzlawick, Beavin, & Jackson, 1967) created by these mixed messages was similar, if not identical, to the one described by a Chinese woman during the focus-group interviews.

In discussing cultural differences, the speaker also resurrected the cultural pluralistic themes heard earlier in the meeting and throughout the dialogue-group discussions. To illustrate, the speaker told an amusing story about his first experience attending a PTA meeting and finding himself lost and confused in a maze of parliamentary rules and procedures:

> I heard a woman say "I move this, I move that." I was very puzzled because I saw she was sitting there. She was not moving anywhere. Why did she keep saying, "I move this, I move that?" And someone

would follow and say "I second that." And I was even more puzzled because I feel you don't have to be so humble. No one claimed to be the first, why do you have to be second?

Again the audience laughed and again the speaker followed with a more serious point:

And that's the culture difference. . . . I think there is a culture gap in between when we talk about diversity here. In the country where I come from the government purposely didn't try to give you democracy, because they knew if they give you democracy people will ask for power. So, we've never been trained that way, . . . Coming here you get all this different language barrier and all this format, all this democratic process. So, I thought it was like someone inside the door waving at people outside, "why don't you come inside and help?", and the people outside couldn't find the door. So that's the situation. I think the most important thing is we have to understand the culture gap and also the tolerance between each other. And that's my comment. Thanks.

By sharing his own personal experiences, the speaker encouraged the audience to treat the differences between Asians and whites as a product of culture, language, and political history. These differences create misunderstandings, or what the speaker refers to as a "cultural gap." The door metaphor powerfully illustrates this point. Cultural barriers are not like walls that must be torn down, they are more like doors that can opened if one is able to find the entrance. These comments were effective within the context of the public dialogue event. The speaker was able to address the potentially threatening topic appreciatively, in a way that promoted intercultural understanding without being polarizing or antagonistic.

Turning Point

A final turning point occurred at the very end of the forum, 10 minutes before it was scheduled to conclude. Two women from an environmental activist group voiced strong opposition against a local cement company and its plans to initiate a tire-burning program. The first speaker said that the company has "put a tremendous burden on the community . . . and with burning tires it [the burden] goes up. . . . I'm concerned that we need to act as a community to not let them get a permit to burn tires." The second speaker followed by urging the audience to contact their environmental group to obtain information and sign petitions against the tire-burning plan. A spokesperson from the cement company responded immediately by defending the company's practices. He cited evidence that the results of a tire-burning test fell "within current air regulations." He gave testimony from the "Bay Area manager of toxicology" that the results were "clearly insignificant." He went on to say that "there is a group, and certainly they're here to be heard, that are asking us to examine it further and we have." He concluded by promising that the company would continue to "examine the risks" associated with the tire-burning program.

This exchange, which clearly followed a debate, attack-counterattack pattern, was more adversarial than dialogic. The environmental group attacked the cement company, who in turn responded by defending their actions and justifying their position. It was also clear that the conflict had sharp edges: it had been formulated well in advance, argumentative battle lines were established, and the disputants recognized each other as adversaries. Their exchange at the Town Hall Meeting simply reproduced the pattern that was already in place. Not surprisingly, the environmental activists and the company spokesperson sat at different tables. Because of the structure of the meeting and the focus on cultural richness and community safety, the activists were not able to voice their opposition in the large-group session until the very end of the meeting, with only minutes left. Once they did, the company spokesperson was obligated to respond; it was the reason he attended the meeting.

The incident was a turning point not only because it introduced an entirely different topic, but because it provided a counter-example to the kind of communication that had previously taken place and that we, the PDC, were trying to facilitate. Had the incident come earlier in the meeting there might have been time to respond in a way that called attention to the form and pattern of the conflict. The best that we could do within the limited time constraints, however, was to integrate the conflict into the larger discussion. A member of the PDC team accomplished this by summarizing the conflict around a shared community vision called "environmental safety."

Episode Seven: Completing the Circle (5 Minutes)

In an attempt to provide closure to the meeting, a member of the PDC team presented a 50-page summary of the focus-group and dialogue-group discussions to the city manager and each of the council members. This gesture was both symbolic and substantive. Symbolically, the summary document represented the voices of the community, with the PDC acting as mediator and narrator in bringing those voices to the attention of city officials. When city officials accepted the summary they were, in a sense, formally acknowledging what community members had said. The summary was also substantive, of course, in that it contained a written account of the concerns, visions, and action plans generated by community residents.

To end the meeting, participants were given a sheet of paper, titled "continuing the conversation," and asked if they wanted to be involved in the project, and if so to give contact information so that they could be notified about future meetings and events. City leaders used the list to gauge community interest in the project and to build a database of project participants.

EVALUATING THE TOWN HALL MEETING

The PDC arranged to have a group of nine outside consultants observe, critique, and respond to the Town Hall Meeting. Consultants were recruited based on their familiarity with the project and/or the work of the PDC, as well as their ability to render critical evaluations from multiple perspectives. The consultant group included public administrators, communication researchers and teachers, college administrators, and communication practitioners. The consultants provided candid and constructive criticism to the PDC in two face-to-face meetings following the Town Hall event. We found their comments to be extremely useful, and we were able to incorporate some of what we learned into subsequent phases of the project.

Two particular criticisms stood out, in part because the consultants, as well as some of the Cupertino residents who participated in the Town Hall Meeting, consistently identified them. The first criticism was that the meeting did not address some of the underlying feelings of frustration, hostility, and conflict that existed below the surface of the cultural richness issue. Several of the consultants suggested that the structure and format of the forum suppressed conflict and precluded people from talking about potentially contentious topics. As evidence, one of consultants noted that participants at his table made a collective decision not to bring up the issue of non-English signage during the large-group report, even though several people in the small group voiced strong opinions about it. Another consultant observed that the conversation at her table included several candid comments about cultural diversity that were not shared in the large-group context.

Some community residents made similar observations, noting that the meeting did not get at the "real issues." For example, one resident who participated in both Phase I and II of the project said that the focus-group interviews were the "most valuable" because "people were encouraged to bring up things they saw as problems." By comparison, he felt that there was an effort at the Town Hall Meeting "to smooth things over" and "not offend anyone." Like some other residents who attended the meeting, he criticized the use of the term "cultural richness" for producing similar effects. "People are really concerned about how this [Asian immigration] is going . . . it's making people upset. That's not the same as saying it has cultural richness. Cultural richness is very politically correct . . . and doesn't make any problems. Hardly anyone is against cultural richness." Another resident told us that discussing the really difficult aspects of Asian immigration is like "lancing a boil." "It's going to be difficult and uncomfortable for some people," he said, "but it's something that has to be done for the good of the community. I didn't see any of that happening at the Town Hall Meeting."

In responding to this criticism, it is important to remember that the Town Hall Meeting was intentionally structured to create a public space in which residents felt "safe" to discuss cultural and demographic changes in their city. Remember that people said they were threatened by the issue and generally avoided talking about it in public. In order to create a nonthreatening environment, we felt it necessary to design a public context that avoided calling forth adversarial patterns of conflict. Although we certainly did not intend to suppress the honest airing of issues, we were convinced that a level of comfort and trust needed to be established for residents to dialogically engage the difficult issues of Asian immigration and cultural change. The fact that some of these "difficult" issues did indeed surface during the table discussions suggests that at least some of the conditions for public dialogue were met, even though they were limited to the small-group context. Moving this process into a large public forum takes time to develop; it cannot be rushed.

Box 4.5. The Facilitators Learn New Skills

The Town Hall Meeting was an important event in the development of the PDC. Among other things, it demonstrated that we could successfully design and execute a large public dialogue event. Going into the project most of us were confident that we could successfully facilitate small-group discussions on sensitive and controversial issues using the microskills of public dialogue. Few of us, however, had any experience working with large groups. Whatever uncertainties some of us might have harbored before the meeting quickly vanished once it was over. It was not a perfect event, as the criticisms described here indicate. On the whole, however, those of us in the PDC were pleased with our efforts and anxious to work again on another large-group event.

A second, related criticism concerned the outcome of the meeting and the fact that a specific action plan did not emerge with a clear consensus and commitment. One of the consultants, for example, said that "there will be people that will wonder if the city is serious about this: 'is this just for show, is this just a PR deal to tell us how great of a community Cupertino is, or is the city really serious about doing something?' Based on this meeting it's difficult to tell." Several community residents expressed similar concerns, claiming that the meeting produced "a lot of talk but no action." In regard to this criticism, we view the Town Hall Meeting as "beginning" the hard work of doing public dialogue. We think it is critical to engage maximum participation in the decision-making process before coming to closure on any given action or policy plan. Similarly, it is important to recognize that the meeting was the first community-wide event in what we hoped would be series of on-going events. By starting small and proceeding slowly in incremental steps we hoped to build interest in the process and trust among the various stakeholders in the community. With more participation there would be greater commitment and buy-in for the decisions and outcomes that developed out of the public dialogue process.

Both of the criticisms just described point to the notion that the Town Hall Meeting was structured to disrupt undesirable patterns of conflict and to create the conditions for public dialogue and deliberation. Putting the really difficult issues on the agenda at the outset and pushing the community toward a final decision at this point would have been premature. As Ellinor and Gerard (1998) state, fostering dialogue in organizations and communities involves careful thought and considerable planning:

> Dialogue represents a significant shift in the way we communicate with one another. Trying to move too fast can provoke a response that is not unlike indigestion—you may even get "thrown up." Injecting dialogue in too many places at once or taking on a project that the group/organization isn't ready for will be counterproductive. Keep your focus on identifying opportunities where it would be of value for people to talk more openly about what is important. Then be ready to support whatever next steps emerge. Dialogue is based on inviting people to move to deeper levels of conversation, to expand their thinking and skills. You can't push people to listen more deeply or to be more curious. Think strategically about what small steps will create opportunities for people to derive value and you will build sufficient momentum. (p. 226)

LOOKING BACK-LOOKING FORWARD

Two general conclusions follow from the various activities comprising Phase II. First, the communication processes involved in the dialogue-group discussions, intergenerational interviews, and the Town Hall Meeting provided opportunities for residents to talk about the issues related to Asian immigration and demographic changes in the city. What was once considered to be an undiscussible topic was brought out into the open and became part of hundreds of conversations throughout the city. This is not to suggest that the issue was resolved. In fact, as the issue moved into the public domain, more and more people came forward to express their views and opinions. So instead of closing the issue down, the project actually created more complexity by eliciting a wider array of opinions and perspectives.

Second, the content of the discussions throughout Phase II revealed a preference to frame diversity within a cultural pluralistic model as opposed to an institutional racism model. The dynamics of Asian immigration in Cupertino made it difficult to claim that the Chinese newcomers were oppressed or economically disadvantaged by existing structural arrangements. As a result, there was little motivation for action plans that redistributed power and resources to minority groups or less privileged members of the community, an approach that would be in keeping with models of institutional racism. What we heard instead was a great deal of talk about the need for educational activities that promote cultural understanding and knowledge. Consistent with the pluralistic model, participants focused on cultural celebrations, intercultural interaction, and cultural information dissemination as a way of learning about the cultural groups who live in the city. It is important to note that both pluralistic and critical models of diversity are amenable to public dialogue processes. Cultural pluralistic models, however, were more easily integrated into the Cupertino Project and the work of the PDC because they approach cultural diversity first and foremost from a communication perspective, as opposed to an economic, political, or historical perspective.

As the Cupertino Project unfolded the difficult issues that were submerged during the Town Hall Meeting were openly addressed and discussed in a variety of public meetings. It is possible to trace the success of these later efforts to the work completed here in Phase II. We are convinced that had we not carefully nurtured and protected public dialogue at this stage of the process, it would not have taken root and grow as it did. At the same time, we listened carefully to the outside consultants and community residents who said that the activities and techniques used in Phase II suppressed conflict and obstructed genuine disagreement.

What the PDC learned from this feedback and from our own critical reflections was that we overestimated our responsibility. By controlling the process and structuring events to the extent that we did, we failed to fully enlist others in the process. And by failing to fully enlist others we gave them tacit permission not to take full decision-making responsibility. The public dialogue process was fragile at this point in the project, in part, because it was not jointly owned. For better or worse, the PDC took primary ownership responsibility. At the time this seemed like a natural and logical thing for us to do. We were, after all, the ones who initiated the process. To gain entry we touted our various credentials in public communication. To establish ongoing credibility we designed events and facilitated discussions. As a result, city leaders and community residents looked to us as the "experts," and we more or less obliged them by assuming that role.

As the project unfolded we attempted to move ourselves out of the expert position by working with others to design the project and to build capacities in public dialogue. By sharing more responsibility for the process and by teaching communication skills to others we found that the community was in a much better position to engage the really difficult aspects of the cultural diversity issue.

NOTES

1. In their review of 12 large-group intervention methods, Bunker and Alban (1997) found that the methods varied considerably in terms of how many participants they could accommodate. Future Search, for example, can handle 150 people successfully, although 70 to 80 seems to be a more ideal number. Open Space technology disregards numbers all together and works off the principle that "whoever comes is the right people." Although exact numbers are not important, we have found that large public dialogues work best with 50 to 100 people. Anything much higher is too unwieldy and anything lower is not usually representative of the stakeholders in the community.

2. The Town Hall Meeting, like the dialogue-group discussions and intergenerational interviews, covered both the cultural richness and community safety topics in roughly equal proportion. The analysis of episodes and turning points as described here, however, is focused exclusively on the cultural richness issue.

3. Although the focus-group discussions from Phase I were summarized at the beginning of the Town Hall Meeting, no one from any of the groups was asked to officially report at the meeting because of the confidential nature of those discussions.

5

WORKING THROUGH
CITY LEADERS

This chapter is organized around the three principle activities that comprised Phase III of the Cupertino Project. The first two activities were designed to give voice to the members of the Cupertino city council and to include them more directly in the project. The third activity, and the one given the most attention in this chapter, consisted of a large Training and Team Building Program for community leaders in Cupertino. The primary organizing theme of this chapter is how the PDC worked with city officials and community leaders to refine and extend the concerns, visions, and action plans identified by residents in Phases I and II.

GOALS AND PURPOSES OF PHASE III

WORKING WITH THE CTY COUNCIL

In the Public Education model of decision making, leaders adopt the conventional top-down method for winning public support. The leader-

ship makes decisions, assesses public opinion, and then wages a persua-
sive campaign to convince the public to go along with the decisions
(Yankelovich, 1991). The model of public dialogue used in the Cupertino
Project rejects this approach by giving the public greater decision-making power. This was clearly evident during the first two phases of the
project in which community residents took the initiative in identifying
concerns, visions, and action plans. Even at the Town Hall Meeting,
where the council publicly participated in the project for the first time,
their response was to simply acknowledge that they had indeed heard
what residents had said.

Phase III was designed to involve the council at a deeper level of
engagement. It was important that the context for this engagement not
be defensive. That is, the council should not feel as though they were
being criticized for shirking their responsibility or, worse yet, that they
were expected to somehow arrive at the solution to the problem. The
context, as we envisioned it, would be one of inviting the council into a
conversation with residents. We agree with Ellinor and Gerard (1998)
that for a dialogue project like this one to have lasting impact within a
community or organization, leadership must demonstrate an on-going
commitment to share decision-making responsibilities. To that end, the
council was asked to find ways of working together with residents to
solve community problems and concerns.[1]

The work we did to bring elected officials into a collaborative
decision-making relationship with citizens can also be construed as an
attempt to align local government with the principles and practices of
participatory democracy. Barber (1984, 1998) notes that even though
government itself is often an obstacle to a strong democratic civil society, it is essential nevertheless in helping to facilitate positive solutions.[2]
According to Barber (1998),

> To re-create civil society on the model of strong democracy does not
> entail a novel civic architecture . . . civil society requires us to recon-
> ceptualize and reposition the institutions already in place. Where a
> civic sector already exists, we must deploy strategies and laws to
> give it room to grow and flourish. Where it exists only as an ideal,
> we must suggest new strategies that help to seed civic institutions
> and then help them to grow. (p. 67)

The activities in Phase III demonstrate how elected officials and
others involved in Cupertino's city government worked within existing
institutional structures to promote a strong, participatory form of
democracy. Their involvement provides a practical demonstration for
how city government can be responsive to the needs of the community
and the contingencies of public dialogue.

SHARING RESPONSIBILITY FOR THE PROCESS

During Phase III a subtle shift occurred in the working relationship among the PDC, elected officials, and community residents. Instead of assuming most of the responsibility for organizing events and facilitating activities, as we did during the first two phases of the project, the PDC became much better at practicing community-based action research and sharing responsibility for the dialogue process.[3] According to Stringer (1996):

> As facilitators assist participants in organizing and implementing activities, they should consciously enact the key concepts and principles of community-based action research, constantly providing participants with information about what is happening, maintaining positive working relationships, and including all stakeholders as active participants in planning and decision-making activities. (p. 134)

By sharing responsibility, elected officials and community residents became more deeply involved in the project. To illustrate this point, community members, not the PDC, initiated most of the activities in Phase III. As the project unfolded the PDC continually searched for ways of disseminating public-dialogue sensibilities and skills throughout the community. These efforts to institutionalize new patterns of public communication became the primary focus of Phase IV of the project and are covered more fully in the next chapter.

ADDRESSING DIFFICULT ISSUES

Community residents, city leaders, and the consultants at the Town Hall Meeting all agreed that the more serious conflictual issues underlying cultural diversity needed to be brought to the surface. These issues were addressed in a large-group setting for the first time in Phase III at a two-day Training and Team Building Program. Importantly, the topics were introduced within the context of learning the principles and skills of public dialogue. As participants practiced dialogic ways of communicating they were simultaneously dealing with such volatile issues as the Chinese Little League, non-English signs, and the potential backlash by whites against Asian members of the community. The event represented a breakthrough in the Cupertino Project in that it established a context that encouraged community residents to publicly discuss difficult and controversial topics.

STRATEGIES FOR IMPLEMENTING ACTION PLANS

Throughout Phase III the PDC continued to organize discussions and design activities using the CVA model. Although this created a certain level of redundancy, we felt it was important to provide on-going opportunities for participants, especially those new to the project, to refine, modify, and add to the concerns, visions, and action plans previously identified in Phases I and II. In addition to expanding the parameters of the CVA model, participants in Phase III were also encouraged to actually choose action plans and to begin developing specific strategies for implementing them. By the end of Phase III a number of action plans were selected, each of which was addressed in one form or another in Phase IV of the project.

CITY COUNCIL INTERVIEWS

The first activity of Phase III involved interviewing the five Cupertino city council members. To start this process, a senior member of the PDC conducted separate, in-depth interviews with each of the five council members approximately three weeks after the Town Hall meeting. The interviews covered both cultural diversity and community safety issues. Council members were asked in an open-ended fashion to comment on their concerns, visions, and action plans for each of the issues. The PDC member summarized the interviews and gave copies to the individual council members for corrections. The revised interviews were then given to all members of the council a week later. The interviews were intended to be an internal document for the council to use at a future council team-building meeting. In order to encourage maximum candor, it was agreed that the interviews would not be made available to the public or used for official city business.

After the final interviews were distributed, the PDC member who conducted the interviews offered the following three observations to the council, each of which was expressed through appreciative language. First, he noted how impressed he was "by the seriousness of purpose" and "fund of knowledge" that each of the council members brought to their work. Second, he noted that there were significant "differences" among the council concerning their views of cultural richness and community safety. These "differences offer a rich array of possibilities for you to explore and develop." Third, he expressed curiosity about the relationship between each of the council's views and the views of residents who participated in Phases I and II of the project. "There are some issues about which you have quite different opinions; some issues which the community seems to feel are more crucial than you do; and some which you nominate as more important than do members of the community."

The interviews served a number of important functions. First, they provided the first opportunity for the council to talk directly and candidly about cultural richness and community safety. Although the council surely had many different kinds of conversations about these issues in the past, it was unlikely that they had ever been formally interviewed in this way and for this purpose. Second, they provided an initial indication of how the views of the council members, both individually and collectively, coordinated with each other and with the citizen participants in Phases I and II. Third, they provided a springboard for the second major activity of Phase II.

CITY COUNCIL TEAM BUILDING AND ISSUE FORMATION MEETING

A day-long City Council Team Building and Issue Formation meeting was held a few weeks after copies of interviews were distributed to each of the council members. It was held on a Saturday at an off-site location owned by the city, in part, to create a more informal, retreat-like atmosphere. The stated purpose of the meeting was to assist the council in formulating a response to the community and what they heard citizens saying in Phases I and II of the project. The PDC developed the agenda for the meeting and facilitated the discussion. As part of our facilitation, the PDC also assumed the role of the community. This involved summarizing to the council what was said in the focus groups, dialogue groups, and intergenerational interviews, and, in some cases, actually speaking for a particular individual or group in the community.

RECONSTRUCTING A HISTORY OF CULTURAL DIVERSITY

The meeting started with an activity called a Timeline, or what Stringer (1996) refers to as "temporal mapping." The five council members were paired off, with the city manager serving as the sixth member. Each dyad was instructed to identify what they perceived as the significant events shaping the community's understanding of cultural diversity and to locate these events temporally within an on-going sequence of events. Each dyad then wrote or drew out their cultural richness timeline on a large piece of butcher paper taped to the wall. The idea here was for the council to be as creative as possible in presenting their timeline and to introduce an element of playfulness into the activity. To that end, the

PDC facilitators encouraged the council to use images, figures, and pictures, as well as words. Each dyad was also given a variety of different colored markers to use. As the dyads presented their timelines to the whole group, it became readily obvious that there were differences and similarities in the narrative flow of events. This led to a wide-ranging discussion among the council concerning the nature of particular events and how they fit together.

The theoretical position supporting the timeline activity is based on the assumption that "remembering" and "forgetting" are inherently social activities carried out through social practices (Middleton & Edwards, 1990). When people join together to remember past events, what is recalled is dependent on the context of the recollection and the ways in which those present talk about the past. As such, remembering is more than the product of each person's individual memory. For example, at the Council Team Building Meeting events long since forgotten by some members were brought back into focus by other members. In other cases, discrepancies in the timelines led some of the members to reinterpret events differently than they had originally remembered them. This type of activity not only encourages a collective remembering of the past, it also establishes a basis for constructing the future. According to Middleton and Edwards (1990), "in the contest for varying accounts of shared experiences, people reinterpret and discover features of the past that become the context and content for what they will jointly recall and commemorate on future occasions" (p. 7).

The PDC facilitators who moderated the discussion of the timeline activity were less concerned with the accuracy of events and more interested in working with the council to explore the underlying narrative flow of the timelines. The goal was to focus attention on recurring features and dissimilarities as a way of assisting the council in building a framework for interpreting the community's concerns with cultural diversity. Perhaps the most striking conclusion was that all of the dyads treated the issue as series of positive and negative events, indicating that from the council's perspective at least, cultural diversity in Cupertino was a product of both constructive and destructive forces. Interestingly, there was little overlap among the dyads in terms of the specific events recalled. So although the narrative flow of the timelines was similar, the content differed substantially.

THE COUNCIL'S VIEW OF CULTURAL DIVERSITY

As the dyads completed presentation of their timelines, discussion turned to the present situation. Given the variety of events recalled from the past, it came as no surprise that the current situation was characterized by difference and complexity. Specifically, the view of cultural diversity that emerged from the council's discussion revolved around three related levels, each of which was thought to exist in dialectical tension with the others. *Cultural identity* refers to events, programs, and activities that enable ethnic groups to maintain a sense of individuality and distinctiveness, such as the Chinese language school and the Chinese Little League Baseball program. *Cultural difference* refers to the experiences and day-to-day encounters people have with cultures different from their own. Some of the examples mentioned here included a conversation between two neighbors from different ethnic backgrounds and reading an article about a particular cultural group in one of the local newspapers. *Common ground* refers to events, programs, and activities that create shared values among members of the community. Examples given included the city's Emergency Preparedness Program and the annual 4th of July celebration. PDC facilitators diagrammed the council's vision (see Figure 5.1) and summarized it back to them at the team building meeting in an attempt to create a common set of understandings about the situation.

RESPONDING TO THE COMMUNITY

Having reconstructed the past and characterized the current situation, the council then considered what the next steps in the sequence should be. In making this transition from past to present to future, the PDC facilitators encouraged the council to see how their response to the community was itself an event in an on-going series of events. Moreover, whatever response the council chose to make would further shape cul-

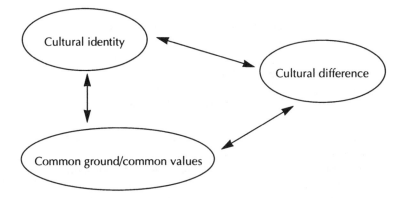

Figure 5.1. The city council's vision of cultural diversity

tural diversity issues in the community, much in the same way that past events shaped the current situation. Out of this discussion the council generated nine action plans. Six of the plans focused on cultural diversity; three centered on community safety (see Table 5.1 for the list of action plans). Council members were careful to note that these were not "official" recommendations because they had not gone through a formal hearing process and vote.

As the council reviewed their action plans, a number of common characteristics were noted. First, the action plans were inclusive of all the groups in the community. Second, they were based in both bottom-up and top-down processes. Third, they focused on local organizations and activities, some of which were already in place. Fourth, they were consistent with, and in some cases identical to, the plans offered by residents during Phase II of the project. In fact, each of the council's plans was mentioned either directly or indirectly in either the dialogue groups or Town Hall Meeting. Additional follow-up discussion revealed that the action plans were weighted heavily toward common ground and unity rather than cultural identity and cultural difference. Put differently, the council's plans called for community residents to work together on civic projects that benefited the whole community, as opposed to events that highlighted a particular cultural group or the differences between cultural groups.

Table 5.1. The Council's Action Plans.

1.	Use training sessions to get input into the next steps of the project (this action item was the impetus for a two-day training and team building program described later)
2.	Expand the city's annual Fourth of July celebration to include a more explicit multicultural component
3.	Develop a community-wide garage sale that might tie into a neighborhood block party program
4.	Have a welcome wagon committee that would distribute materials and establish relationships with new residents
5.	Develop an emergency preparedness program
6.	Expand the Chamber of Commerce's Summer Arts and Wine Festival to include a more explicit multicultural component
7.	Create a Cupertino Community Leadership Council to serve as an advisory group and to train future city leaders
8.	Develop a neighborhood safety fair, perhaps sponsored by the Public Safety Commission
9.	Increase public safety information about community safety

In terms of a specific response to the community, the council decided that their contribution to the project should come in the form of a training and team building program for community leaders (see council's first action in Table 5.1). The last part of the Council's Team Building meeting was thus spent planning for this community-wide event. The PDC worked with the council to develop a set of goals and outcomes for the meeting, including decisions about who should attend, how participants would be contacted, and what role the council would play. A core theme emerging from this discussion was the need to build social capital and communication networks in the city. By identifying community leaders and linking them together in a public communication skills training session, the council sought to create an on-going pool of resource people for managing the city's cultural diversity.

TRAINING AND TEAM BUILDING PROGRAM

The Training and Team Building Program was a two-day event, beginning on a Friday afternoon and ending on Saturday. Over 300 people were identified by the council members and sent invitations through the city manager's office. More than 100 attended. Similar to the Town Hall Meeting, participants were seated approximately eight to a table. These tables served as the work units for the meeting. Unlike the Town Hall Meeting, a PDC facilitator was assigned to each table in order to help guide the group through the various exercises and activities. We also chose to meet on the De Anza College campus instead of the Quinlan Center, where the Town Hall Meeting was held. This location was selected as a way of highlighting the training component of the team building program and the links that exist between learning institutions, civic organizations, and city government.

EPISODES AND TURNING POINTS IN THE TRAINING PROGRAM

Similar to the analysis of the Town Hall Meeting in Chapter 4, the Training Program is described in terms of nine episodes and several related turning points. As previously noted, episodes punctuate the meeting into a series of distinct segments; they are organized sequentially to reflect the development of the Training Program and how it evolved over the two-day period. Turning points refer to specific communication acts that altered the nature, course, and direction of the Training Program and/or the Cupertino Project in some meaningful and significant way.

Episode One: Demonstrating Collaborative Leadership (15 Minutes)

Although it was important for the council to take a visible leadership role at the Training Program, it was critical that they not be viewed as controlling the agenda or the meeting. Consistent with the principles of public dialogue, the council demonstrated collaborative leadership throughout the Training Program. This collaborative orientation, which reinforced the council's performance at the Town Hall Meeting, was established at the outset, before the event even began. For example, in the initial invitation letter sent to participants the council emphasized the need to "increase citizen participation in policy-making decisions" and to "enlarge citizens' influence in shaping the future direction of the city." The council member who was serving as Mayor at the time, John Bautista, expanded on these points in his opening remarks at the Training Program.[4]

Turning Point

The mayor's opening remarks were significant because they helped create a context of shared responsibility, cooperation, and collaborative leadership. To begin, he informed participants that the council was sponsoring the meeting as part of the city's on-going efforts to address issues of cultural change and community safety. This was a subtle yet significant marker in the evolution of the Cupertino Project and the council's role in it. Up to this point, primary responsibility for the dialogue process rested with the PDC, whereas community residents took responsibility for generating content in terms of concerns, visions, and action plans. Having the council step in and assume some of these responsibilities demonstrated their commitment to the project and to the principles of public participation. The mayor also emphasized the need for participants at the meeting to create networks and relationships among themselves and with other leaders in the community. Furthermore, this appeal was framed within the larger context of the Cupertino Project, which the mayor described as a "unique" and "innovative experiment" in public communication.

The mayor concluded his opening remarks by offering his own opinions about the Cupertino Project:

> I would just like to mention that I think we are really embarking on something new in this city. With the cooperation of the Public Dialogue Consortium . . . we are finding new channels of communication in the city. I think we are doing something really different from other cities. We are actually taking steps to build networks between community leaders, and I'm not just talking about council

members and leaders of organizations. . . . So this is a very grass roots type network of individuals . . . and I think this is what democracy is all about and its also what building community spirit and fostering broad community goals is all about.

It should also be noted that each of the five council members sat at separate tables and participated equally with other community residents throughout the two-day Training Program. This further reinforced the collaborative orientation of the council in regard to working with community members.

Box 5.1. Leaders are Citizens Too

Dialogue ought to provide opportunities for leaders to "take off their official hats" and participate along with everyone else as everyday citizens.
—Michael Chang, Cupertino city council member

Episode Two: Creating a Learning Context (15 Minutes)

Immediately following the mayor's opening statement, two PDC members provided a brief summary of Phases I and II of the project and introduced the objectives and agenda for the meeting. Four objectives were listed: (a) get to know other community leaders, (b) learn communication skills for discussing difficult community issues, (c) learn about the city council's action plans for cultural richness and community safety, and (d) respond to the council's action plans and decide the next steps in the process.

Episode Three: Mess Mapping Activity (1 Hour)

The first formal exercise of the meeting consisted of a mess mapping activity, or what is sometimes referred to as concept mapping (Stringer, 1996). It was designed to help participants recognize that cultural richness in Cupertino is shaped through a complex system of events, circumstances, and personal experiences. Participants were first asked to think of a concern they have regarding cultural richness and to explain why the concern is important to them based on their own personal experiences. They were next asked to identify one action plan that would address their concern. As each person at the table discussed their concerns and actions, the PDC facilitators diagrammed their responses on a large piece of paper. This enabled participants to visualize the variety of perspectives that go into defining cultural richness.

The "mess map" was arranged so that each person's concern was written in a large circle, with each action plan diagrammed as a single spoke connected to the circle. An example of a mess map from the Training and Team Building Program is provided in Figure 5.2. Notice the range of concerns identified in the circle and the corresponding action plans emanating from them. Notice too how some of the concerns and actions overlap with one another, depicted by connecting circles and lines, whereas others remain distinct and separate. Finally, there was little attempt to draw the diagrams in a neat and orderly fashion. The idea behind this "messiness" was to show, through visual imagery, the complexity of the cultural richness issue.

Turning Point

Among other things, the mess mapping activity provided an opportunity to address the most sensitive concerns and delineate the more serious problems with cultural diversity in Cupertino. In setting up the mess

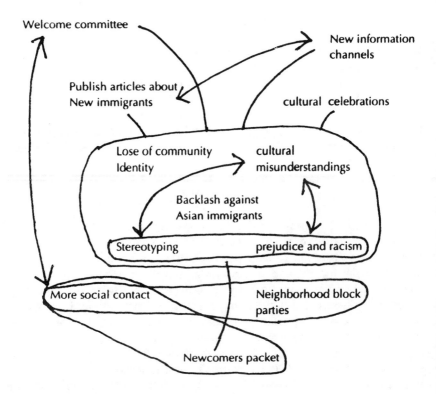

Figure 5.2. Example of a mess map

mapping activity, a member of the PDC team explicitly acknowledged some of these difficult topics. "When talking about issues of cultural richness," he said, "participants . . . talked about Cupertino's lack of sensitivity toward . . . recent immigrants, the presence of monolingual signs, newcomers feeling unwelcome to Cupertino, and the implications of a Chinese Little League." The speaker also acknowledged the challenges some people face in discussing their concerns:

> There are also a number of factors that influence our ability to talk about these issues. For example, a theme that emerged from earlier conversations was that people felt excluded and not invited to participate in such conversations. Some expressed fear that simply talking about the issues of cultural diversity may lead to polarized and competitive conversations. Others voiced concerns that if they raise these issues they may be perceived as being "politically incorrect" and are open to charges of being racist.

This marked the first time in the Cupertino Project that these particular concerns and problems were addressed openly at a large public event. The significance of this was not simply that the speaker articulated the concerns, but that he did so within a context designed to foster awareness and critical reflection. In the focus-group interviews participants were asked to express their concerns, nothing more or nothing less. The context of the mess mapping activity differed substantially in that participants' concerns were situated within a complex system of personal experiences and action plans. In this way, the activity enabled potentially difficult problems to surface in ways that extended peoples' understanding of the situation. This focus on addressing difficult issues within a learning context continued throughout the two-day Training Program.

Episode Four: Learning Conflict Styles (1 Hour)

The next activity entailed teaching participants different communication styles for handling conflict. A PDC member first described a standard model of communication and conflict composed of four styles: avoidance, confrontation, accommodation, and dialogue. Two other PDC members then demonstrated the first three styles in separate role-play scenarios. In each of the scenarios, the two conversants, a white male and Asian female, discussed the topic of the Chinese Little League in Cupertino. In one role play they discussed the topic using the avoidance style, in another role play they talked about it using the competitive style, and in the third they used the accommodation style.

The issue of the Chinese Little League, previously identified as a concern by focus-group participants in Phase I of the project, was pur-

Box 5.2. Beyond "Happy" Talk: A New Cross Cultural
Experience

Before the Training Program I had many casual conversations
with white people, but not about issues or problems. Mostly
we talked about happy things. But at the Training Program I
talked with non-Asians for the first time about issues and
community problems, like the Chinese stores and how they
have signs in Chinese. And I was able to tell the others in my
group that some of these people are actually afraid to speak
to others in English. I told them that inside they are scared
themselves. Talking to others about these things was a new
experience for me.
—Ann Woo, Cupertino resident and 5Cs member

posefully selected. Perhaps because it was fueled by a perception of the
Chinese community as exclusionary and separate from the rest of
Cupertino, it was defined by community members as a difficult and
potentially volatile issue. Using the Chinese Little League as the primary
topic in the role-play scenarios not only demonstrated that the issue
could be talked about in public, but that it was possible to talk about it
in more than one way. A critical point here was to draw attention to the
different forms of communication and styles of conflict management for
discussing controversial community issues. Additionally, the demonstration showed that the conflict styles are not equally effective in managing social conflict. A conversation that follows an avoidance pattern,
for example, produces something quite different from one built on competition or confrontation.

In the next part of the exercise participants were given an opportunity to role play the avoidance, competitive, and accommodating conflict styles (the dialogic style was addressed later in a separate exercise).
Participants at each table were assigned one of the three conflict styles
and coached to role play that style in interaction with the others at their
table. The specific role-play task called for each group to come to a decision by choosing one of the action plans from the mess mapping activity.
The purpose behind this activity was to let participants experience, from
a first-person position (Pearce, 1994), what it feels like to enact one of the
styles. Additionally, we wanted participants to assess the influence that
each of the styles has, both individually and in combination, on the quality of the conversation. Not surprisingly, participants found the role-play
conversation to be less than satisfying, both in terms of the how their
group made their decision as well as the specific action plan selected.

Episode Five: Learning Public Dialogue (2 Hours)

The remainder of the Friday afternoon session was organized around two interrelated activities designed to teach participants the principles and skills of public dialogue. In the first activity, two PDC members performed a role-play demonstration of the dialogic style of conflict, again focusing on the topic of the Chinese Little League. After the demonstration, participants were given a copy of the dialogue role-play script and asked to identify specific points in the conversation that made it a dialogue rather than some other form of communication. The purpose of this activity was to help participants become familiar with the characteristics of dialogue and to enable them to identify how these characteristics are played out in an actual conversation (see Table 5.2). As indicated in the directions, the activity required careful attention to the details of the conversation and the recognition that the seeds of dialogue are contained in specific words, actions, and phrases.

Table 5.2. Dialogue Script.

The purpose of this role play is to demonstrate specific communication actions that are characteristic of dialogue. These include:

- Staying in the tension between standing one's own ground (or holding one's own position) and being open to the other
- Using descriptions and nonverbal behaviors that express trust and respect
- Showing the other that they have been understood

In the dialogue that follows, Rita (R) and Michael (M) are Cupertino residents. Rita is a Chinese American and Michael is a white American. As you read through the following dialogue, identify specific words and phrases that are indicative of the three characteristics identified above.

R: Hi! remember me?

M: Sure! We met at the Town Hall Meeting in November. How are you?

R: Fine thanks. Do you have a time to talk for a minute?

M: Sure, what's up?

R: At the Town Hall Meeting you said some strong things about the Asian community and I'd like to understand them better.

M: I do have strong opinions on the subject. What specifically do you have in mind?

R: I was really uncomfortable when you said that monolingual signs should be made illegal and that the Chinese Little League should be disbanded.

M: Well that's what I think! I'm sorry if you are uncomfortable with that but I have the right to express my opinion.

Table 5.2. Dialogue Script. (con't)

R:	Of course you do. In fact, I'm glad you talked so openly. A lot of people who feel the way you do wouldn't say so in front of an Asian American. But I'd like to understand the reasons for your opinions—if you don't mind explaining them to me.
M:	Well, I'll try. I've lived in Cupertino for a long time but sometimes I feel like a foreigner because I can't read the sign on the store.
R:	So are you feeling that the community is changing in a way that excludes you?
M:	Yeah. Since I don't know what the sign says, I don't feel welcome.
R:	Yeah, I think I understand that. I also think that a lot of new immigrants might feel excluded too if they see English-only signs, even though English is the standard language.
M:	Maybe . . . but I just don't want to feel like I'm a stranger in my own community.
R:	I bet there are other residents who feel that way too. What are some things that you'd like to see happen so that people feel less excluded?
M:	I guess I just don't want to see the city divided between "us" and "them."
R:	So monolingual signs are one way that you see a division between "us" and "them."
M:	Yeah. I also feel this way about Chinese Little League.
R:	Say more about that.
M:	My nephew plays little league in Cupertino. Since he's been playing, I've learned about Chinese-only little league. It really bothers me to know that he—or my own kids—can't play in this little league because they're not Chinese. That's discrimination, and it divides the community.
R:	I think I can really understand how that can seem like discrimination, especially if you're the kid who wants to play on the team. But I think there are good reasons for the Chinese Little League.
M:	Please tell me . . . I'd like to hear them.
R:	My brother plays in Chinese Little League and I'm glad he does. When we moved to Cupertino he wanted to play the American game with the American kids, but he was intimidated. He didn't know the rules or have the right equipment. The whole time he was growing up he never even played baseball like most of the other kids who grow up here. So he dropped out until he found Chinese Little League. He's much happier now; he likes participating in team sports and I don't think he would if it wasn't for the League.
R:	So you think the Chinese Little League is the only way for him to be active in sports?
M:	Well, it's the only way for him to play baseball. He could play soccer—he's probably better at it than he is at baseball, but he wants to play the American game.

Table 5.2. Dialogue Script. (con't)

R:	So in a strange sense, the Chinese Little League is a way for him to act like an American; to fit in even though it's only for Chinese.
M:	Yeah, and there's a kind of paradox in that. On the one hand, those of us who have recently moved to Cupertino want to preserve our culture and make it a part of the city. At the 4th of July celebration last year one of the speakers made the point that America is rich because it has included so many diverse cultures. Well, we have a very old and wonderful culture and it is our American duty to bring it with us as we become Americans. But on the other hand, we don't want to be foreigners, and you know that those of us from Asia are almost always perceived as foreigners, no matter how long we have lived in this country. So there is something of a paradox there, and everything we do is both right and wrong. If we preserve our own cultural identity we are seen as separating ourselves from the community; if we don't we have failed to enrich our new country with our cultural heritage.
M:	So are you saying that monolingual signs and the Chinese Little League are ways of trying to deal with the paradox of trying to preserve your culture and fitting into the community?
R:	Yeah . . . it's all part of the tension.
M:	You know, I hadn't thought of that kind of tension before. It gives me a whole new appreciation for the people in our community who do come from other countries. But I still don't like monolingual signs and the Chinese-only Little League. Actually what I don't like is that it may make it more difficult for us to be a "community."
R:	Hum, I think I understand your position. Although we see these issues differently, I value Cupertino as a "community" too. I'm glad we understand each other better.
M:	Me too. Let's talk again.
R:	OK. See ya later.

In the second dialogue training activity participants were given the opportunity to practice public dialogue in their table discussions. Groups were again assigned the task of selecting one of the action plans from the mess mapping activity, but in this case they were instructed to use a dialogic pattern of interaction in making their decision. The activity was framed as an opportunity for participants to develop and practice their public communication abilities. In order to draw attention to the process of dialogue over the content, participants were told that the group's decision was not as important as their ability to put dialogic principles into practice. Participants were again encouraged to attend to the specific actions and meanings of their discussions and to reflect on these with the facilitators at their tables and in the large group debriefing.

Turning Point

The communication training portion of the Friday afternoon session was significant because of its explicit capacity-building function. Consistent with the principles of community-based action research (Stringer, 1996), this focus on dialogue-skills training was designed to enable participants to extend their understandings of the cultural diversity issue and their abilities to work together to develop action plans for resolving community problems. On a larger scale, the training and capacity-building orientation represented an important shift in the Cupertino Project. Previously, the PDC assumed responsibility for facilitating the public dialogue process. By training community members in these skills, and by providing opportunities to apply the skills in situated contexts, the possibility for developing a self-sustaining, community-wide dialogic process was enhanced.

The pedagogy underlying the dialogue-skills training is covered more fully in the next chapter, but it is worthwhile here to take a look at this approach within the context of the Training Program. In learning the various conflict styles, including dialogue, participants moved back and forth between first-person and third-person positions (Pearce, 1994), each of which involved some form of critical reflection. For example, the demonstration of the conflict styles by the two PDC members and the analysis of the dialogue script in Table 5.2 placed participants in the third-person position; that is, as outside observers looking in on a conversation. Each of these demonstrations was followed by an activity that moved participants into a first-person position by having them actually participate in a role-play situation themselves. Participants were thus encouraged to assess specific communication actions within the process of enacting them. These activities were followed by debriefing sessions at the tables in which participants were led by the PDC facilitators to reflect on their experiences and to evaluate what they learned. In sum, skills and abilities were acquired through observation of others, performing communicative actions, and by critically reflecting on the process.

Episode Six: Council's Presentation of Action Plans (1 Hour)

The Saturday morning portion of the meeting began with a presentation of the council's action plans. The plans, previously generated at the council's team building meeting, were displayed on an overhead projector at the front of the room. Facilitators read each of the plans separately and asked the council members to talk about them. Nothing else was scripted beyond this general format. This meant that council members could speak to one or all of the plans, or not speak at all. This was an open discussion and the council could choose to participate in any way they so desired.

Although it was critical at this point for the council to offer their suggestions, it was also important that their action plans not be privileged in any way. The idea was to avoid the perception that the council's plans were more credible simply because they came from the council, who as elected officials obviously have more political power and resources than other members of the community. To help circumvent this perception, the council presented their plans without advocating them or implying that they be given special consideration. Moreover, the council agreed at the last minute to use the term "conversation starters" when referring to their action plans as a way of encouraging people to respond to the plans. All of this was designed to bring the council's action plans into an equitable and parallel relationship with those generated by community residents.

Episode Seven: Deliberation Activity and Discussion (2 Hours)

Following presentation of the council's action plans, participants were given an opportunity to respond at their tables using the CVA model. Specifically, participants were asked to discuss three questions in response to the council's action plans:

1.   Which of your concerns and visions are addressed by the council's action plans?
2.   What concerns and visions do you have that are not addressed by the council's action plans?
3.   What actions would address these concerns and visions?

Once the groups had a chance to work through these questions they were then asked to select one action plan to present to the larger group. This, of course, created a context that called for a deliberative form of decision making.

Each group was instructed to write their action plans, along with the corresponding concerns and visions, on flip charts that were posted around the room. These were diagrammed similar to the CVA model in Figure 2.2. A spokesperson from each group briefly described the results of their deliberations to the large group. A PDC facilitator followed this with a "harvesting" or group summary session. Discussion focused on the following questions: What have we learned? What values have surfaced? What new action plans are necessary? What issues still divide the community?

Importantly, the deliberation activity was not framed as a role-play activity. Participants were told instead to pay close attention to the content of their discussions because some of the decisions emerging from the groups, in the form of action plans, would actually be implemented in the future. The deliberation activity was also framed as an extension of the communication training that took place the previous day. The expectation was that participants would gain additional practice and experience by applying dialogue principles and skills in their deliberations. This approach, practicing skills in "real" contexts that have social, political, and practical implications, is also part of our pedagogy. We believe that teaching and learning public dialogue skills must, at some point, be tied to contexts and situations that matter in the life of the community and are meaningful to the people who live in it.

> Box 5.3. Understanding Does Not Equal Agreement
>
> When I first heard about the Training Program, I was very pleased to know we had an opportunity for people to speak up about life in Cupertino. I've been in the United States for 25 years and consider myself to be an American, but in my daily interactions with people nobody seems to recognize this. So I was pleased to have a public session to talk about these things. The discussions at my table were very helpful. I think towards the end we kind of understood each other. We may not have completely agreed with each other, but we understood each other's point of view and why we thought the way we did. So I thought it was very good.
> —Roger Peng, Cupertino resident

Turning Point

The presentation of the CVA models and the discussion that followed was vigorous, energized, and remarkably candid. It was during this episode that the difficult issues of Asian immigration—those with the most potential to divide the community—were openly addressed in a large public forum for the first time. This was significant as a response to previous criticisms and claims that conflict was suppressed during the Town Hall Meeting and that the Cupertino Project as a whole was not adequately dealing with underlying feelings of frustration, hostility, and resentment. The episode was also significant in terms of establishing a context that enabled difficult topics to be discussed in ways that were productive and affirming rather than polarizing and antagonistic. By addressing the more serious concerns with cultural diversity within a learning context, participants demonstrated, in practice, the possibilities public dialogue offers for resolving community problems.

The first speaker set the tone. She said that the "major concern" for her group "is the backlash that's prevalent in this community and that nobody seems to want to talk about. We all know it's there; we hear it in the grocery stores, on the soccer fields, but it's very dangerous to discuss." She went on to say,

> The people who have lived in this community for a long time are very frightened about the changes. And while the new immigrants coming into the community have questions and concerns, they really are not the ones doing the most complaining about being uncomfortable about the changes. It's really a lot of people who look like me [reference to being white].

Another speaker made similar points, reporting that the major concern among her group was the "anti-immigration feeling" among long-time residents in the community. She said:

> I think it's obvious to everyone here that long-time residents have these feelings, fearful feelings, and threatened feelings. And probably the immigrants also may feel threatened by this anti-immigrant sentiment. So there's this two-way uncertainty on how to approach this issue. We felt this was the fundamental . . . undercurrent of everything we're here for.

A third speaker reported that his group also expressed concern with the anti-immigrant sentiment. As an Asian male, he discussed the concern from the perspective of the new immigrants, noting that "Chinese in the community are getting mixed messages, which we [the group] think is tied to some of this backlash we are talking about."

Turning Point

The discussion that followed the presentation of the CVA models was similarly candid and spirited, although considerably less focused. One unexpected incident came in response to the question, "What issues still divide the community?" Two participants stood up together. One of them began by saying,

We heard a lot of talk yesterday about Chinese Little League here in Cupertino and how some people say "I don't understand why those Chinese people elect to form their own league" and how some people are not welcome to attend. Well, I am President of Chinese Little League and this person beside me is the President of Cupertino National Little League and we would like to address this issue.

The two speakers went on to explain the rationale for the two leagues and how both presidents supported each other's efforts. In interviews conducted several months later, a number of participants who attended the Training Program identified this exchange as significant. For them, it demonstrated the practical benefits of public dialogue and open communication for clarifying misunderstandings. "It showed how people didn't really know what was going on and that a lot of the division was because of misunderstandings," said one participant. "If people have the opportunity to explain why things are done they might be a little more understanding of it." When asked what the most valuable aspect of the training program was, another participant responded by saying, "we openly closed the Chinese Little League issue."

Box 5.4. Enabling Concerns to be Discussed

I never knew that some people were so upset about the Chinese Little League. However, the concerns of those people who were against it were allayed when the misconceptions about the league were explained. The public dialogue process enabled the concerns to be discussed.
—Claire Omura, Cupertino resident

The unscripted exchange between the two league presidents transformed the context of the training program. In addition to learning how to talk about difficult problems using the skills of public dialogue, participants also witnessed how public dialogue can produce understanding and empathy around a real issue of serious concern to the community. This relatively small success demonstrated the positive effects of open communication, and in doing so it created opportunities to further the public dialogue process. If it is possible to achieve some degree of mutual intelligibility on the issue of Chinese Little League, then the possibility exists for applying the process to other divisive topics as well.

Episode Eight: Selecting Action Plans (1 Hour)

Decision making in a public dialogue process cannot be reduced solely to formal voting procedures and majority rule, at least as they are practiced in traditional electoral politics and those that follow parliamentary rules of order (Barber, 1984).[5] What is needed for public dialogue is the development of alternative formats that emphasize voting as a collective activity, not as a series of discrete acts performed by isolated individuals in voting booths. Moreover, voting should be flexible and the options malleable so that participants can be involved in developing the choices themselves through on-going conversation and discussion. In a public dialogue process voting cannot be construed as an endpoint or terminus, but as a particular type of action that exists within a series of actions leading toward a common decision and an action-oriented consensus.

There are a variety of ways of incorporating voting into a public dialogue event. The format developed for the Training Program went like this. During the lunch break, PDC members quickly summarized the various action plans generated from the deliberation activity and corresponding CVA models and listed them on a large sheet of paper posted on a wall at the front of the room. After lunch, participants were each given four stick-on dots and asked to place them next to the action plan(s) they considered most important. Any voting combination was allowed. A person could use all their dots on one action plan or spread them over several action plans. The voting itself was conducted as a group activity. All 100 participants made their way to the front of the room together, talking with each other and watching the tally as they waited their turn to post their dots.

The purpose of the dot voting was to rank order the action plans in order to assess the preferences and judgments of the group. Based on the results, five categories of action plans emerged as the top choices. The first category, *education*, included a number of action items designed to increase peoples' awareness, understandings, and experiences in dealing with different cultural groups. The second category was named *high tech*. Among other things, it called for the development of a city web page that would include information on Cupertino's cultural richness and be inclusive of the city's diverse population. The third category, *neighborhoods*, called for residents to sponsor highly localized activities for creating community, such as neighborhood block parties and garage sales. The fourth action plan category, called *low tech*, emphasized the need to promote cultural richness through local television, newspapers, and civic organizations like the Rotary Club and the PTA. The final action plan called for participants to develop a *cross-cultural consortium* that would serve as a steering committee for organizing and implementing the various action items suggested during the Training Program and throughout the project.

These action plans are, for the most part, consistent with those developed by the dialogue groups in Phase II of the project. Recall that the categories generated in Phase II were education, community celebrations, neighborhood events, and cultural information dissemination. Clearly, the dominant theme connecting the two sets of action plans is education. Beyond that, there is considerable overlap in other areas as well, with each set of plans identifying different mechanisms for achieving intercultural understanding. For example, there is a clear focus on informal channels of communication that are situated around neighborhood events and existing civic organizations. There is also a preference for utilizing mediated forms of communication that capitalize on recent communications technologies as well as traditional media channels.

There are differences in the two sets of action plans as well. The first is the focus on community celebrations, which figured prominently in the dialogue-group discussions and surfaced in the council's action plans, yet were rarely mentioned by participants at the training program. The second difference is the development of a cross-cultural consortium, which emerged as a major action plan at the training program but was not considered in the dialogue-group discussions.

Turning Point

In deciding on the five categories of action plans, participants at the training program were, in effect, completing the work that began in Phase II of the project. This was a fairly lengthy process involving a number of iterations and refinements. Put differently, the action plans that emerged during the Training Program resulted from an on-going series of conversations and public events involving a variety of different stakeholders in the community. It is critical in a public dialogue process to secure maximum participation when making decisions, whatever they might be. The selection of the action plans during the Training Program was significant in this regard because it represented the culmination of a lot of hard work on the part of community residents, city officials, and the city council.

The action plans were also significant because they outlined specific steps that could be taken in order to resolve problems with cultural diversity and Asian immigration. Recall the criticism from Phase II that the Town Hall Meeting did not lead to a specific action plan, and the related claim that public dialogue is "all talk, no action." While recognizing the reflexive and dialectical relationship between product and process, it is important to recognize that public dialogue can, and ultimately should, produce concrete decisions that lead to specific forms of action. (In the following episode we pushed this idea even further by focusing attention on the strategies for implementing the plans.) Finally, the action plans generated at the training program provided an agenda for subsequent activities in the Cupertino Project. As indicated in the next chapter, considerable efforts were made to bring the action plans to fruition.

Episode Nine: Implementing Action Plans (1 Hour)

Following the voting, the focus turned to identifying the next steps toward implementing the action plans. Participants selected the category of action plan they were most interested in pursuing and joined with others in forming groups in order to develop implementation strategies. One group was formed for each of the five action plans. Discussion revolved around the following question: "Who should do what, when, and in what way?" Facilitators in each group recorded comments on a flip chart. Following the discussion, all the participants reconvened for a final plenary session in which a spokesperson from the group reported their findings. All of the participants who attended the Training Program received a list of those in attendance along with a summary of the five action plans in a follow-up letter sent by the city council a week later.

EVALUATING THE TRAINING PROGRAM

By most accounts, the Training and Team Building Program was a success. In a letter to the PDC, the city manager reported that feedback was "consistently positive" and that a number of the participants made "personal commitments to remain in the dialogue." One of the council members, Michael Chang, the first Chinese American ever elected in the city, called the Training Program "a watershed event in Cupertino's multicultural history" (Cronk, 1997a, p. 1B). One of the participants was quoted in the same *San Jose Mercury News* article as saying, "I was surprised and pleased that they [the city council] even brought it [the topic of Asian immigration and cultural diversity] into the open. An easy thing to do is to deny that there's a problem. It happens all the time, but our city council showed a lot of fortitude in calling a bunch of people together to tackle this very difficult problem" (Cronk, 1997a, p. 4B).

More objective evidence can be found in the answers to a questionnaire administered immediately following the training program. Sixty-eight participants completed the 23-item questionnaire by indicating their level of agreement on a 5-point scale: strongly agree = 5, agree = 4, neutral or undecided = 3, disagree = 2, and strongly disagree = 1. As indicated in Table 5.3, the percentage of responses that fell within the strongly agree-agree and strongly disagree-disagree categories are provided for each item along with the mean score and standard deviation. The final two items (#22 and #23) are particularly relevant in evaluating

Box 5.5. Moving the Project Forward

The Training Program was very interesting in that it brought together so many different community factions. I felt that it was a very strong event, and the fact that many people wanted to take something tangible away from it was a good indication that people wanted the project to move forward. I believe some residents will always think the past was better than the current situation in Cupertino. But I also believe there are many who see the city as more enlightened than other communities, and more willing to face the "tough" issues head on. This kind of event will always inflame those who see "diversity" as a threat to a former way of life, but I think open communication is always better than festering discontent.
—Donna Krey, Cupertino city employee

the overall effectiveness of the training program. We can see from Table 5.3 that over 94% of the participants strongly agreed or agreed that the training program was a "valuable experience" and that they "would recommend" it to other members of the community.

LOOKING BACK-LOOKING FORWARD

Phase III of the Cupertino Project focused on activities designed to involve city leaders in the public dialogue process. The PDC first conducted individual interviews with each city council member and then facilitated a team building meeting with the entire group to help them process and respond to the visions and action plans generated by community residents in Phase II. Phase III concluded with a large Training Program for community leaders. This event represented yet another shift in the project, both in terms of promoting public-dialogue training and moving the community closer to a specific set of action plans.

Perhaps most gratifying to the PDC and the public dialogue process was the sense that the community had taken ownership of the project and an active role in shaping its development. As Phase III developed, for example, there was a subtle yet noticeable shift in language as both the council and other community leaders began referring to the project as "our project," not "your project." In keeping with this notion of shared ownership, it is important to recognize that the city council, who initiated the idea for the training program in the first place,

Table 5.3. Evaluation of the Training Program.

	Strongly agree-agree (%)	Strongly disagree-disagree (%)	Mean	SD
1. The ideas presented in this training program were interesting.	97.1	0	4.48	0.56
2. The length of this training program was appropriate.	69.1	16.2	3.77	1.04
3. The training materials were helpful.	72.1	2.9	3.97	0.79
4. This training program was well organized.	98.5	1.5	4.51	0.58
5. The presenters were able to maintain interest and stimulate participants.	92.6	1.5	4.37	0.64
6. The presenters gave clear instructions.	89.7	1.5	4.40	0.69
7. The pace of this training program was effective.	79.4	4.4	4.05	0.80
8. The skills I learned in this training program will be beneficial to my personal life.	75.0	4.4	4.00	0.82
9. The skills I learned in this training program will be beneficial to the Cupertino Community.	88.3	4.4	4.16	0.74
10. This training program helped me learn how to interact with people who are culturally different from me.	66.1	11.7	3.75	1.01
11. This training program helped me learn how to talk publicly about controversial issues.	70.6	14.7	3.69	0.98
12. This training program helped me become more aware of my own and others' communication.	82.4	4.4	4.08	0.78

Table 5.3. Evaluation of the Training Program. (con't)

13. This training program will enable me to manage public conflict more effectively in the future.	77.9	4.4	3.92	0.72
14. This training program taught me effective listening skills.	67.6	5.9	3.77	0.77
15. This training program taught me that there are different ways of discussing any one public issue.	75.0	4.4	3.97	0.81
16. This training program helped me to better understand the issues facing Cupertino.	85.3	2.9	4.22	0.77
17. This training program will be beneficial to the city council in responding to the concerns of citizens.	82.3	0	4.22	0.73
18. I feel that the city council heard what the community leaders were saying in this training program.	88.3	3.0	4.22	0.77
19. I believe the city council will act on the information they heard at this training program.	80.9	4.4	4.01	0.81
20. I learned new information about the Cupertino community at this training program.	78.0	2.9	4.09	0.79
21. The discussion at our table during this training program exemplified the characteristics of dialogue.	89.7	4.4	4.25	0.76
22. Overall, I found this training program to be a valuable experience.	94.1	0	4.38	0.59
23. I would recommend this training program to other members of the Cupertino community.	94.1	1.5	4.48	0.65

pushed for a collaborative leadership approach in addressing the community's concerns over cultural diversity. Coming out of Phase III there seemed to be a shared recognition that the success of public dialogue could only come when the community as a whole participated in the process. This recognition carried forward into Phase IV as participation expanded and city leaders and community residents found new ways of working together on the project.

To underscore this point, articles were published in the *San Jose Mercury News* and *The Cupertino Courier* several months after the training program identifying cultural diversity as a primary issue in the city council election (Cronk, 1997b; Marino, 1997). One of the candidates was quoted as saying, "Everywhere I go, the subject of racial tensions comes up. I do believe the ethnic makeup of the city has changed dramatically . . . and it may be the speed and quantity that has people frightened" (Marino, 1997, p. 7). All five candidates agreed that "city government needs to play a strong role in helping Cupertino's cultures communicate with each other" (Marino, 1997, p. 8). "It's a nontraditional area of government," another candidate said, "but it's a real important thing for our city to play an active role in" (Marino, 1997, p. 8). This willingness to engage the issue served as both a response to community residents on the part of city leaders and an invitation to continue the dialogue.

NOTES

1. It should be noted that not all city officials participated equally in the project. Fortunately, there were a number of officials who not only supported the public-dialogue process, but also added to it and enriched it by demonstrating the skills of collaborative leadership and good communication. Don Brown, the city manager, provided resources and institutional support throughout the entire project. The members of the city council also voiced support for the project, although the level of actual involvement and commitment varied from member to member. As the project unfolded, one council member, Michael Chang, stepped forward and became an active participant in the process. Both Don and Michael's collaborative leadership style and ability to articulate and enact public-dialogue processes enhanced the project considerably.

2. Not everyone agrees with Barber (1984, 1998) about the role of government in bringing about participatory forms of democracy. Bachrach and Bostwinick (1992), for example, argue that the kind of reform necessary for participatory democracy in the workplace "cannot be accommodated within the present political system . . . the system itself must be changed in the course of class struggle to achieve workplace

democracy" (p. 15). When they apply their approach to the community level, the authors assume at the outset that a radical restructuring of political institutions is required as a precondition for participatory democracy. By contrast, public dialogue makes no such presumption. It begins by working within common institutional structures that are capable of facilitating a critical-reflective discourse that calls into question traditional forms of democratic decision making. Public dialogue might indeed lead to structural changes at some future point; however, that type of change is not assumed at the outset.

3. Being placed in the "expert" position put the PDC in a paradoxical situation. We certainly wanted to include others in planning events and designing activities and did not intend to be exclusionary, but we were just learning these skills ourselves. If we were experts it was only because we did not know enough not to be. Another reason why we assumed more of an expert position than we intended was because of our tenuous relationship with city officials. Although we clearly had the support of the city manager and at least some of the city council, it was also clear that these city officials were waiting to see how the project developed before committing to any long-term relationship, particularly one that involved city resources. We felt as though we had to demonstrate a level of expertise in order to be seen as credible and yet, paradoxically, if we acted too much like "experts" we would be acting counter to the dialogic principles we were trying to promote.

4. Because there is no executive branch in the council-manager system of government, the role of "mayor" is somewhat unique in that the person is not elected by the public to serve in that capacity (Burns, Peltason, & Cronin, 1987). In Cupertino, for example, council members are rotated into the mayor and vice mayor positions based on seniority and the number of votes received in the most recent election. These individuals then serve along with the rest of the council as equal voting members. Council members themselves are elected at-large to 4-year, overlapping terms. Elections are held every two years, with council members being limited to a maximum of two consecutive terms. During the four phases of the Cupertino Project described in this book, the city had seven different council members; three of them served a term as mayor.

5. Given Barber's (1984, 1998) advocation of strong democracy, he is naturally critical of formal voting procedures as a viable form of public participation. "Our primary electoral act, voting, is rather like using a public toilet: we wait in line with a crowd in order to close ourselves up in a small compartment where we can relieve ourselves in solitude and in privacy of our burden, pull a lever, and then, yielding to the next in line, go silently home. Because our vote is secret—'private', we do not need to explain or justify it to others (or, indeed, to ourselves) in a fashion that would require us to think publicly or politically" (Barber, 1984, p. 188).

6

SUSTAINING THE PUBLIC
DIALOGUE PROCESS

This chapter covers the variety of different activities and events undertaken during Phase IV of the Cupertino Project. It begins by describing the development of a volunteer citizen action group called the 5Cs (Citizens of Cupertino Cross Cultural Consortium) and their efforts to promote public dialogue in the community. Among other things, the 5Cs sponsored a follow up Training and Team Building Meeting, formed project teams to work on action plans, participated in a public dialogue training program, and facilitated a public forum on controversial cultural diversity issues. The chapter also describes collaborative efforts by the PDC to extend the public dialogue process into other segments of the community, including the public schools and several community service organizations. The primary organizing theme of this chapter is how the PDC worked with city leaders and community residents to sustain public dialogue in the Cupertino community.

GOALS AND PURPOSES OF PHASE IV

The overarching goal of Phase IV was to institutionalize public dialogue in the Cupertino community as a legitimate and viable form of public communication.[1] In order to achieve this goal, the PDC worked closely with city officials and community groups on the following activities: (a) enlarging the domain of the public dialogue process, (b) expanding public dialogue training and related capacity-building opportunities throughout the community, (c) relinquishing control of the public dialogue process, and (d) facilitating discussions about how the community talks about controversial issues and how public communication can be improved in the future.

ENLARGING THE DOMAIN OF PUBLIC DIALOGUE

The first step toward institutionalization was to extend the reach and influence of the public dialogue process.[2] Part of this was achieved by simply building on the activities and events initiated during the earlier phases of the project. This approach, of course, was entirely consistent with the developmental and organic nature of the public dialogue process, which, if successfully enacted, was designed to create the conditions for sustaining and expanding itself. Public dialogue, like social capital (Putnam, 1995), is cumulative and self-reinforcing. It increases in direct proportion to its use. The PDC sought to enlarge the domain of public dialogue by encouraging people who had previously participated to continue with the project by working on action items, attending training sessions, and planning future activities.

In addition to building on previous events, the Cupertino Project expanded to include qualitatively different kinds of activities that attracted a new generation of participants. Most notable among these was the long-term, sustained efforts to involve students, faculty, parents, and administrators from the Cupertino schools into the public dialogue process. Other "new" groups involved in the project during Phase IV included the City's Emergency Preparedness Program and the Cupertino Leadership Council. With each new activity and event the project grew exponentially, attracting hundreds of new residents who participated in the public dialogue process for the first time. As a result of this expansion, the project became much more diffuse and decentralized.

EXPANDING TRAINING OPPORTUNITIES

As part of the institutionalization process, the PDC refined and extended public-dialogue training programs throughout the community. It is important to recognize that the range of influence public dialogue might have on the community is severely limited when restricted to a small group of so-called "experts" like the PDC. The creation of additional sites for public dialogue is dependent on having a network of trained people, representing the full range of stakeholders, who have abilities to assist in creating such places. This is not as simple as it might sound given that public dialogue capacities are varied and complex. They involve, at a minimum, communication facilitation skills and an ability to design activities and events that contribute to the on-going community dialogue process.

Enlarging the circle of participants who were willing and able to engage in dialogic forms of public communication was vital to the long-term success of the project. Although teaching others new forms of public communication was an implicit component in the first two phases, it was carried out primarily through "modeling" the kinds of actions we sought to teach. In Phase III we incorporated an explicit training component into the project for the first time as part of the Training and Team Building Program. In Phase IV we expanded training opportunities throughout the city, both in terms of the range of competencies taught, as well as the number of individuals and groups who received instruction in public dialogue skills. A related purpose of this effort was to make the PDC obsolete by training others to do the kind of interventionist work that we did in earlier phases of the project, thus enabling the project to become self-sustaining in the absence of any outside consultant group like the PDC.

RELINQUISHING CONTROL OF THE PROCESS

Consistent with institutionalization and the focus on public communication training, the PDC attempted to turn responsibility for the public dialogue process over to the community. Note the transition here from Phases I and II, in which the PDC controlled the process, to Phase III, in which we worked to share responsibility for the process, to Phase IV, in which we attempted to relinquish control of the process. This final shift in the evolution of the project could come about only if city officials and community residents had the capacities to practice and elicit public dialogue at both micro and macro levels. This is a challenging task, as Greenwood and Levin (1998) note:

> Though the professional researcher's obligation to let go of the group near the end is difficult, this is easier than the collaborative development of the local participants' capability to control and direct the ongoing developmental process according to their own

interests. For participants to become active players in a change process, they must exercise power. . . . In the end, the process must be taken over by the participants. (p. 119)

Greenwood and Levin (1998) are writing specifically about action research; however, their admonition that outside researchers and consultants must "give up the process" speaks directly to the democratic obligations inherent in developing a public dialogue project. Public dialogue fulfills its democratic mission when the communication capacities for identifying and resolving community problems rests squarely in the hands of those who live in the community and are in the best position to define and shape the problems that confront them.

LEARNING TO TALK ABOUT HOW THE COMMUNITY HANDLES ISSUES

A related goal of Phase IV was to assist the community in adopting a metacommunicative perspective on public communication in the city; one that fosters analysis and critical reflection. The idea was for community residents to reflect on public communication processes as a way to begin planning for future actions that would move the community closer to where it wants to be. This on-going process of reflection and action was designed to develop capacities that would enable the community to continuously adapt to changing circumstances. Consider, for example, that new issues and problems related to diversity surfaced repeatedly during the period the PDC worked in Cupertino. The questions posed to community members during Phase IV of the project were: How has the community responded to cultural diversity topics in the past? When the next set of issues and problems arise, which they inevitably will, how will the community respond?

Our attempts to foster critical reflection on community issues were perfectly in line with the goal of institutionalizing public dialogue. By reflecting back on past issues and projecting forward to future ones, the community could begin to develop proactive strategies capable of transforming the nature of the issues themselves. Like many communities, Cupertino had no institutional structures or processes designed specifically to deal with difficult social issues.[3] This put the city in something of a defensive position in that once issues were formed the best the community could do was to respond using whatever resources they had available. If a public dialogue process was established and in place, however, the community could anticipate problems and take the initiative in addressing them. Part of the work taken up in Phase IV, then, was to encourage community members to begin developing proactive public communication strategies as part of a larger, institutionalized public dialogue process.

> **Box 6.1. In Search of Dialogue Partners**
>
> As the Cupertino Project expanded during Phase IV, more people naturally stepped forward to voice their views and opinions about cultural and demographic changes in the community. Those of us in the PDC were dismayed, but not altogether surprised, that some of what we heard reproduced old familiar patterns of confrontation and debate. While there were thoughtful exchanges about the advantages and disadvantages of diversity, there were also ugly and aggressive attacks made by some residents who held opposing views on the topic. The PDC team made a concerted effort to look between and beyond these shrill voices to those community members who were willing and able to engage in dialogic patterns of communication. We felt that by working through these community members the public dialogue process could be extended to those residents who insisted on advocating positions and attacking those who disagreed. What we found was that community members who were initially resistant to dialogue were more likely to join the conversation if it was initiated by other members of the community.

PUBLIC-DIALOGUE TRAINING MODEL

The competencies involved in the practice of public dialogue are acquired through a multilevel learning process. These levels involve learning about public dialogue, learning how to engage in dialogic actions, and learning how to reflect on public dialogue actions and processes. The learning that takes place at any one level is integrated into the other two so that each provides a context for the others. Acquiring the skills necessary to engage in dialogic actions, for example, is insufficient without also knowing something about public dialogue and how to critically reflect on the process. It is also important that all of the levels be taught within an applied context that is meaningful to the extent that it has direct implications for the participants. In the original Training Program from Phase III, for example, participants learned public dialogue skills with the expectation that they would apply those skills in the context of the training event as they deliberated among the various action plans. The results of the deliberations had "real" consequences for the participants and the community as a whole. Public dialogue competencies, then, are not taught as an end in themselves, but as a means to achieve particular outcomes and objectives that impact the participants in some meaningful way.

Figure 6.1 provides a diagram of the training model developed by the PDC and used throughout the Cupertino Project. Learning about public dialogue is accomplished through *demonstration*, which can involve explanation of concepts and descriptions or observations of specific actions and communication techniques. Demonstration places participants in a third-person position (Pearce, 1994), external to and outside the concepts, principles, and processes being taught. In order to learn how to engage in dialogue, on the other hand, participants must assume a first-person position (Pearce, 1994) by actually *practicing* dialogic actions. This is normally achieved through some sort of experiential activity or exercise that requires participants to apply knowledge through situated communication performance.

Learning how to reflect on dialogic actions and processes is achieved by developing capacities in critical reflection. This requires participants to consider and evaluate the actions they and others perform while engaged in the practice of dialogue. Critical reflection naturally moves participants back into a third-person position, yet in a slightly different way because they are reflecting, in part, on their own actions. It is also important to recognize that critical reflection is itself a type of communication practice because it is carried out in interactions involving the trainer and the other participants. Participants, then, learn how to engage in dialogic actions and how to communicate with others about that engagement as part of the learning process. Finally, each of these levels is taught within contexts that have consequences for training participants.

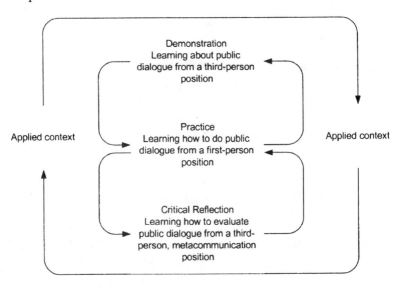

Figure 6.1. PDC training model

THE 5CS

Based on recommendations made by participants at the training program, a group of citizen volunteers organized a steering committee to help coordinate implementation of the action plans generated at the meeting. The 5Cs held their first meeting in May 1997 with 15 people in attendance. Members of the PDC team facilitated the meeting at the request of the group, but that role was quickly taken over by a volunteer from the 5Cs. The PDC continued to work with the group in a resource, advising, and consulting capacity, helping them in whatever way we could to achieve their goals. The city manager (Don Brown) and one council member (Michael Chang) actively participated in the group along with resident members. In addition to supplying administrative and physical support for 5Cs meetings and events, these two public officials enacted collaborative forms of leadership that, in our estimation, greatly assisted the group and the public dialogue process.

The first three meetings were devoted to defining the nature and purpose of the 5Cs. A mission statement was developed ("To create an organizational infrastructure, and to promote a harmonious, yet diverse, community") and a set of goals were defined. As this process developed it became clear the group had aspirations that extended beyond what would normally be expected of a steering committee. In addition to coordinating implementation of action plans, participants envisioned the 5Cs as an on-going resource group for the city, one that would actively take up cultural diversity issues, diffuse problems, deal with grievances, and counteract rumors. Several members saw the group serving as a model for the community in demonstrating how residents can work together to achieve racial harmony and cultural understanding. This latter point was particularly salient given the group's diverse ethnic composition. There were roughly equal numbers of white and non-white members, both among the original group of participants as well as those who joined later.

CONSTRUCTING GROUP IDENTITY AND PURPOSE

The question of group identity and purpose was an on-going source of tension among the 5Cs. A major reason for this, we believe, can be attributed to the rather unique and unconventional nature of the group itself. Held together only by the voluntary efforts of its members, the 5Cs occupied a public space that, although affiliated with city government, operated outside its formal structures. None of the members, with the exception of the city manager, council member, and later the community relations coordinator, were employed by the city or affiliated with the city government in any official capacity. The group was not bound by the procedures and by-laws set forth for other volunteer city organizations, such as the city planning commission or any of the other advisory boards. The 5Cs had no official designation, formal governing process, or prescribed duties to perform. They were, in a sense, self-defining in the absence of any institutional authority or shared history.

The group's efforts to develop an identity and purpose were further compounded by their stated mission and focus. As a civic organization ostensively committed to public dialogue and cross-cultural relationships, it was not readily evident what exactly they should do in order to fulfill their mission or, for that matter, how they should do it. This was, after all, a nontraditional area of city government so there were few, if any, models for the 5Cs to follow. The PDC assisted the group in working through some of these questions, of course, but we were careful to follow the lead of the group, intervening only when we felt we could help participants achieve their own stated purposes and goals. Don Brown and Michael Chang provided valuable guidance as well, yet they too were feeling their way through the public dialogue process and, consistent with collaborative leadership practices, were careful not to impose their authority on the group. All of this created a dynamic and fluid group context that forced members to continually negotiate their identity, purpose, and rules of operation.

> **Box 6.2. "A Lesson in Patience"**
>
> Participating in the 5Cs meetings has been a lesson in patience. We seem to have pulled together a collection of people with a wide variety of experiences working in groups and at meetings—everything from very capable leaders and knowledgeable participants to neophytes who are just learning how to operate in this kind of setting. The most interesting thing for me is the variety of cultures we have represented in the group. I'm also encouraged that so many people have stuck with the process for so long. Their perseverance must mean that we have something valuable here.
> —Roberta Hollimon, Cupertino resident and 5Cs member

It is important to note that the 5Cs experienced many of the problems seen in other voluntary civic organizations and groups (Gastil, 1993). Although attendance at the monthly meetings was remarkably constant, ranging between 20 to 25 people, actual membership at the meetings fluctuated, making it difficult to develop a shared history and common identity. There were personal and ideological conflicts as well. Some members had strong opinions regarding particular cultural diversity issues that were at odds with others in the group. Another frequently debated question was whether the 5Cs should take official positions on issues, or whether the group should assume a neutral stance. Working through these differences was difficult, at least initially, because it called into question whether the group shared a common vision and purpose.

In what follows I describe the major activities undertaken by the 5Cs and comment throughout how these activities contributed to the identity of the group and their on-going efforts to define and redefine their purpose.

FOLLOW-UP TRAINING AND TEAM BUILDING PROGRAM[4]

One of the more tangible goals first identified by the 5Cs was to sponsor a Follow-up Community Training and Team Building meeting. Members felt it was important to host the event in order to carry through on the action items generated at the first training program. Additionally, the group wanted to reach a wider audience beyond the community leaders who were invited to the original event. The meeting was thus announced through the local media as a public event—all Cupertino residents were invited to attend. The 5Cs also expanded the list of city leaders from the first training program, and with the help of the city manager's office mailed them personal invitations.

The second Training and Team Building Meeting was held in October 1997, seven months after the original event. Over 100 people attended the two-hour event, which was jointly facilitated by the 5Cs and the PDC. A member of the 5Cs introduced the meeting and gave a brief report on the history of the group. As with previous public events, it was important that participants recognize how their efforts fit within the larger framework of the Cupertino Project. To that end, a member of the PDC team summarized the earlier phases of the project, giving special attention to the previous Training and Team Building Program.

The working segment of the meeting revolved around the action plans generated at the original Training Program. Recall that five categories of action plans were identified. One of those plans called for the development of a cross-cultural consortium to help coordinate implementation of the plans. The 5Cs obviously represented that action plan, and the Follow-up Training meeting was evidence that results from the first Training Program were indeed being implemented. The remaining four categories of action plans (education, high tech, neighborhoods, and low tech) were then summarized by members of the 5Cs. In addition to reporting on areas of progress, the speakers also suggested items within each plan that still needed attention. This set the stage for the participants at the meeting to begin working on the action plans themselves.

Participants selected one of the four action plans they were interested in working on, and with the help of the table facilitators formed groups around them. There were multiple groups for each plan due to the large number of participants and the small number of plans. Two other groups were formed in order to accommodate those participants who wanted to pursue different topics and action items. During the table discussions, the groups were asked to decide what particular item within the action plan category they wanted to pursue. For example, one of the neighborhood groups chose to work on developing a city-wide neighborhood block party program. Having selected a given action item, the group was then asked to outline the procedures for implementing the plan. The goal here was to be as specific as possible. For example, groups could begin by identifying the steps necessary to implement the action item, they could assign members particular tasks, and/or they could develop a timeline for completion of the action item. At the end of the meeting a spokesperson from each group reported the results of their discussion to the large group.

The facilitators carefully recorded each group's implementation plan and collected the names, phone numbers, e-mail addresses, and so on of the group members. This resulted in a list of at least 15 specific action items along with a list of people willing to work on them. Given that these actions were taken up by a group of citizen volunteers with limited resources, some measure of attrition was to be expected. To be sure, not all of the action items developed at the Follow-up Training Program were considered, much less completed. Nevertheless, the 5Cs did work on four of the items, eventually completing each of them (see Table 6.1 for the list of action plans undertaken by the 5Cs). It is worth noting that the 5Cs did not consider some of the specific items under the education category because they overlapped with efforts already underway at the two local high schools. It is also worth noting that some of the action items from the first Training Program, such as the formation of a cross-cultural consortium and the development of a city web page, were completed before the Follow-up Training Meeting even began.

Table 6.1. 5Cs Action Items.

1.	Develop a neighborhood block party program.
2.	Develop a database of neighborhood leaders.
3.	Develop an information packet for new Cupertino residents.
4.	Develop a series of videos chronicling the Cupertino Project and work of the 5Cs.

The Follow-up Training Meeting was an important event in the development of the 5Cs. It gave the group visibility in the community and served as a catalyst for attracting new members. Not coincidentally, membership in the 5Cs doubled to 30 people immediately following the event. A few months later the group boasted a membership of over 50 people. Instead of moving the dialogue process into an unforeseen area, the event built off existing themes and resources and thus deepened its impact. There were, in fact, no obvious turning points or critical episodes during the meeting that shifted the project onto some new or different trajectory. It was, in the literal sense of the term, a "follow-up" meeting. One of the most important outcomes of the meeting was that it provided the 5Cs with a specific set of action items to pursue and a list of designated people willing to put in the time and energy necessary to implement them. Work on these action items commenced immediately after the follow-up meeting and continued for the next several months.

IMPLEMENTING ACTION ITEMS: STRUGGLES AND SUCCESS

In the first 5Cs meeting following the second training meeting four project teams were formed to work on the action items. The first project team worked on developing materials for a neighborhood block party program; another took up the task of identifying neighborhood leaders to serve as resource people for future cultural diversity events; another began conducting research and gathering data for a newcomers packet to be presented to people who recently moved to Cupertino; and the final team worked with the city's Telecommunications Commission to develop a series of video programs on the 5Cs and Cupertino's cultural diversity. A coordinating team made up of 5Cs participants, city officials, and two members of the PDC team supported these project teams. The coordinating team met off-line to help facilitate and assist the project teams in achieving their individual goals and the overall goals of the 5Cs.

There was a good deal of interest in the action items when the project teams were first formed. One of the challenges the group faced was in sustaining that interest. "Much enthusiasm and energy are generated as plans are articulated and people set off to perform their designated tasks," writes Stringer (1996). "The best of intentions, however, often run up against the cold, hard realities of daily life" (p. 104). One particular episode illustrates this point. A few months after the project teams had been working, several 5Cs members expressed frustration over what they perceived as a lack of progress. There was a general feeling that the group had lost track of their original mission and had very little to show for their efforts. This prompted a PDC team member to go back over the original list of goals identified at the first 5Cs meeting. Reading the list aloud it became clear that the group was indeed doing much of what it set out to do and that a number of tasks had been accomplished along the way.

The decision was made to use the next meeting to review the progress of the project teams and to evaluate the work of the 5Cs generally. As Stringer (1996) notes, review sessions not only motivate and reassure participants, they also provide opportunities to recreate the sense of group identity and purpose. "As people strive to perform their tasks and report on their successes and struggles, they share their worlds in a real, direct way and, in the process, extend their understandings of the contexts in which they are working" (p. 111). In the stocktaking meeting that followed, each of the project teams reported on concrete steps that had been taken and identified specific strategies for completing whatever tasks remained. It was clear at the end of the reports that a good deal of progress had indeed been made, which in turn provided a renewed sense of enthusiasm and interest for continuing the work of the 5Cs.

Box 6.3. A Group Without Guidelines

What's impressed me most about the 5Cs is the way the members get actively involved in working on projects. They continue to volunteer even though we don't have any set goals. It amazes me how we can continue to hang on to people and pique their interests and evolve constantly with no clear cut guidelines.
—Laura Domondon Lee, Cupertino Community Relations Coordinator

In the following months each of the project teams completed work on their action items. The neighborhood block party team developed a self-help packet and brochure that included all the directions, forms, permits, and applications necessary to complete the approval process. This was a major undertaking resulting in a rather lengthy and detailed document. The neighborhood leader project team, in coordination with the neighborhood block party team, developed a map of the city indicating where potential leaders live. Working together, the two project teams sponsored an informational meeting with neighborhood leaders and successfully launched their first block party shortly after. In the following year alone close to 20 block parties were held in the city.

The newcomers group collaborated with the Cupertino Chamber of Commerce and two other newcomers clubs in nearby cities to develop a reference guide to the city. This guide was then made available to all new city residents. Finally, the telecommunications project team produced a video on the changing demographics in Cupertino and the work of the 5Cs to address cultural and ethnic issues in the community. In addition to working on these action items, members of the 5Cs also helped coordinate the cultural diversity segment of the city's annual 4th of July celebration, which featured music and dance performances from the various ethnic groups living in the community.

On the surface, these action items may look somewhat trivial, especially when considering the amount of work that went into selecting and implementing them. It is important not to become overly fixated on outcomes and products, however, without fully recognizing the underlying communication processes that were involved in their creation. Looking at these products retrospectively, we would suggest that the work that went into the action items was as valuable as the final products themselves. For example, each of the 5Cs project teams consisted initially of strangers with diverse backgrounds, interests, and experiences. By pooling their resources and coordinating their efforts, the project teams were able to arbitrate their differences in the creation of a common product designed to benefit the community. Work on the action items also required each of the teams to collaborate extensively with other individuals and groups, thus creating links between the 5Cs and other civic organizations in the community. This is participatory democracy in action, carried out by citizens in pursuit of the public good.

5CS PUBLIC DIALOGUE TRAINING

As the project teams finished their work on the action items, the 5Cs once again found themselves reexamining their role and mission in the community. Two suggested activities converged to give the group a new sense of purpose and direction. One called for the 5Cs to conduct an annual cultural diversity forum as part of the group's on-going efforts to serve the community. The other was an offer by the PDC to do an indepth public dialogue training for 5Cs members, many of whom joined the group after the original training program and thus had never participated in a formal dialogue training. Once these two activities were put on the table, so to speak, an overall plan began to emerge that combined elements of both. Specifically, the plan called for the PDC to train 5Cs members in facilitating table discussions at a large public forum that the group itself would help design as part of the training program.

Twenty-five people participated in the 5Cs training, which lasted 10 hours and was spread out over five separate sessions. The training adhered closely to the model described earlier in the chapter (see Figure 6. 1). It involved a combination of demonstrations, communication practice, and critical reflection in situated contexts that were meaningful and consequential.

Session #1

The first session consisted of various demonstrations designed to teach participants about public dialogue from a third-person position. A member of the PDC opened the session with a description of the social constructionist theory underlying the work of the PDC, and then introduced four models of public decision making: public education, debate, deliberation, and dialogue. Working in small groups with PDC members serving as facilitators, participants compared and analyzed the four models using a matrix designed for this activity (see Table 6.2).

Following the small-group activity, participants were provided with a general overview of group facilitation principles and a fairly detailed description of three facilitation skills: neutrality, listening, and questioning. This set the stage for the next activity. Participants were given a list of different small-group scenarios and asked to imagine how they might respond in each of the situations. Table 6.3 gives the instructions for this activity along with some sample situations. The activity, although designed to demonstrate facilitation principles and techniques from a third-person perspective, also served as a stepping stone to a first-person position in that participants were told to imagine themselves in the role of the facilitator and to consider the situations from that perspective.

At the end of the first session the PDC circulated an open-ended questionnaire asking participants to share their visions and ideas for the cultural diversity forum (see Table 6.4). Results from the questionnaires were incorporated back into the training program during subsequent

Table 6.2. Matrix of Public Decision Making Models.

	Public Education	Public Debate	Public Deliberation	Public Dialogue
1. What are the advantages?				
2. What are the disadvantages?				
3. What skills are required of the facilitator?				
4. What is the desired outcome? What "gets made" in this form of decision making?				

Table 6.3. 5Cs Training Exercise.

Listed below are some situations that you, as a facilitator, might encounter. As you discuss these situations with others in your group, keep in mind the following questions:

- What do you hope your response will elicit from the group? That is, what is being created as a result of your response?
- How else might you respond in these situations, and what effect might those responses have?

Situation #1: The group you are facilitating is talking about the influx of new Asian immigrants to the city, and they are concerned about the possibility for backlash and retaliation by some Cupertino residents against the newcomers. One of the members of the group turns to you and says, "So what is your opinion, do you think we're going to start seeing more backlash?" How might you respond?

Situation #2: A person in your group has just expressed a fairly strong opinion about cultural and ethnic diversity in Cupertino. You disagree with the person's opinion, and in fact have some rather strong views on the subject yourself. Should you respond to this person, and if so, what would you say?

Situation #3: A person in your group says the following: "I don't understand why the city is spending so much time and energy trying to make us all feel good about these foreigners moving into the city. I came to this forum to see what this diversity stuff is all about, and let me tell you, you're all wasting your time!" The rest of the group is silent as all eyes turn toward you. What might you say or do?

Situation #4: Two of the members of your group are disagreeing about whether cultural diversity in Cupertino is benefiting the community. One person sees diversity as having a positive influence; the other person views it as creating problems. The more they discuss their differences the angrier they seem to get. Should you intervene in this situation, and if so, what might you do?

---

sessions and used to assist the group in developing the format and activities for the diversity forum.

Session #2

During this session participants practiced applying group facilitation principles and skills from a first-person position. To set the stage for this

Table 6.4. Eliciting Ideas for the Diversity Forum.

1.	What are your hopes for the diversity forum? What would you like to see happen as a result of the forum?
2.	What specific issues, topics, or concerns would you like to see addressed at the forum?
3.	What kinds of activities would you like to see included in the forum?

activity, the PDC first conducted a role-play demonstration of a group facilitation for the entire 5Cs group. At various points we stopped the demonstration and asked participants to comment and evaluate on the process. We also rotated some of the 5Cs participants into the facilitator role, at each point stopping the activity so participants could reflect on the process. Following the demonstration, participants broke into small groups and conducted extensive role-play simulations, with each of the participants being given an opportunity to practice facilitating. PDC members assumed the role of coach or teacher, offering instruction and joining with participants to reflect and evaluate on the process. These kinds of mutual reflections were designed to move the participants into a third-person, metacommunicative position.

During the role-play activity, participants discussed their ideas for the cultural diversity forum using the results from the questionnaires circulated at the first session. The content of the role play, then, had practical outcomes for the participants, which in some ways transformed it from a simulation into a substantive or consequential activity. Moreover, participants were aware that the facilitation skills practiced during the role play were the same skills that would be used at the forum. This created an added incentive to learn the skills because there was a clear and direct link to their eventual application in a non-role-play situation.

Session #3

This session was designed so that participants could practice communication facilitation skills while simultaneously planning the cultural diversity forum. To accomplish this, results from the questionnaires were organized into three categories: outcomes, topics, and activities. Several options were included for each category, the content of which depended on what participants indicated on the questionnaires. Working in small groups, with 5Cs members facilitating, participants deliberated among the options for each category. So while participants were gaining additional practice in group facilitation, they were also developing the agenda for the forum by deciding what the outcome should be, what topics would be covered, and what activities would be included.

As each of the small groups reported the results of their first deliberation, it became clear that they did not share a common vision about what the forum should accomplish. Given this lack of consensus, the plan to continue deliberating among the various choices was abandoned. Participants were simply not ready to move to that level of specificity; they needed more time to process the choices and explore the ramifications of the various options. Instead of breaking into small groups, as the PDC planned, the full group embarked on a lengthy and wide-ranging discussion about the various options. Eventually, some agreements began to emerge. These were summarized by the PDC at the end of the session and fed back to the group a few days later via a written document.

Session #4

5Cs participants met during this session to review and amend the draft plan for the diversity forum. The draft plan and the meeting itself were designed by the PDC to draw attention to the kinds of decisions that go into planning a public dialogue event. On one level, participants were asked to make specific decisions about the forum; for example, deciding what topics and issues should be addressed, what should be included in the opening plenary sessions, and how participants would be organized into small groups. On another more general level, the decisions were framed to introduce participants to the inevitable tensions and contradictions that facilitators encounter when designing public dialogue events. For example, when considering the specific activities planned for the forum, we asked participants to reflect on the tension between structure and openness. Is there sufficient structure to ensure an efficient use of time? Is there sufficient openness to ensure opportunities for creativity and spontaneity? Do the planned activities provide an appropriate balance between the two?

By the end of the meeting the ideas presented in the plan were finalized, loose ends and unanswered questions were clarified, and decisions concerning specific tasks were made. Even though this was not a formal communication skills training, it was nevertheless important for involving participants in the planning process and introducing them to some of the challenges involved in organizing and designing public dialogue events. Consistent with our training model, the session also illustrates how our attempts to teach particular capacities, skills, and abilities were carried out in an applied learning context. That is, participants learned how to design a public dialogue event by actually designing one.

Session #5

All 5Cs participants attended this session, which in essence was a dress rehearsal for the diversity forum. After reviewing the full agenda for the event, participants were given a facilitator's guide that included step-by-step instructions for the small-group, table discussions. Those 5Cs members who signed up to facilitate were then given the opportunity to practice working through the facilitator's guide as part of a small-group "walk-through" activity. The purpose here was to create the conditions that 5Cs members were likely to encounter at the forum and to give facilitators practical experience in leading a group discussion. The 5Cs members who elected to record the table discussions, rather than facilitate them, were also given an opportunity to practice as part of the dress rehearsal.

CULTURAL DIVERSITY FORUM

Over 100 Cupertino residents attended the Cultural Diversity Forum, which was a 2-hour event held exactly one week after the final 5Cs training session. As developed by the 5Cs, the forum centered around three issues related to cultural diversity: (a) the city's multicultural July 4 afternoon celebration, (b) a Mandarin Language Immersion Program proposed by the Cupertino Union School District, and (c) non-English signs on local business establishments. These issues were selected by the group because they were hotly contested topics during the previous year and because they revolved around ethnic tensions between established white residents and Chinese and Asian members of the community. The purpose of the forum was to use the issues as case studies for exploring how the community responded to controversial topics in the past, and how public communication about such issues could be improved in the future.

PROMOTING PUBLIC DIALOGUE AND CRITICAL REFLECTION

With the help of the 5Cs facilitators, participants at the forum were invited to adopt dialogic forms of communication while talking and reflecting on the three case study issues. This contrasted sharply with the adversarial forms of conflict that the issues had previously evoked. In fact, each of the issues were so bound up in negative patterns of cultural conflict that some of the 5Cs members were concerned these patterns would dominate the forum, in spite of the efforts of the facilitators to

Box 6.4. The Risks Involved

When asked about the risks involved in the Cupertino Project, city council member Michael Chang said, "the one that comes to my mind is the Cultural Diversity Forum. I was somewhat uncomfortable with it because all the issues were focused on one ethnic group [Chinese], and it was almost like we were going to beat on this group. I thought that it was not balanced. But it was like well, we'll go with it. We should accept a variety of perspectives."

foster alternative forms of communication.[5] So why was the case study approach selected? By focusing on how the issues were handled, as opposed to arguing about the advantages and disadvantages, the forum was designed to call attention to underlying communication and decision-making processes. Rather than exercising rhetorical skills of persuasion and argumentation, participants at the forum were encouraged to use dialogue and critical reflection to seek a broader and deeper understanding of the issues and the communicative processes on which they are built.

What might a broader and deeper understanding entail? First, it might mean that participants would come to see that issues related to cultural diversity are shaped and molded through patterns of public communication. Because other more desirable forms of communication exist and can be readily practiced, negative patterns of cultural conflict are not inevitable. Second, participants might come to the understanding that issues do not enter the realm of public consciousness fully formed and prepackaged. Because they are constructed through particular patterns of public communication they can be transformed if taken up in a different pattern of communication. Finally, a broader understanding of the issues might reflexively assist in opening up additional space for public dialogue. If participants are able to use public dialogue to enhance their understandings of community issues, perhaps they will be motivated to seek out additional ways to engage this form of communication in the future.

SECURING A SAFE PLACE FOR STRONG DISSENT

In addition to promoting public dialogue and critical reflection, the forum was also designed to attract community members with particularly strong views on the case study issues. Those who publicly expressed the most intense opposition and support for the city's multicultural July

4 celebration, the Mandarin Immersion Language Program, and non-English signs, for example, did so primarily by writing letters to the editor of the *Cupertino Courier*. In the case of the Mandarin Language Program, critics and supporters also made their opinions known during an emotional three-hour Cupertino Union School board meeting.[6] Many of these views, although certainly not all of them, created hostility and fueled ethnic tensions among members of the community, in part, because they represented the most extreme positions on the issues. The 5Cs felt it was important to invite these vocal critics and supporters to the forum, and they made a concerted effort to do so. Based on both informal conversations with facilitators immediately following the forum, and in a more formal debriefing at a follow-up 5Cs meeting, there was general agreement that the group was successful in this regard.

> **Box 6.5. Some Came Prepared to Argue**
>
> Two of the 5Cs facilitators at the Diversity Forum, Nadine Grant and Don Allen, reported that a person in their group brought a copy of the U.S. Constitution and was prepared to use excerpts from it to argue against making the City's July 4 celebration a multicultural event. He clearly had strong opinions on the issue. At the end of the forum, however, he made a special effort to thank Don and Nadine for giving him the opportunity to express his views. He didn't change his opinion and he didn't think he changed anyone else's either (he also didn't quote from the Constitution). But he said he appreciated that others in his group listened to him and at least tried to understand his position.

Opening: Context Setting Remarks (30 Minutes)

The opening plenary session consisted of four speakers, each of whom helped set the context for the forum.

Introduction and agenda. The city council member who belonged to the 5Cs, Michael Chang, gave the official welcome. Because he was actively involved in designing the event, Michael was able to comment on the general format and overall purpose of the forum, in addition to accomplishing other more ceremonial outcomes (he was also serving a term as mayor at the time). Two points were especially helpful in setting the context. First, he described the forum as an opportunity for the community to reflect on past controversial issues. This approach, he said,

was different than arguing once again *about* the issues. Second, he de-
emphasized the saliency of the issues themselves by asking participants
to treat them as "past issues," as part of the city's social history. The
more immediate challenge was for the community to use the past issues
as a way of learning how it might better respond to new issues in the
future. "How do we conduct the issues as they surface?" he asked.
"How do we conduct ourselves?"

   Overview of the case studies. Following these opening remarks, the
city manager, Don Brown, gave an overview of the three case study
issues. The purpose here was to provide a factual description of each
issue, with as little interpretation and evaluation as possible. This information was included in a packet and made available to all of the participants at the forum. The packets also included comments representing
the range of different views expressed by community members about
the issues. The full text of each case study description is included in
Tables 6.5, 6.6, and 6.7.
   The focus on the public communication processes surrounding
the three case study issues was not intended to exclude other more
informal and private channels of communication. To that end, the city
manager noted that the public comments included in the packets, most
of which were obtained from newspaper articles, letters to the editor,
and public meetings, did not cover all that was said about the issues.
"You all probably have examples of your own where you or other people have talked about these issues," he said. "Please share these during
your table discussions, share how you heard about the issues and how
they were discussed. That will add to the discussion." By reflecting on
both private conversations and public comments, participants were
encouraged to consider how the case study issues were developed
through the intermeshing of different patterns of communication.

   History/description of the 5Cs. Following the presentation of the
three case study topics, a member of the 5Cs, Fari Aberg, briefly
described the history of the group and their role in developing the
Diversity Forum. This background information, although designed primarily for those unfamiliar with the group, also helped to establish the
relative autonomy of the 5Cs and their neutrality on the three case study
issues. The speaker concluded by saying, "What we [the 5Cs] want you
to do tonight is to get actively involved in your table discussions and
honestly talk about your visions and concerns." Given that many of
those in attendance held opposing positions on the issues, it was critical
that the 5Cs establish themselves as impartial facilitators. The speaker
accomplished this, in part, by focusing on the quality of the table discussions and not the issues themselves.

Table 6.5. Case Study #1: July 4 Multicultural Celebration.

The 1998 July 4 Celebration became a day-long celebration this past year. The day's activities began with the Optimist Club Pancake Breakfast at 7 a.m., followed by the Neighborhood Children's Parade. Patriotic Singing at the Quinlan Center followed the parade.

From 11 a.m. until 3 p.m., a Community Showcase: "Honoring our Diverse Heritage," featured music and dance from a variety of cultural and church groups (Crystal Children's Choir, United Methodist Choir, Payvand Dance and Music from Iran, Korean Tae Kwon Do, Indian Folk Dance, Chinese Performing Artists, Hawaiian Dance and Vocal Group, Baha'i Youth Workshop, Filipino Songs and Dance, Pacific Islanders Choir, Aikido Demonstration, Indonesian-American Friendship Association).

In the evening, prior to the fireworks show, the San Jose Metropolitan Band played traditional American music that included a Patriotic Sing-A-Long. The entire day came to an explosive conclusion with the gala fireworks show synchronized to patriotic music.

What People Said

"The Fourth of July is not a holiday to honor skin color or ethnicity or national origin. It is instead a holiday to honor and remember the concepts contained in the Declaration of Independence."

"America is all about change. . . . Why can we not preserve our founding fathers' beliefs and at the same time welcome our diverse heritage that we have today in our city? Why can't we extend life, liberty, freedom, and rights to all? To do otherwise, now that would be un-American."

"The celebration on the Fourth is about being an American, not German, English, Chinese, or African."

"Since when is the Fourth of July a time not to celebrate people? Who fought for our independence? . . . Indians, French and British! Not just Americans."

"We are all tired of this preoccupation with diversity. . . . Why don't we concentrate on ways we are all alike?"

"Intercultural understanding and appreciation are essential to the realization of principals encompassed in our nation's founding documents."

"Wouldn't it be refreshing if all this cultural diversity could be a two-way street? Just think, maybe we would see characterizations of George Washington or Abraham Lincoln marching in the Chinese New Year parade. Sure we will."

"The American experience has always been about people. . . . Let us on July 4 celebrate our liberties based on a 'government of the people by the people and for the people,' all of the people."

Table 6.6. Case Study #2: Mandarin Immersion Language Program.

School districts in Redwood City, San Francisco, Palo Alto, Fremont, and others have adopted various types of dual-language immersion programs. These programs range from "total immersion" where 50% or more of instruction time is devoted to learning the native language of the minority students (Spanish, a Chinese dialect, French), to "enrichment/maintenance" where one period, per day, of the native language is taught, supplemented by vocabulary development in core subjects.

Educational research shows that language-minority students acquire a second language (English) best when their first language is firmly grounded. Majority-language students (English) also learn a second language best when immersed in that language. Finally, long-term studies of students who have completed K-6 dual-language immersion programs perform better in all academic areas.

The Cupertino Union School District adopted a pilot enrichment program after extensive public hearings.

What They Said

"Children of immigrants need to learn English first and their native tongue second. Parents of children who only speak their native tongue at home are doing their children a grave injustice."

"Asserting that too much of one language or another is being spoken in our community is to ask that people deny who they are and to restrict their right to freedom of expression. Anyone in this country is free to choose how and where they use their preferred language."

"This program's real advantage is to English-speaking students. . . . Forward-thinking parents who recognize the value of their kids developing a tongue for an Asian language won't mind paying for that opportunity."

"No one is disputing the fact that English is the most important language to learn. In addition, for students who also want to be proficient in a second language, it includes early immersion in both languages."

"This subject of Mandarin immersion being introduced to the school board is a crime. It is obviously an ethnic proposal that has some general merit, but I wonder how the proponents would feel if, instead of Mandarin, we proposed Vietnamese, German, French, or Spanish as the immersion language base."

"Surprise—The cost for immersion programs is about the same as regular programs!"

"The expenses are far-reaching and should only be paid, as they are today, by those who desire this or any other special interest-type program."

Table 6.7. Case Study #3: Non-English Signs.

As Cupertino's demographics have changed to represent more diverse cultures, so have the businesses in the community. Over the last few years, a number of businesses have elected to display the name of their business in languages other than English. The most noticeable signs use Chinese characters for advertisement and identification.

A survey was completed by the City to determine how many signs were exclusively non-English (e.g., if signs had only Chinese characters and no English text they would be considered exclusively "non-English"). At the time of the survey, there were only one or two exclusively non-English signs in Cupertino. All other signs contained English text, albeit in a smaller size. Some shopping centers, such as Cupertino Village, require all tenants to have signs that contain English as a part of the primary building signs.

The City Attorney of Cupertino has determined that the City has the authority to regulate the size and colors of signs, but not the content (U.S. Constitution: Freedom of Speech). The business owner has the right to determine the content and language of his or her business signs.

What People Said

"There's a sense of closeness when (Chinese-speaking) people see Chinese writing. We want our customers to feel welcome."

"People feel less isolated or uncomfortable when they see signs written in English characters."

"It is hard to always read the street numbers (when) rushing to a scene. It makes it easier for emergency crews, who mostly speak English, if they can read the store sign."

"Signs let people know they speak Chinese and carry Chinese products."

"The community may be more harmonious if everyone can recognize the name of businesses."

"When signs incorporate both languages, English wording seems smaller than Chinese. . . . A single Chinese character can represent a whole word."

Directions for table discussions The final presenter in the opening session, a member of the PDC, outlined the specific purpose and outcome of the table discussions. He began by reviewing the agenda:

The mayor mentioned the agenda for tonight, which is for the community to come together and reflect on controversial topics and issues. . . . Not to rehash the issues in terms of debating them again, but to talk about how the community handled the issues and, very important, how the community can improve the way it handles other issues in the future.

The speaker then briefly described some of the characteristics of face-to-face public dialogue, with the expectation being that participants would practice this form of communication in their table discussions. Specifically, participants were told that dialogue involves: (a) an emphasis on listening as much as speaking, (b) the free and honest expression of views and opinions, (c) the ability to openly consider other peoples' views and opinions, no matter how different they might be from your own, and (d) a focus on mutual understanding and coordination, not winning and losing. The speaker concluded by delineating the outcome of the table discussions. "One of the last things you'll talk about at your table discussions are proposals. . . . Can you as a group develop a set of proposals for how the community can best discuss controversial issues related to diversity?"

Table Discussions (60 Minutes)

Following the opening plenary session, participants selected one of the three case study issues and, with the help of the 5Cs facilitators, formed small groups with others interested in the same topic. A total of 11 groups were formed, each with approximately 8 to 10 participants. One of the advantages of this format was that multiple groups were formed for each case study issue (i.e., four groups discussed the July 4 multicultural celebration and Mandarin Immersion Program, and three groups discussed non-English signs). The format for the table discussions followed a sequence consisting of six interrelated segments, beginning with introductions and ground rules and moving progressively toward specific proposals for action. A brief description of each segment follows.

Ground rules. After group members introduced themselves, the 5Cs facilitator identified three ground rules for the table discussions: respect differences, one person speaks at a time, and keep remarks brief and concise.

Descriptions of the case study. In this segment participants discussed the events surrounding the case study issue by utilizing observational accounts and factual descriptions rather than evaluative statements. In a sense, this was an opportunity for the groups to construct an agreed-upon story of what happened. Many of the groups were in fact able to arrive at a common set of facts and observations, although in some cases there were discrepancies that went unresolved. Facilitators were careful not to insist that their group reach full agreement, and they simply noted areas of factual disagreement before moving forward into the next segment.

What do we like about the way the issue was handled? In asking this question, facilitators encouraged group participants to focus on appreciative evaluations. In spite of the often heated rhetoric surrounding the case study issues, most of the groups were able to generate a common list of positive outcomes. Not all of the groups reached full agreement, of course. Again, facilitators did not push their groups toward consensus, although a more concerted effort was made here to probe and explore the underlying nature of the disagreements.

What concerns us about the way the issue was handled? By focusing on critical evaluations, this segment represented the flip side of the previous one. Not surprisingly, the groups had little difficulty identifying concerns and criticizing the way the issues were handled, although not all of the groups achieved full consensus. Similar to the previous segment, facilitators explored areas of disagreement with group participants before moving forward.

How could the issue have been handled differently to promote greater community unity and harmony? There was a noticeable shift in the direction of the table discussions during this segment. Instead of evaluating the issues solely as historical case studies, the groups were now asked to consider the kinds of changes that would need to take place in order to bring about more positive outcomes. There is an implicit comparison embedded in this question between a reconstructed past and an imagined future, with the focus of the discussion being on the differences between the two. Most of the groups responded in this segment with little assistance from the facilitators. In those cases in which the groups needed guidance, the following probes were used: Who would be involved that was not involved? Who would act differently? What differences would there be in timing? What differences would there be in the process? What would be done or not be done? Where would things be done or not done?

What specific proposals do you have for improving the way we deal with issues like these? After considering how the case study issues could have been handled differently, the groups now worked to codify their responses into a specific set of recommendations. Facilitators encouraged group participants to put their ideas for improving public communication into concrete terms and actions.

Box 6.6. More Risks Involved

The Diversity Forum seemed risky at first, and much of the discussion at my table was centered on negatives. In the end, however, our group was able to enlist positive contributions and solutions from everyone. I think everyone appreciated being able to talk about sensitive issues in an open, non-judgmental atmosphere.
—Donna Krey, Cupertino City employee

Closing: What Was Learned? (30 Minutes)

During the final session of the forum spokespersons from each of the 11 small groups reported their findings to the larger group. A member of the 5Cs, Jonathan Ma, moderated the discussion. Following the reports, the moderator briefly summarized and reflected on the overall findings, focusing specifically on the commonalties and differences in the proposals. Fari Aberg, the 5Cs member who presented a description and history of the group in the opening plenary session, concluded the forum by inviting participants to join the 5Cs and thanking them for their participation.

RESULTS OF THE DIVERSITY FORUM

The PDC collected notes and flip charts from each of the groups, summarized the results, and reviewed them, first, with the 5Cs coordinating team, and later with the entire group at a follow-up meeting. The final summary document was then mailed to all forum participants, and made available to the larger community through a full-page advertisement in the *Cupertino Courier*.[7] The document, titled "Summary of diversity forum proposals: A blueprint for public communication," is organized into three sections: (1) appreciations, (2) concerns, and (3) proposals. The complete text of the document appears in Table 6.8

EVALUATING THE DIVERSITY FORUM

An open-ended questionnaire was used to obtain feedback from forum participants. As indicated in Table 6.9, the first two questions provided participants with an opportunity to comment on the case study topics that were covered during the forum. The third item focused specifically on assessment and evaluation. Based on responses to this item, the

Table 6.8. Summary of Diversity Forum Proposals.

Appreciations: What Was Handled Well?

Not Avoiding the Issues: All three issues received considerable public attention, primarily as a result of articles, editorials, and letters published in the *Cupertino Courier*. Participants noted that media coverage of the issues signaled a willingness on the part of the community to engage issues rather than avoid them.

Voicing Opinions/Raising Issues: In addition, media coverage provided an opportunity for people with different and often competing views to voice their opinions. As a result, important questions about the issues were raised.

Creating Awareness: And because people on different sides were heard and able to express their views, the community as a whole became aware of the issues and the various positions on them. Without public airing, the issues would have gone unnoticed by a large segment of the community.

Bringing People Together: Similar appreciations were noted for the School Board Meetings where the Mandarin Immersion Program was publicly discussed. These meetings gave people a chance to voice their opinions and talk openly about the issue. Moreover, the meetings brought people together who felt strongly about the issue, even though there were intense differences of opinion.

Concerns: What Was Not Handled Well?

Overemphasizing Extremes: Participants at the forum appreciated that the issues were discussed openly and in public, but they were concerned that discussion was limited primarily to editorials and letters in the *Courier* and School Board meetings. They were concerned that the people who participated in these forums reflected the most extreme views in the community, and that discussions elicited defensiveness and provoked attack. People with other views might have been reluctant to join the discussion or were simply unable to get "air time" for more moderate views.

Few Opportunities: The public had few outlets other than the *Courier* and School Board meetings for publicly expressing their views on the issues. While well adapted for other purposes, such as creating interest in a topic or making a decision, these outlets are not necessarily the best for good listening and mutual learning about the issues.

The Need for a Common Set of Facts: The public was not adequately informed about the issues in terms of factual background information. There was concern that the goals, purposes, and facts behind each of the three issues were not communicated as clearly as they could have been, which in turn led to some misconceptions and confusion.

More Timely Information: Similarly, there was a lack of timely information that would have alerted the public to the issues before they became

Table 6.8. Summary Document of Small Group Discussions.

contentious, inflamed, and polarized. There was concern that the public was not informed about the issues as early as they should have been.

Proposals: How Can Public Communication About Issues Be Improved?

Involve the Public Early: The public should be involved in framing issues and planning events before decisions are made or are about to be made. The public will become vested in whatever decisions are made if they participate in shaping them. The process for framing issues and planning events should be open so that it encourages broad public participation, including children. Suggestions for accomplishing this are to use a variety of communication channels for involving the public, including town forums, traditional news media, as well as the internet and city web page.

Inform and Educate the Public: Factual information about issues and events should be made available to the public early and often. Information should be repeated over and over again and a variety of communication channels should be used. In presenting information, the media should try to educate the public, in addition to providing a forum for people to voice their opinions.

More Town Forums: The community should hold more town forums so that people have opportunities to discuss issues and events in face-to-face discussions. Other types of forums might be developed in response to specific issues or to meet the needs of particular groups. For example, the city might develop a "quick response" capability for holding a well-facilitated forum on potentially volatile issues as soon as they emerge. Other forums might be designed as one day or two day events, permitting in-depth discussion and deliberation of issues in more varied formats than those mandated by the responsibilities of a city council or school board meeting.

Create Opportunities for Open Communication: Along with the town forums, the community should advance open communication on issues related to culture and demographic change. This type of communication can be promoted through ground rules that encourage listening, honesty, and respect, and through training programs that teach people the skills of public dialogue.

Find Common Ground: When discussing issues of culture and demographic change, people should be encouraged to explore common interests and common goals in addition to whatever differences they might have. This can be accomplished by developing communication activities and events that focus on community unity and harmony.

Choose Words Carefully: The words and language used to describe issues and events should be chosen carefully because they trigger responses in people that have unintended consequences. The particular words used to label an issue can create resistance in some people even though they might not disagree with the underlying principles and goals of the issue.

forum was an unqualified success. Over 90% of the participants described the event using adjectives such as "superb," "great," "excellent," "beneficial, "good," or "useful." Interestingly, the few participants who did not respond favorably took issue with the title of the event, and not with the case study topics or the quality of the discussion. Typical of this was the participant who wrote: "We should not call this a diversity forum, but a unity forum."

A closer analysis of the responses reveals that the forum achieved a number of stated outcomes. First, several participants commented on the way the case study topics were discussed, indicating that they were able to reflect on the form of communication in addition to the content. "It was a great way of communicating with others," wrote one participant. Others commented that the table discussions provided "an excellent opportunity to listen to others" and sufficient "time to communicate." Some of the participants reflected on the value of dialogic forms of communication in bridging relational and cultural differences. One participant said that the "most beneficial aspect was the opportunity for communication. An opportunity to honestly and frankly discuss the issues with others who hold other points of view." Another wrote, "I think it is an important way to get to know and understand people of different cultural backgrounds."

Another successful outcome of the forum, as reported by participants, was that a variety of views and opinions were expressed and a deeper understanding of the issues emerged. "It was superb," wrote one participant. "It helped me understand the issues and both sides of the story much better. Thanks to all who are behind this forum." Another person commented that she was "surprised at the breadth of viewpoints presented," and concluded by saying, "I learned a lot from this forum." Along these same lines, another participant wrote that the forum was "very successful" because "people got to hear opinions from others."

A third outcome of the forum was a recognition among some of the participants that the public dialogue process is flexible and can be adapted to a variety of community issues. This is an important finding

Table 6.9. Diversity Forum Feedback Questionnaire.

1.	Do you have comments or suggestions about the other case study topics not addressed at your table?
2.	Is there something you would like to add here that you were unable to comment on during the meeting?
3.	What is your evaluation of the Diversity Forum? What do you think was beneficial? What can be improved in the future?

given our focus in Phase IV on institutionalization. Among other things, it demonstrates that some of the participants recognized the value of public dialogue outside of the specific issues of cultural diversity, Asian immigration, and demographic change. One participant, for example, wrote that the forum was a "great opportunity for public/community dialogue! Forums like these could be employed to address any proposals that might have the community in an uproar, before any actions are taken/approved." Another participant said that it would be "useful to continue these discussions in some fashion without coming across as being overly concerned about diversity." The person went on to suggest that "other topics can be generated from letters to the editor, school board agenda items, and city council items."

NEXT STEPS: REVISITING QUESTIONS OF GROUP IDENTITY AND PURPOSE

Following the Diversity Forum, the 5Cs met to review the feedback questionnaires and plan the future agenda of the group. The first half of the meeting was spent on evaluation and assessment as group members reflected on the forum and talked about their experiences facilitating and recording the table discussions. Reviewing the results of the feedback questionnaire during this portion of the meeting corroborated the group's mostly positive evaluations and heightened their sense of accomplishment. In the second half of the meeting attention turned to next steps. There was naturally a good deal of enthusiasm and interest for continuing the work of the 5Cs. The challenge was deciding exactly what the group would do.

Although several proposals were offered, the range of activities suggested was not nearly as pronounced as in the early stages of the group's formation. In fact, there was far more agreement than disagreement. It seemed as though the process of reflecting on and evaluating the Diversity Forum, and using that event as a springboard for planning future activities, created a common framework for determining the direction of the group. By the end of the meeting there was consensus that the group should focus its efforts on four types of activities. A summary of these activities was compiled by a member of the PDC team and reviewed by the 5Cs at their next meeting. A copy of the final summary is included in Table 6.10.

Table 6.10. 5Cs Agenda.

---

1. *Networking and outreach activities* (with community groups and representatives from the schools, media, service clubs, city commissions, law enforcement, Chamber of Commerce, etc.). The 5Cs will initiate conversations with community groups to explore common interests, concerns, and opportunities for future collaboration. One suggestion is to start by inviting groups who were identified at the Diversity Forum and in the proposals generated by the participants. For example, representatives from the various media organizations might be invited to attend a 5Cs meeting to talk about ways the two groups can work together to improve public communication.

2. *Capacity-building workshops in intercultural communication.* The 5Cs will learn principles and acquire skills for effective cross-cultural communication through ongoing training activities. Three members of the group have volunteered to initiate the workshop series, the first of which will take place at the next 5Cs meeting and continue on a regular basis.

3. *Organize and plan future town forums* (to be sponsored and facilitated by the 5Cs). The idea here is not to be locked into any one type of format, but to be flexible in developing different types of forums that respond to what best fits the community at any given time. Forums might be held annually, semi-annually or more depending on the need; they might be developed quickly in response to a single issue and/or they might take a long-range perspective covering a variety of issues; they might be designed for a particular community group (e.g., the schools) and/or they might be inclusive of the entire community. It was also suggested that the 5Cs might host a community potluck for more informal types of interaction.

4. *Respond to specific action items.* The 5Cs will continue to work on specific action items in collaboration with other civic organizations. The group will begin this effort by responding to the specific plans generated at the Diversity Forum.

WORKING IN THE PUBLIC SCHOOLS

In addition to the 5Cs, another major set of activities conducted during Phase IV involved training students at the two Cupertino high schools, Monta Vista High and Cupertino High, in public dialogue and group facilitation techniques. The move into the local school system fit both the broad goals of the project generally, as well as the immediate goals of Phase IV. First, schools are ideal sites for children, young adults, and teens to learn the kinds of communication abilities that lead to active and responsible citizenship (Barber, 1997; Battistoni, 1997).[8] Schools are also important centers of community life (Lappé & Du Bois, 1994). They bring diverse stakeholders together around issues that often reflect the larger concerns of the community. This was certainly the case with the Cupertino Project. The public schools were a constant source of discussion in the focus groups, dialogue groups, at 5Cs meetings, and large public events. This should not be surprising given that schools are a vital part of community life.

The approach taken by the PDC to working in the schools was to train cohort groups of students in small-group facilitation skills and to create opportunities for these students to lead discussions with their peers on important issues facing the campus community. Consistent with the PDC training model, we believe that the microskills of public dialogue and facilitation are best taught in contexts that are meaningful to students; that is, when students have an interest in shaping the learning process. One of the ways we accomplished this was to create opportunities for students to practice the skills of public dialogue and facilitation with other students. An approach similar to this is used in the thousands of peer mediation programs currently in place in schools across the United States in which students, trained in conflict resolution skills, act as mediators in helping to resolve disputes among their peers (Crawford & Bodine, 1996). By comparison, our work in the Cupertino schools, although also employing a peer learning component, was focused more on group facilitation skills and community development than it was on the resolution of interpersonal conflict.

THE CUPERTINO HIGH SCHOOL (CHS) PROJECT

The CHS Project, titled "Making Connections," was designed to teach students citizenship skills and to provide opportunities for the members of the campus community to address important topics and concerns. The project developed over a series of phases, each corresponding roughly to the phases of the larger Cupertino Project.

Phase 1: Listening to All the Voices

The PDC initiated the project by training 15 De Anza College and San Jose State University students over a 2-day period in communication facilitation techniques. This training focused primarily on basic facilitation skills (neutrality, listening, questioning asking), and also included some instruction in advanced communication practices (appreciative inquiry and systemic questioning). Working in small groups with PDC members serving as facilitators, participants also compared and analyzed the four models of public decision making used in the 5Cs training (see Table 6.2). The college and university students then facilitated 12 small-group discussions over a two-day period with 150 CHS student participants about their concerns for the campus community. The focus-group discussions lasted approximately 90 minutes and covered a variety of different topics.

Four issues stood out as particularly important. The first concerned the quality of teacher-student relationships. The second concerned the way funding decisions for extracurricular programs were made. The other two issues focused on a large-scale CHS initiative called the Expected Schoolwide Learning Results (or ESLRs). Students in the focus groups expressed concern about the language used to describe the ESLRs as well as how the ESLRs would be taught. Interestingly, the issue of cultural diversity did not surface in these discussions even though the student population at CHS, like most other Cupertino schools, is more ethnically diverse than the community at large.

Phase 2: Visions and Action Plans

In the next phase of the project, the PDC and the De Anza College and San Jose State University students provided a six-hour facilitation training program for 20 volunteer CHS students. The purpose was to teach the CHS students specific communication skills that would enable them to facilitate small-group discussions with their peers. The content of the training mirrored the skills taught in the first training program from Phase 1, with the material being adapted to fit the high school audience. This training was followed by a second round of small-group discussions held on the CHS campus. The purpose of the discussions was to generate proposals and action plans relating to the four issues identified in the first round of discussions. Over 60 CHS students participated in one of the 10 discussion groups. Importantly, the 20 trained CHS students co-facilitated these discussions with the college and university students, thus giving them practical experience in the skills they were learning.

The variety of different action plans generated in these discussions were summarized by the PDC and framed as a series of choices, with each choice corresponding to one of the four issues previously identified in Phase 1. For example, under the topic "teacher-student relationships," three action plans emerged as the choices: (a) bring the teachers into the conversation, (b) provide additional support for the teachers in doing their jobs, and (c) identify specific issues for special attention. The rationale underlying each of these choices was provided along with a detailed description of the action plan (see Table 6.11).

Table 6.11. Example of Action Plans/Choices.

Topic: Student-Teacher Relationships

Choice 1: Bring the teachers into the conversation

Rationale: Students want to be active in their own learning and to have good relationships with teachers. They find some forms of instruction more engaging than others, and they find some teachers more willing and able to help them than others. As the teachers are vitally involved in these issues, there should be an opportunity for students and teachers to explore together ideas about how to improve or maintain existing levels of teacher relationships.

Action Plan: CHS should sponsor special meetings for students and teachers to talk about how their relationships can be improved and/or maintained at a high level.

Choice 2: Provide additional support for the teachers in doing their jobs

Rationale: The work done by teachers is difficult. Many teachers are assigned to large classes that make them less able to give individual attention to students. Students differ in their abilities and in their learning styles. To the extent that teachers emphasize the "A" students, they do not give adequate help to students who have more difficulty with their studies, and to the extent that teachers use just one or two modalities for instruction, they make learning difficult for students whose learning styles favor other modalities.

Action Plan: Provide opportunities for summer courses, peer evaluations, and additional teaching aides for teachers.

Choice 3: Identify specific issues for special attention

Rationale: CHS students appreciate the efforts of the school and the efforts of their teachers. However, there are some specific areas that present unusual challenges. Students, teachers, and school administrators should identify these areas and take steps to improve them.

Action Plan: A team of students, teachers, and school administrators should identify courses with which students are dissatisfied. Working together, they should explore the reasons for the dissatisfaction, make recommendations for improvement, and monitor the effects of the changes that are implemented.

Phase 3: Deliberations

The PDC conducted another training with the college and high school facilitators in preparation for the third round of discussions. A major part of this training focused on the principles of public deliberation and the communication skills used to facilitate these kinds of discussions. The 78 CHS students, parents, faculty, staff, and student resource officers (SROs) who participated in these final deliberations were divided into 10 different groups. Each group was assigned one of the four issues and deliberated among the choices (or action plans) developed for that particular issue. Again, the 20 trained CHS students facilitated these deliberations with the college and university students. In some cases, the high school and college students co-facilitated together; in others cases high school students co-facilitated with other high school students.

Following the deliberations, the Cupertino School Site Council, composed of students, parents, and teachers, met to review the results and decide the next steps in the process. The meeting took place in June at the end of the school year. The Council identified student-teacher relationships as the topic to pursue for the following school year.

Phase 4: Implementing Action Plans

One of the action plans for student-teacher relationships identified by students in Phase 2 was to bring the "teachers into the conversation" (see Choice #1, Table 6.11). The implementation of this plan was accomplished, in part, at a meeting held in November 1998. Approximately 100 teachers and students met in 10 groups composed of 10 or so participants. Trained students and teachers co-facilitated each of the groups. The facilitators guided the group participants through the following three questions: (a) When you think of teacher-student relationships, what comes to mind? (b) When you think of the ideal teacher-student relationship, what do you think of and how is that different from other teacher-student relationships? (c) If Cupertino High School were to move closer to the ideal, what would need to happen and who would need to be involved?

The PDC complied a written summary of the group discussions and shared these with the School Site Council at a follow-up debriefing meeting. There was a good deal of similarity across groups; however, some of the more interesting comments came out of the two "fishbowl" discussions held immediately after the group discussions. In one fishbowl session, the teachers sat in a circle and shared their reflections on the meeting while the students looked on and observed. In the second fishbowl, the students shared reflections while the teachers observed. In both cases, teachers and students said that they were surprised by what they learned from each other. Teachers were surprised, for example, that students wanted to get to know them on a more personal basis and that students rarely approached them in that way because they felt intimidated. Students, on the other hand, said they were surprised to learn how hard and frustrating it is for teachers to establish relationships with students. Both groups concluded by saying how beneficial it was for them to hear what the other had to say. Other results from the meeting were taken up by School Site Council and the PDC and used in subsequent activities the following semester.

Box 6.7. "They Felt Important"

The most interesting part of the Cupertino High project was the way that students were included in the process. Students were trained and used as facilitators, as well as participants. The process made them feel that their thoughts and opinions were significant and valid. They felt important. Asking the students what their concerns were, and then actually structuring programs around these concerns, said a lot to the students about their value. Students have told me that when someone asks their opinion about something they usually never hear anything about it again. This was a different experience. The PDC demonstrated to them that there was value and merit to what they had to say.
—Janet Shannon, Student Resource Officer

MONTA VISTA HIGH SCHOOL PROJECT

The project at Monta Vista High developed a bit differently than the one at CHS. This was due primarily to a rather extensive campus-wide program that was already in place at Monta Vista before the PDC arrived. The program, titled "Building Unity While Appreciating Diversity," brought stakeholders from the community and the campus together around a number of on-going projects and events. It was clear that a good deal of commitment and work had gone into developing the program. There was, however, little coordination between the various projects and no overarching plan to connect them to a set of stated objectives or outcomes. Although the PDC was welcomed into the program (the 5Cs were also included but never participated in any activities or events), we were limited to developing activities that corresponded with what the other intact groups were already doing. Such was not the case at Cupertino High, where we were involved in the overall design of the project as well as the development of individual activities and events.

We started at Monta Vista High by training two groups of students in group-facilitation skills. One group consisted of 25 students from the campus Peer Counseling course, which is modeled on the national peer meditation program. The other group, called the "Helpers," consisted of 15 students who were selected specifically for this assignment. Each group underwent several days of training in preparation for a campus-wide student forum on diversity at Monta Vista High. At the forum, a PDC member mediated a "fishbowl" discussion with six students on the question of how well Monta Vista High prepares its students for a diverse society. Over 2,000 students attended the forum and observed the discussion. The following day the two groups of trained students attended over 60 different classes on campus and facilitated small-group discussions with their peers. The small-group discussions were designed to give as many on-campus students as possible an opportunity to respond directly to the issues raised during the previous day's forum.

In a second training and group facilitation activity at Monta Vista High, the PDC worked with 40 students from the campus Link Crew Program. The Link Crew is a group of junior and senior students who are trained in mentoring the younger students on campus. After undergoing a training session with the PDC, the Link Crew students facilitated small-group discussions with 300 students from one of the local junior high schools on issues related to conflict resolution. A similar training and group-facilitation activity with the Monta Vista High School students was conducted the following year. Instead of conflict resolution, however, the topic dealt with group decision making.

Box 6.8. Developing Lifelong Skills

The project at Monta Vista was unique in that our students had the opportunity to be trained by the PDC in communication facilitation skills. This is not a skill that one would learn in an "academic" class, but it's a lifelong skill that they will be able to use after they graduate, go to college, and enter the world of work.

—Joanne Laird, Vice Principle, Monta Vista High School

The training programs conducted at Monta Vista High were similar to the ones at CHS in that they provided students with practical experience in facilitating group discussions with their peers. The programs thus placed students in the position of having to learn from each other.

THE CUPERTINO MULTICULTURAL INTERAGENCY COLLABORATIVE

One of the benefits of working in the schools was that the PDC became a visible resource for various educational institutions seeking to address topics related to culture, race, and ethnicity. Such was the case with the Cupertino Multicultural Interagency Collaborative, or Collaborative for short. Initiated by a local Asian American Parents Association (AAPA), the Collaborative was formed to explore ways of integrating multiculturalism into the public school system and to forge links with the larger community to help sustain these efforts. A number of influential educational and civic leaders participated in the group, including the superintendents from the two local school districts, the president of De Anza College, the mayor and city manger of Cupertino, and representatives from the 5Cs. The PDC assumed a rather unusual role in the Collaborative. In addition to designing and facilitating a Collaborative meeting, one of the members of the PDC team was also asked to participate as a contributing member of the group.

During Phase IV of the Cupertino Project the Collaborative held two formal meetings. The first meeting was mostly informational with each of the participants reporting on how their various agencies were addressing multicultural issues. Dr. Derald Wing Su, Professor of Educational Psychology at California State University Hayward, attended the meeting at the request of AAPA and offered suggestions for how the group might consolidate their individual efforts. Based on Dr. Su's recommendation, the group held a second meeting to identify common core values and develop a working definition of multiculturalism. The PDC was enlisted to design and facilitate this five-hour meeting. The format, which included a combination of large and small-group discussions, called for participants to generate a list of core values, deliberate among them, and use the results to develop a definition of multiculturalism (see Table 6.12). The meeting concluded with participants discussing how they planned to work with faculty, staff, and students to integrate the definition into the various aspects of their respective campus communities.

Table 6.12. The Collaborative's Definition of Multiculturalism.

- Multiculturalism includes, appreciates, and respects the complexity and richness of our community and the various lived experiences and perceptions of our residents.

- Multiculturalism is a dynamic, evolving and complex process which is based on a powerful set of core values. These are: (1) understanding differences in ways that promote unity, not separateness; (2) promotes inclusion, cooperation, and movement toward mutually shared goals; and (3) respects the unique characteristics of individuals as well as commonalties among culturally diverse groups that make up our community and reflects all aspects of who we are (race, class, gender, ethnicity, religion, national origin, etc.).

- A realistic working definition of multiculturalism recognizes that conflict and disagreement, as well as collaboration and consensus, are essential parts of a rich dialogue and necessary to achieve the goals of a culturally rich community.

- In our multicultural community, an action plan is developed to influence behaviors and organizational structures to nurture the common good and integrate the positive contributions of all members of the community.

ADDITIONAL COMMUNITY TRAINING ACTIVITIES

In our on-going efforts to teach public dialogue skills to community residents, the PDC conducted several trainings with different stakeholder groups. The content and format of these trainings varied in response to the particular group and circumstances. Because public dialogue is a multifaceted and flexible process, it can be applied to a variety of different contexts, issues, and outcomes. Part of our task in institutionalizing public dialogue was to adapt our training model and teaching practices to the unique needs of various stakeholder groups.

EMERGENCY PREPAREDNESS TRAINING

The PDC conducted a six-hour training for the 32 neighborhood leaders involved in the city's Emergency Preparedness Program. Given that this group is responsible for coordinating neighborhood activities in response to natural disasters, the training focused on leadership skills. More specifically, it covered five communication skills associated with collaborative forms of leadership and facilitation: (a) mobilizing resources, (b) empowering participation, (c) listening, (d) dreaming (or visioning), and (e) deciding (or deliberation). Consistent with the PDC training model, each of the leadership skills was taught using a combination of demonstrations, communication practice, and critical reflection. For example, in the first session dealing with mobilizing resources, participants worked in small groups to brainstorm ideas for inviting neighbors to an emergency preparedness meeting. The ideas generated were then put into practice through a role-play exercise, with the group reflecting on the techniques and evaluating their effectiveness.

LEADERSHIP CUPERTINO TRAINING

The PDC conducted a three-hour training for 20 participants in Leadership Cupertino, a program designed to prepare residents for various leadership positions in the city. Given the expressed civic function of the program, the PDC focused the training on public communication and democracy. Unlike the other training programs conducted by the PDC, this one included a good deal of theoretical and historical information. For example, participants were provided with an historical overview of public communication, beginning with the development of democracy in the ancient Greek city-states and continuing through to the current late-modern or postmodern period. The purpose here was to demonstrate how different forms of public communication give rise to different forms of democratic practice existing in various historical periods. As the focus turned to current conceptions of communication and democracy, participants compared and analyzed different models of public communication using a matrix similar to the one described in Table 6.2.

COMMUNITY RESIDENTS TRAINING

This intensive, two-day training program involved a cross-section of 20 Cupertino residents, including members of the 5Cs, students from Cupertino High School, and others who had not previously participated in the project. Given the focus on communication facilitation skills, the training was similar in some respects to the 5Cs training and those conducted at the two local high schools. That is, participants learned facilitation skills through demonstrations, communication practice, and critical reflection. The training differed from previous ones, however, in that it represented the first systematic attempt to integrate strategic process planning, event design, and communication facilitation skills into a single training program. In this way, the training demonstrated the fullest expression of the PDC community dialogue process model as depicted in Chapter 1 (Figure 1.1).

In the community training program, strategic process planning was described in terms of designing a public communication project that includes multiple events, each working toward some specified outcome. The Cupertino Project itself, as well as the schools project developed at CHS, are obviously examples of public dialogue projects. Although the focus was clearly on public dialogue, it is important to note that a strategic planning process can also be based on the other models of public communication identified in Table 6.2. In any case, one of the goals of the community training program was to teach participants strategic process skills and sensibilities that would enable them to design their own public communication projects. A second goal of the training was to teach participants how to design public communication events, such as a large town forum. The linkage here involved situating event design within the larger context of a public communication project. That is, particular events should be consistent with and contribute to a larger process. Finally, the community training program was also designed to teach participants communication facilitation skills, such as listening, questioning, and the like. These microskills are, of course, enacted in the context of a particular event and should thus contribute to whatever outcomes are specified for that event.

ON-GOING WORK WITH LAW ENFORCEMENT

Beginning in Phase I and continuing through Phase IV, the PDC facilitated numerous small-group discussions with members of the Sheriff's department about ways to enhance community safety. As previously noted, a common theme expressed by Sheriff's officers was the need to connect with citizens at the neighborhood level through "community policing" efforts. The Sheriff's Department, in collaboration with the city, took a major step toward implementing this action plan by creating a "community programs liaison" position. The primary responsibilities of this position, which was staffed at the Sergeant's level, was to develop and coordinate neighborhood outreach activities involving beat officers and community residents.

The new Sheriff's position was created in response to both community safety and cultural diversity issues. The Sergeant hired for the position, Steve Angus, articulated the connection between the two issues in a briefing meeting with the PDC and in an interview with the

Cupertino Courier. "I got here as a direct result of what citizens wanted," he said. "As a result of the work of the Public Dialogue Consortium and interaction with the community, we found out that public safety and cultural enrichment were the city's two biggest priorities" (Enders, 1998, p. 5). He went on to say,

> In Cupertino, there's a large, culturally diverse community, and each brings in their own views and biases and backgrounds to how they view and relate to law enforcement. We want to serve better, and the city does, too. So we want to find out what concerns different cultures have toward law enforcement. (Enders, 1998, p. 5)

Box 6.9. A Law Enforcement Conduit

The impact of the project is beginning to take shape. In my case, I have had very good responses from the people I've interacted with. These include citizens, city staff, and deputies. The citizens are starting to realize that they have someone they can call directly with concerns and comments. The city staff has utilized the resources of the Sheriff's Office with more ease and frequency than in the past. The deputies are enthused that they have a contact person who can deal directly with the public. The goal of my position, being a conduit between citizens, the city staff, and the Sheriff's Office, is becoming reality. I think this is a significant contribution from a law enforcement perspective.

—Steve Angus, Sergeant, Santa Clara County Sheriff's Department & Cupertino Community Programs Liaison

The new Sheriff's position represented an another important step toward institutionalizing public dialogue in Cupertino. First, by recognizing the linkages between cultural issues and law enforcement issues, the position created possibilities for new collaborative relationships between stakeholders in the community. Second, Sergeant Angus himself participated in PDC training programs and helped to facilitate various public dialogue events. After going through the 5Cs training program, for example, Sergeant Angus served as one of the table facilitators at the Cultural Diversity Forum. He continues to be an active member of the 5Cs.

LOOKING BACK-LOOKING FORWARD

The activities comprising Phase IV were much more diffuse and varied than earlier phases, due in large part to the expanded nature of the project. Some of the activities, such as the 5Cs, grew directly out of the work completed in Phase III. Other activities, such as the school training programs, moved the project and the PDC into new areas of civic participation. Importantly, the PDC assumed different roles in these various activities. In the case of the 5Cs, for example, we served primarily as a resource in helping the group design their own activities and achieve their own stated outcomes. At Cupertino High School, on the other hand, we took the lead in designing and facilitating the training program by submitting a formal proposal to school administrators. The expanded focus on communication facilitation skills and event design training is particularly important in Phase IV given the emphasis on institutionalization. By disseminating public-dialogue skills and capacities to a range of stakeholders in the community, the PDC went a long way toward relinquishing control of the project.

There are a number of encouraging signs to suggest that Phase IV of the project was successful in helping the city develop a social infrastructure capable of sustaining the public dialogue process. One significant institutional development was the formation of the 5Cs. The group's initial success in sponsoring public dialogue events and attracting new members provided on-going opportunities for residents to engage cross-cultural issues and the city's changing demographics. This kind of citizen involvement was essential in sustaining the public dialogue process in Cupertino. Even though it might have been possible to advance the project working solely through city commissions and existing community organizations, those of us in the PDC have come to realize that the process will have a deeper and more lasting impact when there is an identified group of citizens whose main responsibility is to promote and facilitate good communication. In Cupertino, that group is the 5Cs.

Another key development was the city's decision to hire a community relations coordinator to provide staff support and assistance to community groups, such as the 5Cs and the various project teams that developed to work on action items. In addition to staff support, the person hired for the position, Laura Domondon Lee, also took an active role in learning how to design community events and facilitate dialogic forms of communication. To assist in this effort, she participated in the two-day PDC public dialogue training for city residents. Having a staff person available to coordinate activities and provide communication support helped considerably in advancing the public dialogue process.

The on-going work of city officials represents another marker of success. Throughout Phase IV, Don Brown and Michael Chang expanded their role in the project by facilitating and sponsoring events and activities. They regularly attended 5Cs meetings, served as city representatives on the Cupertino Multicultural Interagency Collaborative, and actively promoted the work of the PDC with grant agencies, the Cupertino Unified School District, and other civic organizations in Cupertino. Their involvement helped to solidify the city's commitment to the project, providing the leadership necessary for citizens and others on the Council to support it as well. The project also attracted the attention of elected officials and public professionals outside the city. Shortly after Phase IV ended, the League of California Cities recognized Don Brown with its statewide city manager's award for the advancement of diversity.

The efforts to expand the project into other segments of the community was another crucial step in moving the public dialogue process forward. As intended, the training programs in the schools and with different civic groups, and the on-going work with law enforcement, produced a "ripple effect" that reverberated throughout the community. Not only did these activities serve a capacity-building function, they also created networking opportunities for groups and individuals. A public-dialogue process must operate at multiple levels of the community in order to become an institutionalized practice. By reaching out to different community groups, organizations, and institutions, the project took important steps in that direction.

Box 6.10. Keep the Conversation Going

Addressing issues does not mean solving them, therefore the dialogue must continue.
—Jenny Purushotma, Cupertino resident and 5Cs member

EPILOGUE

There have been a number of significant developments in the Cupertino Project since Phase IV ended. Taken together, they provide additional evidence that public dialogue is becoming an institutionalized form of public communication within the community.

First, the 5Cs have firmly established themselves as a vital community resource in the area of cross-cultural communication. In addition to sponsoring public dialogue events and working on diversity-related projects, the group is frequently called on by other organizations to assist in dealing with diversity issues. At a recent goal-setting session, for example, the council asked them to help sponsor Cupertino's first multicultural festival. Another on-going part of the 5Cs mission is planning, designing, and executing the city's annual diversity town forum. One year after the last forum, described earlier in this chapter, the 5Cs sponsored their third large public meeting, titled "Building Community." Over 130 community members attended.

Second, the schools project at Cupertino High School is still in process and continues to show signs of success. In the most recent iteration of the project, currently underway, the PDC has refined the training program and extended it to the middle-school level. Recently, a cohort group of 20 CHS students trained 40 middle-school students to facilitate discussions on peer pressure and cliques. The results have been so successful that the Cupertino Union School District is currently working with the PDC to fund an upstream, multiyear communication facilitation and conflict management program.

Three, the council has taken steps to ensure that the city government continues to use public dialogue processes in the way it conducts its business. The current Mayor, John Statton, is working with the PDC to develop a "community congress," which is designed to bring together leaders from various civic groups and organizations, including the 5Cs, to engage in a long-term planning process. Among other things, this event will widen the scope of issues beyond cultural diversity and ethnic change. One of the goals of the event, for example, is to identify the various issues facing Cupertino and how residents and city officials can best prepare for them before they become problematic or divisive. This move toward a long-term, collaborative planning process is significant because it demonstrates how public dialogue has become an accepted communication practice within the city. It is also significant because it indicates that diversity is no longer the overriding issue of concern that it once was when the Cupertino Project first started.[9]

The city made another major commitment to employ public dialogue processes when Don Brown recently announced his retirement. In a clear demonstration of support, the council stipulated that one of the duties of the incoming manager was to continue the city's involvement in the project. Given these recent developments, it is readily apparent that public dialogue in Cupertino is alive and well, with every indication that it will continue on into the foreseeable future.

NOTES

1. By institutionalization, we mean that public dialogue is established throughout the various levels of the community such that it becomes

the expected form of public communication for addressing sensitive and controversial social issues. In order to reach the point of institutionalization, we believe that a civic infrastructure supporting public dialogue must be in place, along with a social network of people willing and able to engage in dialogic actions. We are not suggesting that public dialogue be institutionalized as the *only* form of public communication. Rather, our position is that an institutionalized space within the community be made available for public dialogue, which would enable this "new" pattern of public communication to exist along with other more traditional forms of public decision making.

2. The professional motivations on the part of the PDC to expand the project had to be weighed against the resources of the group and what we could reasonably hope to accomplish given our rather limited resources. One of the reasons why the project expanded as it did during Phase IV was because grant funding was made available to the PDC through the City of Cupertino and the David and Lucile Packard Foundation. The funding allowed PDC members to spend more time on the project working with stakeholders, facilitating meetings, and designing and conducting training programs. Although the PDC had previously received two small start-up grants for the project, the increased funding level expanded the resources of the group considerably.

3. Although Cupertino has a number advisory commissions, composed of Cupertino residents, none of them have ever been given the charge of looking at controversial issues related to social values, cultural diversity, or moral conflict. Although rare, some large cities have human relations commissions that deal directly with diversity related issues, often within the legal context of civil rights protections and violations (U.S. Department of Justice, 1998). These commissions are almost always structured around a formal complaint process and thus function in a reactive manner to problems in the community. Before the Cupertino Project was initiated the city did not have a structure or process for dealing with controversial and sensitive social problems like cultural diversity. Outside of forming a human relations commission, there were few other options available to the city.

4. The name of this event, Follow-up Training and Team Building meeting, is somewhat misleading because it did not include an explicit training component. Whereas the original training program included both a dialogue skills component and discussion of concerns, visions, and action plans, the follow-up meeting was focused primarily on action plans. So although the follow-up training program was directly connected to the original event, the focus was much narrower.

5. A few of the 5Cs members were also concerned that they did not possess sufficient skills and abilities in dialogue and group facilitation to prevent adversarial forms of conflict from emerging. To address these concerns, role-play activities were developed for the 5Cs training that

simulated small-group discussions in which one or more of the members insisted on arguing the merits of the issues in one way or another. The goal was for the facilitators to intervene in these situations by responding in such a way as to create the conditions for more dialogic responses and reflections. These simulations constituted the major activity of the fifth and final training session.

6. Several community members also expressed their opposition through nonpublic channels of communication. For example, the city manager's office received numerous anonymous phone complaints (D. Brown, personal communication, July 9, 1998). The *Cupertino Courier* also received dozens of anonymous phone calls criticizing the newspaper's coverage of cultural diversity issues (N. Collins, personal communication, June 17, 1997).

7. A member of the 5Cs coordinating team, Don Allen, paid for the advertisement.

8. This view is not new. Over 70 years ago John Dewey (1927) argued that schools, when reconstituted as laboratories of experiential learning, should prepare students for democratic participation and citizenship.

9. The most recent independent community survey supports this claim ("Survey of residents," 2000). Compared to the previous survey conducted in 1998, more residents now rate race relations in Cupertino as either "excellent" or "good" (from 79% to 84%). This 5% difference approaches statistical significance, according to the authors of the survey (p. 41). Conversely, fewer respondents now rate race relations as "poor" or "very poor" (from 15% to 11%). Importantly, substantially more respondents now say that the city's ethnic diversity has made no change in how they feel toward people of other races (from 15% to 11%). The most recent survey also found that in response to an open-ended question, only 2% of the sample identified "race relations" as an important issue facing Cupertino (this data was not collected in the 1998 survey).

III

PERSPECTIVES ON
THE PROJECT

7

EVALUATING THE PROJECT

FROM THE INSIDE

VOICES OF THE CUPERTINO COMMUNITY: AS HEARD AND REFLECTED UPON

ROBYN PENMAN*

On Wednesday, June 2, 1999, I was privileged to spend the day talking with six members of the Cupertino community who were actively involved in the community dialogue project. In the evening I was invited to participate in a meeting of the 5Cs (Citizens of Cupertino Cross Cultural Consortium). I knew of some of the significant events that had

---

*Robyn Penman is the Executive Director of the Communication Research Institute of Australia and Adjunct Professor of Communication at the University of Canberra, Australia. At the Institute, a nonprofit, independent, research organization, she leads projects designed to improve the quality of communication practices in society. These projects have included improving the relationships between local government and its citizens; facilitating people's understanding of legislation in areas of aged and child care and aviation safety; developing information support programs for people on complex, long-term drug regimes; and enhancing the communication practices between large organizations and their customers.

occurred over the three years of this project from Barnett Pearce, a member of the Public Dialogue Consortium (PDC). Now I had the opportunity to hear at least some of the voices of the community.

The voices heard were those of Laura Domondon Lee, Community Relations Coordinator; Sergeant Steve Angus, Liaison Officer between the Sheriff's Office, the city, and the 5Cs; Don Brown, City Manager; Don Allen, leading businessman and member of the 5Cs; Roberta Hollimon, citizen and member of the 5Cs; and Michael Chang, City Council member and former Mayor. I am extremely grateful for their willingness to talk with me.

I was very keen to understand how these community members had experienced the project and how they thought it could be put into good effect in other cities. I was also keen to understand if, and how, they thought it had brought about changes in the community. In contemplating these conversations later, I thought that there were four important themes. I have organized what I heard and reflected upon around these four themes: faith and commitment, how the process worked, critical moments, and factors that made the process work. I was also struck by a number of poignant remarks and events, and I conclude by offering them to you as a way of showing the "heart" of the project.

FAITH AND COMMITMENT

As expected, each of the people I interviewed offered a somewhat different perspective on the project, arising from their different positions in it and the time when they became involved. But what came through loud and clear from each of them was their faith in, and commitment to, the project.

Don Brown was the initial promoter of the project. He had increasingly realized that so much of community input was formalized and divisive and usually forced the council to choose between sides or make a compromise: a situation he found far from satisfactory when, as he said, "you are trying to work out a real solution." When he was approached by the PDC and heard about other projects designed to facilitate communication, it "set off a light bulb." He could see the possibility of something different and, as he pointed out, "it was a real leap of faith." "City managers are trained to keep a lid on things . . . so encouraging discussion of sensitive topics is counter to their everyday experiences." Michael Chang was the first minority on the city council and he was very concerned about cultural issues. When Don Brown told him about the work of the PDC he saw the opportunity "to build bridges." He knew that the real problem was that people were not willing to talk about cultural issues, and he could see that what the PDC had to offer "was a process for engagement with safety." So he too committed to the project.

Don Allen and Roberta Hollimon were key citizens who supported the project in its infancy. Don Allen knew that racial/cultural issues were becoming increasingly "sensitive," and he also knew that something had to be done. He expressed the same faith in the project from the beginning that Don Brown and Michael talked to me about. Roberta similarly entered the project with a commitment to being a good citizen and a realization that "we all have to learn to live together."

Both Michael and Don Brown had the foresight to see potential problems ahead of them and realize that the conventional approach to community input was not likely to help them through. They also had the courage to take a step into the unknown and a fundamental belief that what they had to do was set up the conditions "for people to be good." And with the support of committed citizens like Don Allen and Roberta, the project was sustained. Without this support it was unlikely that the project would have proceeded.

Laura and Steve, joined the project later: Laura as a council-supported liaison officer in March 1998, and Steve as a sheriff's department officer in August 1998. Both of their positions grew out of the active work of the 5Cs and the PDC. Steve told me how great it has been working with the 5Cs: "It helps to build up long-term relationships" and "offers law enforcement a voice in collaboration." Laura spoke with enthusiasm about the range of projects she is working on and how she felt energized by her work with the community and the 5Cs. Again, these are good, committed people who are actively helping to sustain the community work.

HOW HAS IT WORKED?

A SLOW PROCESS

When I conducted my interviews, the Cupertino Project had been running for three years, with a number of significant events in different segments of the community and other events adapted to the community as a whole. Interestingly, rather than seeing it as a complex or an extended process, it was described as a slow process.

Michael realized that this slowness was necessary because it was:

- "Not a major crisis and the slowness was strategic . . . needed to train . . . and get parameters set up."

Roberta also thought that the process needed to go slow. For her:

- "The 5Cs is still in its infancy . . . it's interesting that they still haven't set up a formal structure . . . but this may be good because as one participant said, 'everyone is welcome.'"

Don Brown thought that the slowness of the process has helped in gradually bringing about change in such a way that:

- "The process itself has never been debated . . . its very important that no one has objected to the process and how the dialogue has developed."

Don Allen, however, thought that:

- "The process was good but too slow . . . we've really just begun this journey."

I think all of these points are pertinent. Bringing about change in a community on sensitive issues without generating unrest or hostilities is an extremely difficult process. In such circumstances, the slower the better. Nevertheless, Don Allen's point needs to be borne in mind—the journey must be continued.

ALWAYS INCORPORATING DIFFERENCE

One of the underlying thrusts of the various activities fostered by the PDC has been to help people understand and accept difference, not as a fundamental threat but as an opportunity. This understanding was reflected throughout the conversations in various ways. More than one person mentioned that in their particular involvements they always tried to include people or groups who opposed the project or who wanted to "stir things up."

- "We kept on trying to find common ground."
- "We had to learn how to invite the 'opposers' into the project."

MEASURES OF SUCCESS

Success of a project of this nature is always difficult to measure. Nevertheless, those I spoke with could point to good examples to illustrate that the process had worked, or is working.

Don Brown talked about how at the beginning everyone was afraid to talk about racial issues but,

- "Now we sit down and say 'what are the differences?' Without the idea that we want to change anyone's mind . . . now we have a way to handle things."

Michael saw things similarly, noting that the process had been good because:

- "We are able to confront real concerns [and] people feel comfortable with talking about diversity."

And Don Allen made a very astute point about the whole process:

- "Success is measured by what didn't happen [i.e., no racial strife]. It's very difficult to quantify . . . and while nothing happens the whole process may stop and then it will happen."

The "failure" of things to happen is perhaps why Roberta said that she was not sure that things have changed. Yet she is still committed, which is surely a measure of a little success. She believes they need more time and more forums and will know that the 5Cs have been successful when they,

- "Are invited [by other members/groups of the community] to facilitate an event or hold a town hall meeting."

The way in which the press reported on community issues and project events was also mentioned as an indicator of changes in the community on diversity issues. In the beginning the press had reported things in quite a cynical manner, but over time that attitude changed to a more positive one. Indeed, the change was so marked that Don Allen was instrumental in recently awarding a prize for "Responsible Journalism" to the *San Jose Mercury News*. Laura and Steve particularly monitor the Letters to the Editor section of the *Cupertino Courier* as an indicator of the reactions to the various activities for which they are responsible. They have noted that negative, anonymous letters to the editor with "racial" comments have diminished markedly.

CRITICAL MOMENTS

This project has been a long and complex process with a number of planned events forming part of a broader communication strategy. Although you cannot expect any particular event to make a momentous difference, it is often the case that an event acts as a critical moment and consolidates the cumulative effects or stands out in some way as significant. For most of the people I talked with, it was the Cultural Diversity Forum, held in October 1998, that was the significant change moment.

For Laura and Steve, it was significant because they felt they had played a very positive role as facilitators in the meeting, and the press response was very positive. But most importantly they believed this marked the moment at which long-term effects could be seen. It was the culmination, offering a "blueprint for communication" that allowed for a diversity of opinion:

- "People at the forum were more apt to say 'OK that's their perception, let's see what is real.'"
- "Finally, there was public voicing of views with names . . . compared with the previous anonymous letters to the editor."
- "Even the problems were expressed more positively instead of the usual negative way."

Don Brown also thought the Diversity Forum was the turning point for the whole project because the general public turned up to talk about hot issues and the discussion included those with negative views and strong opinions. Afterward, Don heard that those people with strong views,

- "Felt good because they got the chance to say what they wanted to say."

Laura also believed that the two-day public dialogue and facilitation training workshop for community members, held before the forum in October, provided another significant moment, especially for her personally:

- "I felt empowered to work on the project [and] there was lots of energy."

For Michael, it was the two-day training program for community leaders held in February 1997 that was the highlight. He identified two critical features of this meeting that made it significant:

- "It was a coming out of the issue . . . diversity was put on the table properly . . . and there was the opportunity to express positive affirmation to make it work."

Obviously, if I had talked to other people in the community, such as the high school students who had participated in different events, I could have found other critical moments. But whichever event is taken as significant, I think it is important to note the common element expressed in the voices quoted here. The event was significant because it allowed the expression of strong views without the conversation degenerating into a divisive diatribe, clearly a key goal of the whole project.

WHAT MADE THE PROCESS WORK?

There was marked agreement among all six people on the three critical factors that made the process work.

SUPPORT FROM THE TOP

In all the public projects I have worked on "support from the top" has been critical, and this project is no exception. Everyone recognized that without this support the project would not even have started, let alone continued for three years.

- "The city manager's support and involvement has been critical."
- "To be effective it [the dialogue process] has to be institutionalized."

This support has come from the faith and commitment I talked about earlier. To implement an equivalent project in another city will also require the same faith and commitment "from the top."

SKILLED OUTSIDE "EXPERTS"

Everyone also mentioned the importance of having skilled, outside experts:

- "We must have people with skills to keep it going and to keep it open . . . or else it is just the old debate."

- "A key component is smart trained people to do the train-ing . . . in fact it is much better if it is an outsider."
- "It takes some of the politics out of it."

Although it was not stated directly, it seems clear that the expertise needed for this type of project is in the capacity to generate the condi-tions for public dialogue and to develop the necessary strategic commu-nication plan to sustain that dialogue.

COMMUNITY INVOLVEMENT

Two interrelated aspects of community involvement were mentioned here. First, it was pointed out how important it was not only to involve the community but to empower the community to act for themselves:

- "We really do need to pay attention to community involve-ment . . . the right balance of support and autonomy . . . that empowers people to do things."

Second, it was important to allow the community themselves to deter-mine the issue of concern:

- "We have to allow the community to choose the topics . . . it's truly a topic of concern that makes it significant."

Both Don Brown and Don Allen pointed to the importance of this self-determination of topic. Don Brown expected that "growth" would be the issue and was surprised when "diversity" was the one to surface. Don Allen thought others believed that "safety" was the issue. If either of those presumed topics had been forced onto the agenda it would only have waylaid the process.

WHAT WAS I STRUCK BY?

When I heard Steve, the liaison police officer, describe his work as "to identify concerns and reach out and touch the people," I was touched at the human commitment. It led me to believe that the Cupertino Project has allowed the space for this one police officer, at least, to show a human face.

When I observed at the 5Cs meeting one of the more vocal, provocative, and difficult members of the group openly supporting

Laura, a person of another cultural background, in her liaison role, I was struck both by the fact that her views could be expressed and accepted in such a meeting and that despite or because of them she could openly affirm Laura.

When the person from an Asian background, designated to lead that 5Cs meeting for discussion, readily pointed to the white American culture as being only one component among many, I was struck by the ease with which she said it and the ease with which it was accepted as a legitimate part of the discussion.

When the people at the 5Cs meeting just incorporated me into their group work as another member, and not the outside expert, I was struck by their ready acceptance of a stranger, one from another culture at that!

When I heard the people I interviewed use words and phrases like "cultural enrichment" and "diversity," I was struck by how far removed that was from the term "racial issues" and how much they had worked to get to that removed position.

When I heard Down Brown, the city manager, talk about how risky it felt to initiate this project, and how after some "very powerful learning" it now "seems so very unrisky because this way is pretty strong stuff," I was struck by how much he really had learned and how committed he must have been from the very beginning.

When I heard Don Allen, a leading businessman and a member of the 5Cs, describe the whole project as "a noble effort," I was struck by his strong moral commitment to the community.

When I heard Roberta, a citizen who facilitates the 5Cs meetings, worry about whether they have made a big difference, and yet she has contributed substantially from the beginning, I was struck by how important the little differences are, such as her contribution.

And when I heard Michael, a member of the city council, say, "some issues in our society that may seem daunting are crying out to be addressed. . . . We have discovered a model that can work. It gives us a lot of hope that with the right tools we can do it," I also knew there was still hope.

AN INTERVIEW WITH MICHAEL CHANG*

SS: What was your reaction when you first heard about the PDC and the proposal for the Cupertino Project?

MC: As you know, the city has been experiencing very significant demographic changes in the last 20 years, which will probably continue for another 10 to 20 years. The community has become tremendously diversified. After my election I talked about this with the city manager [Don Brown], and soon after he talked with Kim Pearce of the PDC. I was intrigued by the idea. I knew that we needed to bring in some level of expertise, and I knew we wanted to try to minimize the politics of it, especially within the city council. We thought the PDC might be the answer. When we learned more about your group both of us felt more comfortable proceeding.

SS: What did you need to know in order to proceed?

MC: I needed to know the approach, the skill level, and when I learned that you're very much a process-oriented group, I felt that was important. Because my assumption is that there might be a lot of well-meaning people in Cupertino, but in terms of really having a lot of experience or expertise with diversity, I think we're much more limited in those areas. So I felt we needed a process to help us talk about these kinds of issues in a constructive way, in a nonthreatening way, and the PDC seemed to fit that.

SS: What influence has the project had on Cupertino?

MC: I think it has been a very important one in terms of dealing with what I think is one of the most important issues in the city. The rapid demographic changes present some pretty fundamental issues about the fabric of the community. When you have demographic diversity there is always a question of whether the community will unravel in some way, and so I think the issue is a very important one. What we know for sure is that the city leadership is now able to

---

*Michael Chang is a member of the Cupertino city council. He was born and raised in Hong Kong and came the United States when he was 18-years-old. He attended San Francisco State University as an undergraduate and earned an MA and PhD in Education from Stanford University. In 1991 he was elected to the Cupertino School Board, and in 1995 he became the first Asian to be elected to the city council. He served a term as mayor from January 1998 to January 1999. Michael has been an active participant in the 5Cs and a supporter of the Cupertino Project from the beginning. This interview with Michael Chang (MC) was conducted by Shawn Spano (SS) in June, 1999.

engage this issue and feel much more confident in understanding where it stands. The project has helped us become more empowered to do something constructive about this issue.

SS: So what I'm hearing you say is that you've been able to take more of a proactive stance, as a city leader, in addressing the issue.

MC: Exactly, and that's very important. I remember at the council team building workshop we were surprised at how many incidents that we have had related to diversity over the last 10 years. We were just amazed. Once you sit down and take stock, it's just one thing after the other. But none of them was a full-scale crisis situation, which means that our community can still be proactive rather than reactive. We weren't reacting to a racial riot, so it gave us the luxury of dealing with it on a different time agenda without the pressure to respond immediately.

SS: You said there are no major riots or anything like that. How would you describe the concerns that people had in the community going back to 1995 when you were elected, and 1996 when the project started?

MC: Well, I mean there were all kinds of issues. Some of them we have overcome pretty well, but one of the more recent issues we know about has to do with the Mandarin language immersion program. Some people said, "if we had a French immersion program, no one would have a problem with that." But since it was a Chinese language program, some people said, "why do we need to do this, why do we need to spend the taxpayer's money on this?" I also remember the first time they had a Chinese business sign in Cupertino, about 10 years ago. It was at a bank, a very artistic sign. I remember city leaders talking about it and asking, "is that OK to have a sign in Chinese?" That was something that was new to people. Four years ago, when Cupertino Village was not doing well, it was sold to a Chinese-American developer who was going to do a Chinese-American theme mall. People reacted to that: "Is it OK to do?" Other people reacted to people coming from different backgrounds into our community with uncertainty. Some people found it troubling. A lot of the issues are school-related, especially the language schools; the Japanese language schools, Chinese language schools, Korean language schools. Some people look at that and say, "is that a good thing, should we be supportive of these extracurricular activities or not?" Everything was a new test to see what people were doing, to see what people think. When people formed sports teams, people said, "is that good or not?" "Do they have a right to form sports teams that are mainly about their own group?" That type of thing. So there were lots of new things that were happening.

SS: How would you characterize the way people in the community were framing the issue? What were people doing when they talked about the issue in these ways?

MC: They were asking, "what's going on here?" and "where are the boundaries?" There were questions about why some people even need to be among themselves. "Is it OK to have their clubs and associations?" And when some of the Asian people wanted to get involved, say in the schools or city council, there were other sets of questions. "Why do they want to get involved, you know, what's their objective?" There is a lot that needs to be understood and a lot to still understand, so we need a vehicle to process some of this. And the PDC provided a very useful vehicle to help us in a somewhat systematic, honest, and constructive manner. So I would say that the city is much better in terms of being able to address diversity issues. I think most people like where our city is. We're stronger as a community, stronger as a city, more together.

SS: That kind of segues into the next question about some of the more long-term residents. What effect has the project had on them?

MC: I might be wrong, but there were probably 500 or so families here when Cupertino first became a city, so long-term residents have not been here for hundreds of years, they've been here only 30 to 40 years. This is an important context to note. And I think that a lot of people, because Silicon Valley is a place of change, have tried to adjust to the different kinds of changes. Cultural change is just another kind of change. But in answer to your question, we were encouraged by the PDC not to isolate or exclude from the dialogue those people who have the most problems with cultural change. If anything, they know they have a place to talk about their concerns, and we've learned how important it is to keep them included in the process. One of the things we've realized is that they're not the majority. We have found that we have a very strong center here in the city in terms of these issues. Those people who feel the most uncomfortable about it are probably a small segment, but we've also made it important to give them a chance to voice their perspectives and their anxieties. And I think some people might have even changed their opinions to a certain degree. Even the ones who haven't, we still keep them in the loop and I think they appreciate it. There were a lot of people at the last Cultural Diversity Forum who saw diversity as a problem, and afterward they came to me and said, "we are glad we were able to get that off our chests and talk about it and not feel you guys in government are just trying to silence us. That you trust us enough to allow us to go ahead and say what is on our minds." And some people actually changed their opinion. They said, "hey, for the first time I talked face to face with that person and understood the reasons for that issue from a different perspective. I never thought about it like that before, and I'm going to give it some more thought."

SS: Has the project benefited the Asian community and newer Chinese immigrants?

MC: I think the project has benefited everyone in the community. I don't know that you can say it benefited one group more than any other group. I do think the newcomers probably had more to lose if the project didn't work well. People who have been here and have negative views of the newcomers have the capability of making life harder for them. So you know I think it benefits everyone, but it is more crucial for the newcomers.

SS: So if the project had gone awry, if something had happened badly, the newcomers would have suffered more?

MC: Probably.

SS: How have the new Asian immigrants to the community fared as a result of the project? Have they benefited?

MC: Oh yes, of course. I think that people want to know where the city stands on certain types of issues, and for a time we weren't sure where the city stood on this issue of growing diversity. And the city wasn't sure if this was the right type of agenda to put on the table. So what the PDC did was to allow that to be put on the table and say that it doesn't mean we're guilty of anything, it just means that this is something that is worth talking about. And we were able to get at the issues, as you remember, at our first community training program. And so because of that we have offered a vehicle where newcomers have a common ground to meet with established residents over an issue of mutual interest, which is, how do we bring our community together? How can we work with each other from this mutual interest? And so it brought people in touch with each other, it allowed people to know each other. As newcomers you really need people to understand where you are coming from. You really need people's understanding. Because of the project our city leaders, and our city in general, have learned more about these people. It has benefited them.

SS: So it's uncomfortable for new immigrants when they do not know what the city's position is on them being here?

MC: Absolutely. And it was a sleight of hand, I thought for a while, because the city was not sure how strongly it felt about this. We talked a lot about growth and development, more libraries, affordable housing, those types of things, but we hadn't had a discussion about this growing diversity. Now that we've had a discussion, I think everybody feels more confident because we know where our city is. From what we can see most people seem to be comfortable with our stance, once we knew what our stance was.

SS: Is it unusual for a city to be out in front of this issue, to be proactive?

MC: I don't know. For very diverse cities, especially large ones like San Francisco and San Jose, to talk about diversity is a given, it's the politically correct thing to do. Whether it means anything beyond talk is a different question, but that's the rhetoric. Here it wasn't just part of the rhetoric. Now we talk about it, and hopefully it's matched by some substance or some commitment rather than the rhetoric of diversity.

SS: What specific activities associated with the project do you think were the most useful?

MC: All the activities were useful in the sense that they built on each other. The sequence was right. I thought that with hindsight the steps that we took really made sense, beginning with the focus groups, going to the council team building retreat, going on to the development of the 5Cs, the training of the 5Cs, and finally the Diversity Forum. All those steps were important. I think the first big break was with the training program for community leaders, when we were able to get 100 opinion makers in Cupertino together and basically put the issue on the table. It was the first time that the issue came out of the closet. We discussed it seriously for the first time. It also reaffirmed the ideas of democracy, that people should have the right to pursue their interests and live wherever they want. But it allowed the opinion leaders to affirm reality too, which is to look at the community and say, "hey, you know, maybe our city council or many of our leading institutions in the city are not very diverse." It forced them to look at it realistically. And then finally to say, well, what do we want to do about it? It put people in a position to solve problems. So it did a lot. I also think that building the 5Cs and allowing the group to become more sophisticated on these issues was important. There are a lot of well-meaning people, but that doesn't mean that they are knowledgeable or skillful. And so through the 5Cs we can build those capacities in terms of attitudes and skills, or just knowledge and understanding of the issues. And then the Diversity Forum was our test to see how we would deal with controversial issues. It took us almost three years to get to that point, but we got there.

SS: One of the criticisms that we received early on, especially with the very first Town Hall Meeting back in 1996, was that we weren't getting at the real issues. People were saying that they wanted the process to move faster. Is it your sense that it was useful not to rush?

MC: Well, yes and no. Yes in the sense that we didn't need to be in a hurry; we weren't reacting to a big crisis. So we had a more flexible timeline. I believe in building trust and that takes time. So yes, I support the idea that we shouldn't rush into things but develop them slowly. No in the sense that I think the PDC's strength is in communication. Diversity is more of a minor field for your group. Had it been more of a stronger major field, then we would still go slow but maybe not as slow. We wouldn't have to think as hard and agonize over how are we going to deal with the real issues. We'd be a little more certain and little more knowledgeable.

SS: What about your own development? What did you learn, if anything, as a result of participating in the project?

MC: Well it's a great process and experiment. On a more personal level, it was amazing to see how it unfolded. It gave me an additional sense that even for very intractable problems, such as race, you need to have the right kind of people to work with. I think that it gave those of us in city government confidence to engage the public and be willing to take some risks. There were many risks I thought along the way.

SS: What were some of them?

MC: Well, the one that comes to mind first is the last forum we did [Cultural Diversity Forum]. I was somewhat uncomfortable with it because all the issues were focused on one ethnic group [Chinese], and it was almost like we were going to beat on this group. I thought that was not balanced. But it was like well, we'll go with it. We should accept a variety of perspectives. Another risk was the 5Cs. Probably because of the influence of the PDC and the emphasis on dialogue (laughs), there were times when the group just let different ideas come out, and some of the anti-diversity comments we heard were hurtful. I think at some point you have to say, "you know, this is 1999 and there are parts of diversity that are beyond discussion." You have to take a stand on this and the question is how do you promote it more. So I think that for some people the 5Cs is a place for them to state their opinions, but there also needs to be a discourse within a commitment to improvement, not a discourse as an end in itself that would go nowhere.

SS: Do you think that some people use the 5Cs and the project as a whole as a forum to complain?

MC: Yes. So we've had to ask ourselves, "is this the place where people bring all their complaints?" We don't want to leave anyone out, but if all we have are complainers then we'll get bogged down, we won't do anything, go anywhere. Some of these people seem to think that we can solve problems by fixing whoever their complaining about (laughs). You know, getting them to change. Or is the question, shouldn't everybody be changing? See what I'm trying to say? So there are risks like these. There are certain occasions where you want that discourse. There are other occasions where you probably do better trying to help the 5Cs, for instance, decide what is the most strategic thing they could do to promote their mission instead of being a place where people come and complain. So I think it's a really back-and-forth process.

SS: What about next steps. Where do you think the project and city should go from here? What still needs to be done?

MC: We have built a number of institutions that provide leadership, like the 5Cs, the involvement of our city manager, city staff, community outreach program, and the school-city collaborative on diversity. The Chamber of Commerce has their own initiative, the Asian-American Business Council.

These are things that have come into place. One of the key things is to keep these vital, keep them alive. So that's one area of challenge. The second is to build the knowledge base and the skills level. There was a time when we didn't know where people stood on these issues. Now we know even if there are people who don't agree with us completely, that's OK, there is a comfort level, we know we can talk about the issues, we know where they stand, and we stand, and so on. But it's very important that we continue to build that capability so that if there is a crisis that hits, we know who in our community will be the strong voices to bring us together. We need to know what the institutions are and how will they react, instead of being caught with our pants down, so to speak. We're not there yet, we're still probably in a pretty rudimentary stage, and we need to continue to work on that. And we need to continue to allow people to assume leadership roles. There are always new people to bring into the program. I myself am looking at different possibilities to serve and so we need people to continue this. We also need to continue to educate the community. And if you think about it there have been many spin-off projects, for instance, collaboration between the telecommunications commission and the 5Cs. They want us to continue working on diversity video projects. Of course, that is community education—it's great—and so all this has a relationship with each other. When we do diversity trainings, that's another way of bringing the community together. So we need to keep it going.

SS: So is it your sense that an infrastructure is starting to develop here in the community for maintaining a climate for good discussion about diversity?

MC: Absolutely. Not only good discussion, but good action. Good action would be integration, respect, feeling comfortable, reducing stress, reducing anxiety. These are the real results of that, feeling comfortable with each other, and more respectful of each other.

SS: Is there anything else you would like to add?

MC: Maybe we've been keeping this among ourselves for too long. Because there are not many other cities doing this kind of thing, even in California. We probably need to be more proactive in sharing what we are doing. It would be helpful to let other people get a sense of what we have done, both successes and continuing efforts, so they can decide if it's something they might be interested in doing themselves. It can be both an educational and informational tool. I would also add that I'm extremely appreciative of the work of the PDC. Great organization, right place, right time, right people.

8

DIALOGUE PRACTITIONERS
AND PARTNERS

there's no critical theory enough [handwritten]

REFLECTIONS AND QUESTIONS:
A RESPONSE FROM THE PUBLIC
CONVERSATIONS PROJECT

SALLYANN ROTH, ROBERT STAINS, JR., AND
RICHARD M. CHASIN*

We want to preface our comments with expressions of appreciation and admiration for what the members of the Public Dialogue Consortium (PDC) team have taken on and have already accomplished. This account is exhilarating in its implications. It demonstrates the possibility of creating environments for constructive conversation and action in

*Sallyann Roth is Founding Associate of the Public Conversations Project and Co-Director of the Program in Narrative Therapies of the Family Institute of Cambridge. Robert Stains, Jr. is Training Director at the Public Conversations Project and also serves as a mediator and trainer for the U.S. Postal Service. Richard M. Chasin is Founding Associate of the Public Conversations Project. The authors can be contacted at 46 Kondazian Street, Watertown, MA 02472 (phone: 617-923-1216, email: info@publicconversations.org).

systems larger than those in which we, at the Public Conversations Project (PCP), have worked directly. It exhibits the transformative power that dialogue can have as its effects ripple through many levels of a geographical community.

We appreciate the thinking that underlies the work, the attempts to consciously and consistently tie together theory and practice, and many technical aspects of the various conversation designs. We are most impressed, though, with the example set by practitioners who were willing to step out into a very large arena, trusting in the wisdom and skills of their participants as well as in the constructive power of dialogic communication. There are few among us who would take such a risk under such a bright light of public exposure.

Because we know the PCP's 10-year ever-evolving approach much better than other approaches in the field, we will use it as the basis for commenting on similarities and differences between the PDC Project and related work.

Our dialogue facilitation and that of our colleagues (Carol Becker, Laura Chasin, and Margaret Herzig) in the PCP shares key aspects with the work of the PDC. We share the intention of fostering dialogue on controversial matters. We share the practical goal of designing conversational structures that make contentious issues genuinely discussible and that invite people to speak about what has been experienced as unspeakable in constructive ways. We share the dream that members of any community can enjoy full, inclusive, and complex conversations about challenging issues, especially issues that are often spoken of in simplified, polarized ways—or simply not discussed. The PDC, like the PCP, regards its project designs as evolving, collaborative, and emergent.

The actual practices of the two groups are different in many respects. The entry point of the PDC's project (in this example) has been the entire community, older people, younger people, elected leaders, and interested citizens, whereas the entry point of the PCP's work has most often been with small groups of first and second-tier community leaders. The PDC project involved mostly public meetings, PCP meetings have been typically small and private (by invitation only); frequently they are also off the record.

Whereas the PDC's foci, as reported here, were on issues generated by groups of community participants, the PCP's various projects have involved a wide range of specific contested issues, each of which had already been identified by the individuals or groups whom we approached or who sought us out. Sometimes we recruited individual partisans who had not known each other; more often we discovered, or were discovered by, groups of people, often activists and leaders, who found themselves unable to have constructive conversations on a public matter on which they had long disagreed.

The PDC focused on creating public contexts for developing fresh ways to have community conversations that previously may have been unproductive or nonexistent. The PCP has mainly focused on facilitating private, relationship-shifting conversations that may indirectly promote constructive community-wide conversation. The difference is not one of aim, but of practice. The PDC concentrated on open, public, group settings. Most of our work has been done in smaller, more protected contexts.

We are always mindful of the trade-offs inherent in choosing a private or a public path and wonder about what is being sacrificed or gained with either choice. Some things are more likely to be spoken in private settings than in public ones, and others are more likely to be said in public settings than in private ones. Some of the very same things will be said in quite different ways in each kind of setting. We feel this tension even as we write this response to the PDC project. A book is very public, and writing is a very fixed and unsupple form of exchange. There is no way to have an easy back-and-forth, no way to check out each other's meanings, our understandings and misunderstandings, and the effects of our speaking as we go along. Anything we say in this text has real and public consequences for us, for the people to whose work we are responding, and for our relationship with them. What we say here is true for us, however, we are aware that we would speak differently in a more private setting, and in that setting it would be easier for us to be in a learning conversational exchange with each other. We imagine that some of this public-private tension was also at play in the PDC convened meetings. Such tensions would also appear, in different ways, in small, closed dialogues.

The PDC's project held public conversations on public issues. Because we have not had much open, public dialogue experience, nor have we had the opportunity for conversations on this matter with the PDC, we do not feel in a particularly good position to comment on the PDC's overall design, or on its macro structure, except to be in awe of the courage, energy, and vision we imagine it took to aim so high and wide. Thus, with hesitation and uncertainty we offer some reactions to specific aspects of the PDC project.

FOCUS GROUPS: GETTING ORIENTED

We are interested in the use of focus groups as a way to get oriented about the issues that might be ameliorated though dialogue. We note the careful thinking behind the participant selection process, the choice of a range of participants, the groupings that were selected, the design for group participation, and the ways the PDC used the data as an initial source of information about the community. We saw how it provided a useful map for further steps.

And we are left with some questions.

As part of a community intervention, we find it important to hear about the experience of the uninvolved majority. Outlying voices, through choice or exclusion, often represent perspectives that are enormously enriching to the centrally involved group. Among those who chose not to go to the focus groups, would any have agreed to discuss with the facilitators how they made their choice and their experiences of its consequences?

Did the team consider engaging focus-group members as consultants in designing the subsequent steps? Our team has sometimes included clients in the design process. When we have, they have shown us how to expand or modify our approaches to increase effectiveness in their context. They have provided us with fresh ideas and have often steered us away from pitfalls that we might not, ourselves, have foreseen. Further, they have told us that co-creating the design increased their sense of ownership in the entire enterprise.

The stated intention for the PDC's focus groups was for community members "to share their personal experiences and stories and to reflect on how their experiences were linked to larger community problems." However, the questions in the guide for focus-group interviews do not specifically ask for experiences. The questions are phrased in a way that might be taken as an invitation to speak of experiences, but seem more likely to invite people to "go into their heads," that is, to talk about ideas, opinions, and positions. We wonder when offering opinions (rather than experiences) happened and when it did not, what encouraged one or the other kind of speaking, and what the differing effects of one kind of speaking and the other were on this ongoing conversation.

The ground rules of respecting difference, not interrupting, and maintaining confidentiality feel to us like beginnings. We believe that additions and clarifications may have prevented some of the concerns that later arose for PDC facilitators. For example, with a general agreement about "respecting differences" in place, a facilitator might be tempted to adjudicate on the spot when a difference arose about what was experienced by some as respectful and others as disrespectful. Developing ground rules with indisputable behavioral descriptions can initiate a group climate of shared responsibility for the safety of the process, hence immediately addressing one of the PDC's stated concerns about wanting to be less "expert" and more collaborative.

THE DIALOGUE GROUPS

The structure of breaking into small groups with specific tasks always presents the dilemma about how to share the proceedings of separate small groups with participants in the large group in a way that is inclusive, generative, adequately protective of privacy, and interesting to the listeners. We know that the PDC team had access to written notes and that the findings of three of the eight groups were presented in the Town Meeting. We learn in a footnote that report-backs were not given from the other small groups because of confidentiality issues. We puzzle over the challenge of effective report-backs in general, and the ways these were handled here specifically. Did the group structure allow for making distinctions between personal speaking and issues that such personal speaking could point to? Did group members have a chance to sort out with each other what they themselves thought was important to bring from their small group to the larger group? Did the actuality of having a participant give a public report from only three groups get framed in a way that reduced a sense of invitation to express differing opinions and ideas? Did group members from the reporting groups whose views were not represented in the verbal report have a way to bring these views (or their response to not having their voices represented) to the group at large?

One especially inclusive (though labor-intensive) solution to the report-back dilemma is to gather written summaries from all participants and distribute them before a second meeting to all other participants. When we ask one person (whether participant or facilitator) to report on the findings of a small group, we take the risks of accidental exclusion of perspectives, insertion of the reporter's own biases, participants not recognizing their voices as they are presented, and, rightly or wrongly, as de-emphasizing what is important to us. Yet alternatives to the single reporter are hard to imagine or laborious to carry out.

A representative from only three of the dialogue groups spoke about their group's findings. Curiously, two of the three speakers emphasized economic inequity, and one of them addressed ethnocentrism. Yet, little of these issues showed up in the facilitator produced "data text." To add to the confusion, one reporter did not mention affordable housing even though it had been mentioned in the spokesperson's group. It seems hard to be sure that concern about racial and economic inequity are limited to a few outspoken individuals and are of little relevance in the community.

We see why the PDC team questioned the usefulness of the terms "cultural diversity" and "multiculturalism" and selected "cultural richness" as one of the two main topics for the dialogue groups. Each commonly used term carries baggage with it. However, so too does the avoidance of those terms. We worried, as did others whose voices are in the text, about the unpredictable connotative and exclusionary impact of the facilitator-designed term "cultural richness." Although we understand the goal of naming issues constructively, we wish the facilitators had been transparent about their goal, named their invented phrase, and invited participants to work with them to see if it reflected what was important to the community members. Here we wondered if the wish to move appreciatively may have also served to make some perspectives undiscussible, for example, experiences of institutional racism which do not involve economic oppression.

EXPERIENCES OF "DISRUPTION"

On several occasions one or another participant spoke in an ideological way, or introduced content that did not seem to fit into the flow of the on-going conversation. Issues like ethnocentrism and economic inequality appear to have caused "disruption" of the apparently growing consensus of optimism on the "cultural richness" issue. In our experience, ideological-positional statements emerge when group ground rules, facilitator questions, or group structure permit or invite speaking that is disconnected from personal experience.

We have also found that rapid progression from dialogue to action plans can suppress dialogic exchange and excite tactical maneuvers and ideological speaking. We note that such a development took place just as the meeting focus was about to shift from open dialogic conversation to the formulation of action plans.

STRUCTURE OF THE TOWN MEETINGS: CITIZENS AND COUNCIL MEMBERS TOGETHER

We were delighted to see the development of a context in which the public presented its wishes to elected officials rather than the other way around. However, we wondered to what degree having city council members present increased the risk that people might become less interested in dialogue with other community members and more interested in presenting their general political stance and specific action objectives to the powers that be. We wondered also to what degree people's willingness to keep attending meetings and work on hard issues was encouraged by the presence of the council members, a sign of being taken seriously by those people who could use their power and position to support plans the citizens developed. To what degree might people have been willing to come because of the exhilarating feeling of being connected with city hall instead of fighting it?

COMMENTS AND QUESTIONS

Given our uneasiness in viewing the PDC project through a lens designed elsewhere, we turn now with relief to more general comments and reactions.

All conversational structures, all accounts of events, make space to welcome and expand some stories, and in so doing, diminish space for others. We are all, always, making such choices. This written account of the PDC's Cupertino Project presents and develops a story about what people did, when they did it, what processes they engaged in, and how the facilitators and planners thought about the development of each element in process. We also hear about how the facilitators shifted their thinking and actions over time. And we know the who (demographic) of the community participants, the how (process), and the when (timeline). We know the why, from the facilitators' theoretical perspective.

After reading all these things, we now want to hear all of the participants' and facilitators' voices; we want to hear about their experience of the process; we want to know what stories they tell about their experiences, and to whom; we want to know what kinds of connections were made among them, and what meanings these connections have. We want to know the details, the juice, the stories, how the ways in which they participated are connected with their hopes, fears, triumphs, intentions, their lived experience of this process in the moments that were officially part of the PDC plans, and in those moments between, when they reflected on what they had participated in and what it meant to them.

What we wish, for the most part, and long for, is to hear the voices of the people in the community. Our interest in hearing from them surfaced early in our reading. As the conceptual foundation was laid by the PDC in its statement of "principles for developing public dialogue in communities," we learned a great deal about the writers' principled perspective on the power of language, the value of difference, their view of systemic processes, the need for support from the top, and their view of dialogue. We found ourselves wondering, however, where the actual experience of individuals fit into this framework. We wished for a chance to talk with everyone involved, to ask them about the rich details of their experiences, of doing, of reflecting, and of carrying fresh actions forward into their lives

This is not idle curiosity. Although we value the highly detailed description of process in the book, we think it is the information in these stories that can guide us in knowing how best to use the rich experience generated by this project for our thinking and our future. Here are some of the questions we wish we could ask the people of Cupertino and the facilitators.

Questions for people who knew about the meetings but did not come, and for people who knew about the meetings and came.

1. What ideas did you have about what you were being invited to?
2. What made you think that any given PDC meeting would or would not be a meeting you'd want to attend?
3. How did specific announcements, invitations, or conversations affect your decision about whether or not to attend? Be as specific as possible about the effects of specific things such as the language used, the sort of person you spoke to, what the person did or did not do, the location where you first saw the announcement, or invitation, and so on.
4. About invitations to meetings, what advice do you have now for anyone else trying to bring community members together to see what possibilities there might be for improving their experience in that community?

Questions for people who did not come (this includes the "missing" council member)

1. How did you decide not to attend? Was it a decision for you or a given? Are you curious about what happened? From what you have heard, do you think you did what was right for you?
2. Did you hope that those who did meet would find ways to include you by filling you in on the content and process of the meetings? Did you—or how did you—want to be included even if you were not present? Did you want to read about the process? In the newspaper? In a letter? To hear about it on radio or TV? What kinds of things, if any, did you want to hear?
3. Was your not participating a statement of some sort? If so, what did you want it to say? What would you like those who attended meetings to know about you and your absence? Could they have done anything that would have

made attending and participating seem more desirable to you? If so, what?

Questions for all people who came to one or more meetings (community participants, members of the city council and facilitators)

1. How did you think of the event(s) you went to before you went to them?

2. Did you prepare yourself for the different events? If so, how? If not, from your present perspective, is there some way you'd prefer to be prepared should you do something like this again? Do you have ideas about what you would suggest to help others prepare to participate productively in such meetings?

3. Were any other people or events helpful in preparing you for what the event was to be, and planning for how you wanted to be part of it?

4. Without violating the confidentiality agreement you made, can you describe the kinds of experiences you heard about that affected you. How did they affect you? What stories did you tell that you were aware were "heard" or received by others as you wanted them to be? What was the effect on you of being heard?

5. What encouraged you to bring yourself to the meeting(s)? If you went to several, what kinds of things happened that encouraged you to keep going? Were parts of any of the meetings challenging for you? How? What made it possible for you to continue on even though some things were hard? What (if any) events occurred at or around the meeting(s) you attended that encouraged or discouraged you to return or not? If you did not come back, why? If you did come back, why?

6. Did you develop or improve or worsen your relationship with any of the other participants over the course of the process? How did such change come about? What effects, if any, do you think that these relational shifts had on what you were able to accomplish?

7. What for you was a high point of the process? What made it so? Who participated and how? What did you do, or not do, that contributed to its being a high point for you? Do others know this was a high point for you? If not, might you tell some of them? Who would you tell, how would you describe what happened and why it was a high point? What do you carry forward from it?

8. Did this or any other experience you had in the process with the PDC team members affect your experiences in any other community contacts you had in the time during or since the process was carried out?

9. Years from now, perhaps 5, or even 10, what might be happening in this community that would encourage you to feel proud and pleased that you had spent the time you did at these meetings?

10. One goal of the PDC team was to make space for all voices. Was this your experience? What was done to ensure equal voice? Facilitator interventions? Structures set in place? If so, what were they? Agreements and ground rules? Did it just happen? Were there times, from your perspective, that freedom to enjoy equal voice did not happen for you? If you think it might not have been that everyone felt there was room for all voices, how would you have known? Were there any times you wondered about this? Were there times when you chose to restrain your voice in the interest of making space for others? Or any times when you chose to restrain your voice because you were concerned about its particular welcome? Can you tell us the details?

Questions for facilitators

We know that the facilitators found a way to take nonexpert stances because group participants eventually took responsibility for the process.

1. What did you do or refrain from doing to make it possible to shift your stance? In the group? With yourselves?

2. What were you aware of group members doing (the 5Cs) that facilitated this shift in you?

3. Looking back, what advice do you now have for practitioners facing similar goals and dilemmas? On what experiences do you base your advice?

4. Did you experience a tension between public and private conversations in this process? Was there movement between public and private conversations that is not detailed in this account? Among facilitators? Between facilitators and various members of the community?

5. Looking back, what actions would you avoid in the future?

6. Looking back, what would you do more of in the future?

7. If you consulted at this time with a range of those community members who participated at any stage in this process about beginning a similar project elsewhere, what do you think the members of the community would suggest?

8. Were there times when you had concerns about the fit between your actions and your theory? If there were, did the actions encourage you to shift your theory or vice-versa, or both? Can you tell us some of these stories?

9. What do you most celebrate about this work? What experience captures the heart of it for you?

9

DIALOGUE AND

COMMUNICATION THEORY

ARTICULATIONS, PRIVATE EXPERIENCE, AND PUBLIC DIALOGUE

RONA T. HALUALANI*

I recall the last annual academic conference meeting of the National Communication Association (NCA) at which a panel of prolific intercultural communication researchers emphasized the need for researcher involvement with surrounding cultural communities. Those of us in the audience, all scholars, nodded our heads and spoke of an idealized

*Rona Tamiko Halualani (PhD, 1998, Arizona State University) is an assistant professor of language, culture, and ethnography in the Communication Studies Department at San Jose State University. Her main research interests include intercultural communication, cultural studies, identity, articulation, cultural communities and migration (or diasporic communities), and the construction of the social subject through historical memory, law and governance, tourism and global capitalism, and popular culture. She is currently conducting two ethnographic studies regarding cultural community: one on Pacific Islanders in the west (California, Arizona, and Las Vegas) and the other on the cultural relations and experiences within an Asian women's shelter in the Bay Area.

vision: quantitative, qualitative, and critical communication researchers working with the public to address issues of cultural contact and understanding. Although some academics bring such a vision to fruition, many suspend engagement as the daily demands of their role become taxing. The Public Dialogue Consortium (PDC), however, enacts the much-touted scholarly principle of public participation and community involvement with its Cupertino Community Project. The PDC researchers fulfill a role at first imagined and later proscribed by early European and American intellectuals akin to Gramsci's (1971) notion of an "organic intellectual." An "organic intellectual" is a scholar-practitioner who seeks to move beyond the confines of the university and improve the arenas of civic life and social freedom.

The team members of the PDC have integrated insightful scholarly communication theory and practice with community participation, public dialogue and process, and real or lived social-cultural relations. It is this productive intersection between a team of academic researchers and the Cupertino community of citizens, students, and city leaders that constitutes the focus of my comments. I discuss the value of such an applied project and its implications for the ways that we in academe should frame, inform, and continually reform our research. I also present several considerations for how the PDC might rethink the notions of "community" and "public dialogue" with regard to cultural experience and articulation.

Through several venues (focus groups, large public forum, interviews, and communication training), the PDC set out to create a setting in Cupertino that enabled open, constructive dialogue about often difficult and confrontational community issues. The project objective is laudable, serving as a model for intercultural scholars to combine our research efforts with community concerns. Moreover, the project revolved around team research and a training model so that a series of "inter-conversations" among scholars, practitioners, citizens, students, and leaders was continuous from beginning to end. Intercultural scholars can learn from this example. As we continue to map out the paradigmatic terrain of the field—functionalist, interpretive, and critical—it becomes clear that we should engage in multiparadigmatic team research on cultural communities and intercultural encounters. I would like to see the PDC serve as an exemplar of research collaboration and community involvement.

In the search for public concerns, one issue that emerged as a significant focus was cultural diversity, or "cultural richness." I found this issue and the initial focus-group data both fascinating and disturbing. Citizens expressed resentment at the "new Asian immigrants" and their growing numbers and insularity. The explosive growth of the

Asian population in Cupertino and the seeming threats of language barriers, competition among the students, and exclusive Asian forums
(Chinese Little League, Asian businesses) are underscored as the main
concerns of focus-group participants. In fact, in many ways, these comments do not seem much different from larger discourses on culture,
immigration, and the struggle to define American identity in the face of
growing multiethnic communities.

The PDC, although concerned with the content of the issues
raised, focus specifically on a communication format, meaning that the
form and process of speaking and discussing such issues carries significant consequences and plays a part on our perspectives, feelings, and
behaviors. This is not disputed. However, we must also remember that
such issues and the ways in which we express them are partly "spoken"
for us. Public dialogue concerns the substance (of what is spoken about)
and the process in which it is spoken. But the dialogue itself is also articulated (meaning structurally and politically expressed) by larger interests such as government entities (local, state, and national), the media,
the law, and popular culture. The comments made by citizens about
"immigrants" and "Chinese" who fail to adapt in terms of language and
cultural relations, echo the discourses constructing immigrants as
"strange aliens" and "noncitizens" who are ill-equipped to adapt (while
the connotation is clearly on assimilation and the focus is solely on what
the immigrants can do differently; see Lowe, 1996). On the "tube," as
news reports of the housing market flash after a story about increased
Asian immigration and Chinese espionage, perceptions of those who are
culturally different combine with sociopolitical constructions of the
immigrant alien Chinese, who have a discursive history in the United
States since the 1800s via legal doctrine, immigration policies, and
Orientalist stereotypes (Lowe, 1996). It will prove useful for the PDC
researchers to expand their focus, not just on the spoken form of the
issues by participants (communication rules, appreciative inquiry), but
also on the discursive, historical, political, and economic forms that
speak the issues around us (Grossberg, 1996; Hall, 1979).

Some questions the group might consider are: How do these
articulated forms frame our speaking practices and logics about such
issues? Is there an exterior point? Or a way to work from within to
reframe the issue? I raise these questions with regard to articulation of
the issues: Can there be a discussion about cultural richness without
being wary of the logic of the seemingly progressive multiculturalism
discourse in the country, which touts cultural diversity while reifying a
form of racialized citizenship? To what extent, does "appreciative
inquiry" and facets of the communication training (like the 5Cs) incorporate and reproduce the larger discourses of multicultural equality,

socioeconomic monopoly, and the polarity of Asian immigrant versus white citizen? A focus on the larger sociopolitical articulations of the issues may provide rich insights about the most impactful way to create awareness and reach some understanding.

In addition to articulation, I cannot help but wonder if some of the dialogic interests have yet to come to the table or have yet to approach, as one participant expressed, the "door." The number of participants is impressive. However, the number of Chinese, Asian Pacific, and other cultural residents (Latino(a)s, African Americans) is glaringly absent. The means to attain respondents is tricky; for the focus groups, moving from the registered voter lists may preclude participation by some residents who have failed to register or focus on other demands (maintaining jobs, watching over extended families). In addition, meeting with some of the Asian community leaders and ministers in Cupertino may help in bringing attention to the project and these needed voices of Asian residents. Conducting focus groups in other languages may help here as well, as this would require including other team members who are culturally and linguistically familiar with specific groups.

Capturing the differently positioned interests within the Cupertino community is important. In terms of Asian residents, the focus on the "new Asian immigrants" should be considered in relation to many Asian residents who first settled in Cupertino through the 1970s and 1980s.[1] These residents represent a different socioeconomic class than those who are more affluent: many live with extended families in apartment homes, work more than one job, and struggle on a daily basis, a lived experience far different from the community perceptions recorded. The various interests and experiences of residents from different cultural groups should be analyzed in the process of public dialogue. Considering the cultural specificities could lend insight into the nature of "cultural richness" and the ways in which it could be more productively approached.

This could be achieved through the PDC team approach; multilingual researchers and/or students can conduct focus groups or interviews with as many differently situated Cupertino residents as possible. The key focus should be on the "private experiences" of residents, the lived stories of those who have lived there for years to those who have just arrived. Such a research process may also break down how "community" and "participation" are perceived and experienced in culturally specific ways. Many may feel that participation is equivalent to residency. Others may conceptualize their extended family and church community as being their primary group and "community" over that of the Cupertino area. Still others may prioritize the needs of their jobs and domestic lives over any kind of participation. Private experiences describe and explain the reasons why residents may be absent from and or resist the PDC process. Again, the most insights will derive from the various articulations of private experiences in terms of making public dialogue and participation more accessible and collaborative.

Reading over the citizen comments about cultural richness, I was reminded of my own intercultural training in cultural contact. The primary foci were: What happens when several culturally different groups enter into conditions of contact? And how can positive intercultural attitudes be created in such conditions? Gordon Allport (1958), a psychologist whose work has informed intercultural communication research, identified several conditions under which positive contact may emerge (better known as the "contact hypothesis"). Two of these conditions stand out as possible challenges to the PDC project. First, according to Allport, interactants should be equal in status for an open, positive attitude to be achieved. In this project, the issue of equal status, specifically with regard to socioeconomic class, constitutes a central concern. The data reflects a conflation of culture with class and the resentment of perceived material wealth by specific groups. Training sessions can temper this issue by conducting several in-group focus groups. The in-group may be constituted by groups who live in similar areas (with similar class markers) and participate in similar activities (church groups, Chinese Little League parents). In this way, although not all uniformly equal in status, residents may feel more comfortable expressing their viewpoints and concerns around people they know and with whom they can identify.

Allport establishes that successful intercultural contact should have the potential to extend beyond immediate and superficial forms and should occur in a variety of contexts and long-term situations. This condition is critical for the PDC to bring about its desired objective. Although the designed action plan recommends that more activities commence between residents, there will have to be a point at which the community must move beyond annual festival events (the one day a year). Clearly, these are important to initiate cultural contact and understanding. But there must be more events and activities that provide ongoing interaction between residents and incorporate their individual interests and concerns (e.g., speaker events, cultural exchanges, mixers for parents—which stands as a potentially rich area—and church mixers, voter information sessions, neighborhood safety meetings, and business and commerce forums).

It is certain that the PDC has achieved in part the condition of institutional support. The strength of the project lies in the cooperation of city leaders and residents with the team. Although the PDC has received monetary support from the city, it is important that this institutional support continue (i.e., monies, meeting sites, materials, and verbal support in City Council meetings) for public dialogue training, forums, and the aforementioned activities. Public and intercultural dialogue requires financial support and a long-term commitment to thrive.

Indeed, I find the work of the Public Dialogue Consortium compelling and significant for intercultural communication research and community studies. Their continual efforts at revising their process and reaching out to as many voices as possible are impressive. With challenges still ahead, the PDC is the rare case in which scholars, practitioners, and residents work together on a larger goal of social and cultural connection. I wait anxiously for their next steps and insights.

NOTES

1. I stumbled on this identity position in several ethnographic interviews with Asian women from Cupertino in an in-process ethnography of Asian women's identities.

DIALOGUE IN THE CUPERTINO PROJECT

JOHN STEWART*

The Public Dialogue Project in Cupertino, California is an outstanding example of integrative action in at least two ways: First, the project integrates "town and gown," civic concerns, and scholarly ones. As every academic and virtually every member of a college or university community knows, it isn't easy to get professors, students, citizens, and public officials reading from the same page. Typically, academic institutions are both appreciated as economically important and resented for the traffic and parking problems they create and the pressures they put on legislative budgets, police departments, and public utilities. Citizens often view scholarly activities as idealistic, impractical, expensive, and politically naive or radical, and many academics resent the pragmatic demands of political realities and consider civic solutions simplistic and ethically suspect. In Cupertino, academics in the PDC, city officials, and citizens are successfully bridging this gap between town and gown and, in the process, they are contributing significantly to the quality of public life.

Second, the project integrates the concerns of several academic disciplines, and this is also not a simple feat. Within the discipline of communication, scholars concerned with interpersonal communication or dialogue are typically separated from—or even at odds with—those studying public discourse, and the PDC begins with the conviction that these two parts of the discipline can be connected. Moreover, as the preceding chapters amply demonstrate, the Cupertino project blends communication concerns with interests of political scientists, action researchers, public journalists, and educators committed to service learning in both high school and college. Given the cultural, social, political, and intellectual crises that are currently being created or exacerbated around the globe by various painful and short-sighted divisions, this project should be highly praised for the ways it brings diverse people and concerns together.

*John Stewart (PhD, 1970, University of Southern California) is Professor of Speech Communication and Graduate Program Coordinator at the University of Washington and works with technical professionals, primarily with architects and engineers, throughout the United States as a communication consultant. He has published numerous articles and books on the philosophy of language, interpersonal communication, and dialogic communication. John has been involved with the PDC since the group first formed. In addition to attending an international conference sponsored by members of the PDC team in 1996, John also served as one of the outside consultants at the Town Hall Meeting during Phase II of the Cupertino Project.

As a person who's been working on the philosophy and the practice of dialogue for almost three decades, I was excited to first learn about the Cupertino Project from some PDC members in mid-1996, and I enjoyed being one of the observer-consultants brought in for the Town Hall Meeting in November of that year. It is gratifying to see how PDC members responded to feedback we offered after that meeting and to learn of the project's on-going successes. The next few pages contain half a dozen of my responses to the ways things have gone so far, all of them expressed from the perspective of an interpersonal communication teacher-scholar and in a frame of deep admiration and respect for everyone who's been involved in this project.

POIESIS AND PRAXIS

Interestingly, I think one of the reasons for the project's success is that the participants have gotten exactly right the implication of the distinction Aristotle made over 2,500 years ago between *poiesis* and *praxis*. Poiesis is a kind of instrumental action, like baking bread or building a house. It has an end in view or an object in mind prior to the time the action begins. Poiesis is an activity that brings about specific products, and it requires a kind of technical know-how or expertise that Aristotle called *techne* and people today sometimes call "technical knowledge" or "technology." *Praxis*, on the other hand, is also directed at a specific end, but its aim is not to produce a particular product, but to realize some morally worthwhile good. As one commentator puts it, "The 'good' for the sake of which [*praxis*] is pursued cannot be 'made,' it can only be 'done.' 'Practice' is a form of 'doing action' precisely because its end can only be realized through action and can only exist in the action itself" (Carr, 1995, p. 68). In addition, the ends of praxis are constantly revised as the goods are pursued. All this means that *praxis* involves both intellectual and moral or ethical work, and it draws on a kind of reasoning and knowledge that Aristotle called *phronesis* or "practical wisdom." *Phronesis* is the kind of knowledge it takes to get a bill through the legislature or to overload a college class. It isn't written down anywhere, partly because it changes with the context, but it's still definitely knowledge because it's *known* by some people and *unknown* by others.

Many efforts to apply scholarly insights fail because the people doing the applying forget this distinction, and many civic projects fall short because they are approached as *poiesis* rather than *praxis*. The problems often are that people try to nail down the end-product rather than letting it emerge, and they try to create a "technology" for achieving it. But not in Cupertino. This project is succeeding in large part, I believe, because the people involved—the PDC, city officials, students, and citizens—are engaged in *praxis* guided by *phronesis* rather than *poiesis* guided by *techne*. This sensitivity surfaced when PDC members purposefully avoided any claim of scientific objectivity at the start of their involvement with the city, when they began their efforts by listening rather than lecturing, when they changed plans and activities in response to feedback, and as they consistently approached the project as a fluid, complex, emergent system of interdependent people and processes.

I noticed, for example, that when the PDC offered communication training to citizen participants, they didn't try to lay out a technology of dialogue or a series of prescriptive behaviors. Instead, they focused their training efforts on specific and relevant topics (Chinese Little League, Chinese signs, etc.) and three general characteristics of dialogue:

- Staying in the tension between standing one's own ground and being open to the other.
- Using descriptions and nonverbal behaviors that express trust and respect.
- Showing the other that they have been understood.

If they were applying a *techne*, they would have specified how speakers should show understanding—by paraphrasing, for example—and that nonverbal cues of trust should include touch, smiling, or open gestures. But they recognized that the dialogic quality of communication they are encouraging is different from situation to situation, and that there are many ways to embody and practice these three principles. As a result, they allowed the communication solutions to fit the specific communication problems, and they encouraged all participants to join them in the serious and focused process of making-it-up-as-they-go-along.

Another feature of the participants' praxical focus is what my co-author and I have called "nexting" (Stewart & Logan, 1998). "Nexting" is possible only when communicators remember that meanings are emergent, that communication is on-going, and that, regardless of how bad things currently are, something helpful can always be tried "next." It seems to me that this awareness has been consistently present during the Cupertino Project. Nexting happened at the Town Hall Meeting when a speaker born in Taiwan spoke of the stereotype of Chinese as "takers, not givers," and then (next) told a story that broke the tension with humor. It occurred again that same evening when a PDC team member responded to the attack and counter-attack between environmental activists and a cement company spokesperson by labeling the shared community vision "environmental safety." And it has happened during the project each time participants, city officials, or

PDC team members have responded to a roadblock, a crisis, or stalemate with a next positive step.

Aristotle wisely emphasized the crucial importance of approaching any task with the right kind of expectations and demands. "It is the mark of an educated [person]," he wrote, "to look for precision in each class of things just so far as the nature of the subject admits; it is evidently equally foolish to accept probable reasoning from a mathematician and to demand from an orator scientific proofs" (Aristotle, *Nicomachean Ethics*, 1941). The Cupertino Project could have failed if PDC members, city officials, or community members had expected crystal clarity, simple solutions, or mathematical precision. It is succeeding in large part, I think, because the people involved recognize—and sometimes even celebrate—the fact that the processes are inherently, necessarily, and appropriately messy, imprecise, changing, and unpredictable.

FOUR SUGGESTIONS

I've also been invited to offer suggestions for improving the project, and four occur to me. First, the PDC's teaching or training model could be enriched by the addition of some simple but powerful findings from research on adult learning. The model the PDC has developed is explained in Chapter 6 and graphically displayed in Figure 6.1. It integrates demonstration from a third-person position, practice from a first-person position, and critical reflection from a third-person position, all as applied to a specific context. The principles the model integrates are well-established, and the model makes good sense.

And (not "but"), there are three findings from adult learning research that can be integrated into this model to increase its power. As Richard F. Elmore (1991) summarizes these findings,

> All learning is contextual in at least 3 senses: New knowledge is acquired by extending and revising prior knowledge; new ideas acquire meaning when they are presented in a coherent relationship to one another; and knowledge becomes usable when it is acquired in situations that entail application to concrete problem solving. (p. xiv)

So far the training has done an excellent job with the third point. All the dialogic communication attitudes and skills have been consistently linked to local applications. At the same time, the first of these principles appears to be the least-observed in PDC training to date. It appears that no efforts have been made to ask either city officials or community members what "public dialogue" means to them as they enter the project, how they have been previously involved in civic affairs, or what experience they have had with the specific issue or context being discussed. All of these would be ways to identify the prior knowledge that participants are using to frame their understanding of the new ideas PDC trainers are explaining and modeling. Training efforts could be more effective if systematic steps were taken to encourage participants to connect dialogue principles and skills to experiences they have already had and to integrate ideas about dialogue into their current understandings about communication.

Efforts could also be made to show how the various principles and parts of the project fit together. For example, it would be useful to explain how the three main features of dialogue (staying in the tension, showing trust and respect, demonstrating understanding) make a coherent whole. Clearly the first feature is about overall perspective, the second focuses on what communicators "say" or "give out," and the third highlights elements of what communicators "hear" or "take in." This structure could usefully be clarified for those undergoing the training, and other parts of various wholes in this project could also be explicitly interrelated. If these two elements were added to the training model, its already-potent features could be even more effective.

A second suggestion is to encourage the involvement of high school students even more fully and consistently. It was a stroke of genius, I think, to have high school students do the intergenerational interviews early in the project. Not only did this move dramatically increase the raw number of people involved in the project, it also integrated a crucial intergenerational component, helped show both teachers and students the benefits of service learning, and developed the high school students' interviewing, conflict management, and listening skills. Especially given this success, I was puzzled by the omission of any reference to high school students in the city council's action plans reviewed in Table 5.1. Here the council committed to having additional training; expanding the Fourth of July celebration; developing a community-wide garage sale; beginning or expanding the welcome wagon, emergency preparedness, and neighborhood safety programs; expanding the Summer Arts and Wine Festival; and creating a Community Leadership Council. Students could have been key participants in several of these action plans, but they could also have been the focus of plans customized to their capabilities and contributions. At this writing (Summer 1999), I can't help but note that one of the lessons learned from the disaster in Littleton, Colorado is how potent—positively or negatively—high school energies can be. I hope project participants will be able consistently to find additional creative ways to enhance and develop involvement from Cupertino's two high schools.

My third suggestion is that project participants brainstorm ways to involve an even more diverse group of Cupertino residents. So far there have clearly been several selection biases. Participants have mainly been community leaders, those with a personal stake in some part of the diversity issue, and those with time to attend meetings or training sessions. But if the project is actually going to encourage new forms of civic communicating and new ways of solving future public problems, it needs to reach an even wider constituency. How might dual-career couples with tight schedules be reached at their workplaces, for example? How might the project link with PTSA, YMCA/YWCA, or service clubs (Rotary, Kiwanis, Lions, etc.)? How might various community forums (Fourth of July celebration, Summer Arts and Wine Festival, garage sales) recruit project participants? Every effort should be made to keep the project from becoming a clique or in-group activity, and this relates to my fourth suggestion.

It is gratifying to read that PDC members are working to, as they put it, "relinquish control of the process." Everybody knows that consultants should ideally work themselves out of a job. But I suggest that this goal not overshadow the more primary and ultimately more important one of "institutionalizing public dialogue in the Cupertino community as a legitimate and viable form of public communication." The predominant current approach to public communication in the United States is anything but dialogic, and even after this project's several years of success, there is still plenty of conflict, debate, and divisive discussion in Cupertino. PDC members wisely recognize that they should not become the "dialogue police," or, as they put it, that public dialogue not "be institutionalized as the only form of public communication" (footnote 1, Ch. 6). But I am not convinced that they fully recognize how long it might take to accomplish the cultural change they have begun. Many enormously powerful aspects of contemporary American culture are resolutely antidialogic, from the court system through labor management negotiation processes, to violence in televised wrestling and cartoons. There are counter-influences that support the PDC's goal in this project, including mediation training in elementary schools, alternative dispute resolution centers, and aspects of no-fault insurance legislation. But it will still take years of concerted effort to achieve, even in this one locality, the transformation that this project promises. I encourage PDC members not to bow out too early.

CONCLUSION

The PDC can be justly proud of this project. It combines philosophically and conceptually solid insights, a high level of ethical and civic commitments, humble flexibility, a great deal of enthusiastic energy, and considerable hard-nosed pragmatism. This book should help the project serve as a model to other academic and community collaborations that can go a long way toward significantly improving the quality of public life in democratic cultures.

10

COMMUNITY DIALOGUE AND PUBLIC ADMINISTRATION

REFLECTIONS ON THE CUPERTINO PROJECT: COMPARING COMMUNITY DIALOGUE INITIATIVES

JOY SALMON AND JOHN HIATT*

The courage and efforts of the Public Dialogue Consortium (PDC) and the citizens and government of the City of Cupertino are commendable. The process of dialogue is a challenging one, with no certainty of out-

*Joy Salmon is the manager of Nevada's Clark County Community Services, which includes the Neighborhood Services and Rural Town Services programs (both of which are described later in this response), and the county's animal control and code enforcement programs. She has worked in client and citizen-centered endeavors throughout her 11 years in the public sector. John Hiatt is a citizen volunteer and active participant in Clark County's community programs. He has been a member of the Enterprise Town Advisory Board for over 20 years, serving as chair for the past 10 years. He is the recipient of the 1999 Southern Nevada Neighborhood Impact Award in the Community Bridge category, awarded to individuals who have contributed substantially to providing a link between citizens and government.

come. In the end, one might either question the wisdom of having initiated a discussion that has "gone bad" or be inspired by a stone that is finally turned. It is significant to note that the Cupertino public dialogue process was ever-emerging and developmental. As each step was guided by the previous, the outcome was uncertain to the PDC as well as elected officials. All parties had to trust that the spirit, intent, and principles on which conversations were built would have sufficient influence to ensure a constructive outcome.

Across many disciplines, including public service, there is a shift from decision making by experts to decision-making partnerships. Historically, the industrial revolution brought with it a compartmentalization of roles—the division of labor—to achieve greater productivity. Much in line with this philosophy, citizens, busy with work and family responsibilities, turned to government to manage community affairs. Government employees, who were, after all, the full-time, paid servants of the people, diligently accepted the delegation of duty by community members to serve as their expert planners and policymakers. Yet, in time, citizens experienced government as single-handedly determining the direction of the community. They became disillusioned by the state of their communal lives and their diminished role in decision making. Similarly, government became discouraged and frustrated by the criticism of citizens who believed government should have done more (or less).

Just as in business, in civic matters there is a healthy renegotiation of relationships underway. There is a desire to ensure that public programs and policies are no longer compromised by this division of labor and accountability. Instead, there is a desire for both citizens and government to contribute to and enjoy the accomplishments of a thriving community.

Our interest in the Cupertino Project is motivated, in part, by our own efforts to initiate community dialogue projects in Clark County, Nevada. In this response, we first offer our reflections on the Cupertino Project and the work of the PDC, and then highlight what we think are some important similarities and differences between their project and our own.

MULTIPLE VOICES

An inherent challenge in any public dialogue is how to ensure a representative cross-section of the public is involved. Because participation is voluntary, even if one begins with a randomized mailing list, a self-selection process influences the diversity of the participants. In a democratic system, it may be inevitable that the active participants are those who are not completely satisfied with the status quo.

As discussed in the Alliance for National Renewal's 1996 publication, "Toward a Paradigm of Community-Making," successful community making involves the active involvement and reciprocal transformation of both the community and government. Local organizations can serve as mediating, mentoring, or intermediary agents to bolster citizen efforts.

The Cupertino Project successfully engaged and educated citizens to give voice to and act on their community concerns. It elicited the multiple voices of the community, substantially benefiting the community by strengthening the sense of community and the city's civic infrastructure. However, the active voice of government was largely absent. The quality communication facilitated by the PDC occurred among citizens more often than it occurred between citizens and government. In the first two phases of the project, the role of elected officials and government was held to a minimum. Although the third phase brought in top policymakers, their role was to craft "a response" to the community.

In the early developmental stages of any partnership in which the parties have unequal power, it is important to ensure that the voice of the less powerful is heard. However, these early stages are often marked by reactivity. The involved parties often see one another—and perhaps act—as victims or villains rather than well-meaning participants jointly caring for their community. As the partnership matures, the valuable roles and contributions of each of the parties are recognized and appreciated. All parties take on responsibility and accountability for the success of the partnership and its desired ends.

In citizen-government partnerships, it is recognized that by joining forces the vision for the community is more likely to be attained. Similarly, one would anticipate that, as it matures, the public dialogue in Cupertino would mirror more reciprocal conversations between citizens and government. If this partnership does not eventually allow both government and citizens to be active, then reactionary responses from both parties are likely to continue, and the full benefits of the partnership will not be realized.

On the other hand, the involvement of Cupertino's elected and appointed public officials is also notable for its restraint. Most government observers would agree that the involvement of "those at the top" is desirable in such a community-wide endeavor. Few would argue, however, that they have obtained such involvement without running the risk or exacting the price of politicizing the dialogue. When conversations are politicized, authentic dialogue is often diminished. The PDC approach appears to have successfully thwarted the political jockeying that often accompanies the involvement of those in positions of power. Perhaps among their chief accomplishments was their ability to inspire the restrained participation of Cupertino's executive body.

MEDIATING ORGANIZATIONS

The PDC considers itself the facilitator of public dialogue whose role would no longer be needed as community members gained needed skills. They view their neutral, external status as a necessary precondition for the successful initiation of public dialogue. They doubt that government could have successfully initiated such an endeavor.

In its broadest sense, mediating agents serve multiple roles—as skilled trainers, neutral facilitators, and passionate advocates of the dialogue process. The context of a public dialogue determines which roles are needed and when. For example, the need for trainers may evaporate as communication skills are learned, but the need for external, neutral facilitators may continue. Although the PDC provided facilitator training to community leaders, it is likely their skills will be used in contexts in which they are deemed neutral experts—those involving their fellow citizens. It is conceivable that other contexts may require external, more experienced facilitators. Furthermore, it has been our experience that either private or public entities may initiate public dialogues or serve as mediating agents. It is more critical that all parties are engaged in a truly authentic interactive process, with the context defining the roles of the parties.

Clark County's Neighborhood Services and Rural Town Services are government-sponsored mentoring and intermediary organizations whose intent is to facilitate citizen involvement in government. The link to government does, in some instances, leave citizens questioning the neutrality of staff. In these instances, it is advisable to access an external mediating organization. However, these government-sponsored programs have also effectively reflected government's intent to engage citizens in community efforts.

Although Clark County's efforts to enhance public dialogue involves and seeks the blessing of our elected and appointed officials, the role of staff cannot be underestimated. Staff are apt to know the issues of both elected officials and citizens, and they play a significant part in the facilitation and institutionalization of participatory decision making. If staff do not make room at the table for citizens, participatory decision making efforts fail. In other words, it is both practical and necessary for staff to serve as mediating agents. By doing so, we transform our governmental institutions.

Similarly, in Clark County, citizen groups serve as mediating agents. In addition to existing community organizations, neighborhood groups and Town Advisory Boards/Citizens Advisory Councils provide important links between citizens and government. Their intermediary roles are supported and promoted through the Neighborhood College and the efforts of neighborhood and town liaisons.

ABOUT CLARK COUNTY, NEVADA

Clark County is the most populous of Nevada's 17 counties and includes five incorporated cities. It spans 7,910 square miles (an area larger than New Jersey) and has over 1,200,000 residents. Over the last few years, Clark County has topped the nation in growth with a growth trend of 78% projected between 1990 and 2000. Over half of its residents are relative newcomers, with 55% residing in the county for less than 10 years. Demographers continue to forecast a 5.7% increase in growth per year.

Clark County government's uniqueness lies in its simultaneous responsibility for regional, urban, and town governments. The county provides numerous regional services to all residents regardless of whether they live in an incorporated city, an urban or rural town, or other unincorporated areas of the county. The county also provides municipal services to more than 450,000 residents residing in urban unincorporated areas of the Las Vegas Valley, as many residents are not located within a city boundary. In its capacity as a town government, Clark County is responsible for 15 unincorporated towns. Although the Board of County Commissioners makes all official governmental decisions, each unincorporated town has a Town Advisory Board (TAB) that provides input on community issues to the board. In addition, five Citizens Advisory Councils (CACs) serve in a similar capacity for communities located outside the boundaries of unincorporated towns.

The responsibility for this multifaceted service delivery is borne by a 7-member Board of County Commissioners, elected from geographic districts. The commission, in turn, appoints a county manager who is responsible for the administrative operations of county government.

The commission authorized neighborhood-based programming in 1996 and implemented the county's Neighborhood Services program in 1997. A multidisciplinary team of employees designed the program with input from an Advisory Council made up of representatives from community and intergovernmental agencies. Its objectives are to improve communication between citizens and government and increase citizen involvement in enhancing their neighborhoods. The program accomplishes these objectives through the following programs and services: citizen training and networking opportunities (e.g., the Neighborhood College and Neighborhood Congress), communication initiatives (e.g., community dialogues), better support to and utilization of TABs/CACs, matching funds for neighborhood projects, and liaisons to facilitate civic involvement. In 1998, these services were extended to rural communities.

DIFFERENT COMMUNITIES-DIFFERENT APPROACHES

Although the approach to involving the public in government and community issues used by the PDC in Cupertino is an interesting one, a different approach has been used in Clark County. Different approaches to public involvement and foci of interest are inevitable in different communities as each has its own unique blend of social factors, such as ethnic make-up and diversity, length of residency, economic circumstances, age structure, and problems.

The principles and values driving the conversations in Cupertino and Clark County are similar. Both initiatives support constructive, civil interaction and community action. Both initiatives seek to create opportunities for authentic, meaningful dialogue; to involve diverse groups of citizens early on in discussions; to educate citizens through information sharing and skill-building; and to go to citizens, meeting them in their living spaces.

The differences between Cupertino and Clark County lie in the strategies pursued. The PDC initiated Cupertino's public conversations by assisting the community to give voice to its concerns through focus groups, intergenerational interviews, and town meetings. It then helped citizens take action by developing visions and action plans and interacting with city officials. And, finally, it sought to sustain the public dialogue process by providing citizen leadership training and developing a core leadership group.

Clark County initiated its community-making efforts in reverse. Our strategies were defined by the differing characteristics of our community. Many residents are relative newcomers, have no ready ties to the community, and have no sense of connection to place, as most home addresses do not reveal the town or jurisdiction they live within. Thus, our primary strategies focus on ways to link citizens and neighborhood groups to existing avenues for communication and identity, specifically the TABs/CACs. By strengthening the sense of place and community, we hope to motivate residents to participate in public dialogue and community action.

As the majority of residents have lived in the community less than 10 years and attended school elsewhere, there is a general lack of understanding of how county government is structured, its relationship to the various city governments, and its multifaceted service delivery. A primary approach to public involvement has been to teach citizens how their government is organized and how they can make it responsive to their needs. Clark County teaches citizens to successfully interact with government and their neighbors through the Neighborhood College, a 10-week, 30-hour leadership training program. The course includes experiential learning activities, such as a mock planning hearing and leadership exercises, and facilitates the development of a neighborhood project vision and action plan. As citizens learn how to partner with government and community groups to address their concerns, they are empowered to become effective members of the community. The issues they choose to address are those that are important to them as individuals and to their community groups.

In addition to educational opportunities, Clark County emphasizes programs that will help forge strong neighborhood bonds. These include issue-specific neighborhood forums, pancake breakfasts, and informal coffee or cyber chats that allow citizens to meet their neighbors, community leaders, and elected officials.

We are also purposefully expanding the role of and support to TABs/CACs. They, along with our Neighborhood College alumni, are a ready-made core group of citizen leaders. Neighborhood liaisons piloted simple strategic planning with two towns, which included town meetings, Community Planning Teams, and Neighborhood Action Committees. Quarterly networking and informational meetings are held for TAB/CAC chairs and quarterly training opportunities for members. At their request, the county mandated that all zoning variance applicants go before the TAB/CAC so local residents could provide input and recommendations to the County's Planning Commission.

In the future, Clark County anticipates implementing a more comprehensive community-making endeavor, which will include broad-based visioning through intergenerational interviews, citizen-driven planning in each town, and strengthening of town identities.

CONCLUSION

If we were to take Cupertino's approach and ask residents in Clark County to identify the major community concerns and issues, the responses would vary depending on where people lived. It is a large and diverse area. However, we would expect many of the issues to be related to growth and development. As the fastest growing metropolitan area in the country, the strains this is causing with regard to housing, schools, traffic, and air quality are among most residents' list of concerns. Because Clark County enjoys a strong economy based on its recent growth, many in the community support growth. As a result, some citizens question whether elected officials and business leaders would be willing to participate in open and frank discussions that address both the positive and negative consequences of growth. We, in Clark County government, view public dialogue as community-making, as action as much as voice, and as the reciprocal transformation of community and government.

Although one of Clark County's four goals refers to the creation of partnerships with citizens, the implementation of authentic opportunities for citizen involvement varies department by department. Those of us in intermediary and mentoring roles are fully aware that we are creating citizen voices that call attention to the fact that the County's institutionalization of the paradigm shift—the decision-making partnership of citizens and government—is far from complete. Although the county has made in-roads to involving citizens—TABs and CACs most notably—the changes are soft and could be dismantled. The possibility remains that officials may feel threatened or see futility in a public dialogue process that is not yet well-honed and may be abused by special interest groups.

As intermediary agents, it is necessary to remind elected officials, colleagues, and ourselves that developing an influential and constructive voice is a developmental process for citizens, and Clark County is in the early stages of this great experiment. On the other hand, making room for authentic citizen participation is also a developmental process for government, as we are reminded when we fall short.

A PUBLIC ADMINISTRATOR'S INSIDER-OUTSIDER ACCOUNT OF THE CUPERTINO PROJECT

MARK LINDER*

I first encountered Cupertino in 1977. At the time I was the staff director for the Santa Clara Valley Coalition, an active community organization that has since ceased operations, and a number of our key leaders lived or worked in Cupertino. I found Cupertino a pleasant suburban community with bright, active residents. I later worked in Cupertino as a management consultant. When I served as the Assistant Town Manager in Los Gatos (also located in Santa Clara County), I became acquainted with Cupertino City Manager Don Brown, a highly regarded professional in local government.

Many of the qualities I first observed in Cupertino are present today, but the city has changed as well. As described in this book, one of the more significant changes has been the influx of new Asian immigrants. Based on my experiences listening and talking with friends and colleagues who live and work in Cupertino, I learned that this influx was causing concern. So I was excited to hear in 1996 that the Public Dialogue Consortium (PDC) had been invited by Don Brown to facilitate a dialogue between residents and government officials on community issues like cultural diversity. Since then I have followed the PDC's Cupertino Project with interest, both as an outside consultant and as a public official interested in improving the quality of citizen participation in local government.

EVALUATING THE PROJECT

It was interesting that the PDC wanted outside evaluations done on the project while it was developing rather than waiting until the end. I found this invitation to critique refreshing and an indicator of the PDC's desire

*Mark Linder is the Director of the Department of Parks, Recreation and Neighborhood Services for the City of San Jose. He previously served as a Deputy City Manager in San Jose, Assistant Town Manager in Los Gatos, and Assistant General Manager for Santa Cruz Metropolitan Transit District. In addition to having ties with Cupertino city officials and residents, Mark also served as an outside consultant for the PDC. He attended the Town Hall Meeting in Phase II of the Cupertino Project and provided feedback to our group in a follow-up meeting.

to learn and continuously improve. At the same time, I was also skeptical about the dialogue process and whether it would actually produce meaningful results. My initial impression was that people would attend the public forums, politely offer some opinions on how nice Cupertino is, and then go home. And although people might talk about the need for good communication, I questioned whether they would actually practice it, and whether it would make any difference even if they did.

At the Town Hall Meeting, I listened to the large-group discussions and participated in the small-group working sessions. I was struck by the diversity of the participants and the way in which they discussed the two topics (cultural richness, community safety). Real issues were being raised; people were wrestling with them together. An advocacy group opposed to the Kaiser tire burning facility tried to push their agenda and determine the outcome of the meeting, but they failed because the people in attendance did not seem to be interested in taking sides. This may seem simple, but it was actually remarkable. In my experience people usually come to public meetings to express an opinion or advocate a position. That was not the case at the Town Hall Meeting. Here was a large group of people, including elected officials, who wanted to listen. The other thing that frequently happens in public meetings is that a few people speak frequently, while others cheer for their side and become critical when an opposing view is offered. In this dialogue event everyone participated, offering their views and listening to others.

In the post-meeting debriefing, I was positive about the dialogue I had witnessed but remained skeptical about whether change would occur. As the project unfolded over the next years I continued to wonder if this would be just another exercise in "feel good" dialogue, or whether real fears and concerns would be put on the table. Would it produce good public policy? Would people actually gain more power over their own lives? Would people use the newfound skills to confront difficult issues? Would people feel that they were a part of Cupertino and had some ownership over the city's future? Would the simmering racial tensions be addressed or remain underground in the hope it would go away?

I found the answer to all these questions to be "yes." The dialogue process produced results. People addressed cultural diversity and racial issues. People felt an ownership in their city's future. People wanted to continue to listen, learn, and act. Elected officials were partners. High school students became active participants and brought their newly learned communication skills into the schools and the community. An on-going process for change was taking place in the local government, in the local community, and the local schools. This was very exciting and went beyond my expectations.

CONFIRMING ASSUMPTIONS

You have to have sufficient confidence in your abilities and in the people with whom you are working to allow a process to find its soul. The Cupertino Project began as a dialogue between residents and government officials on community issues. It ended up with an organization (the 5Cs) and an action plan to address racial conflicts, celebrate diversity, provide for a safer community, and develop the communication skills of students. It would have been easy to have one forum and to call it quits, or to force the process to stay focused on pre-selected questions. The PDC team and the city officials, I feel, had the confidence in the process and in people to let it go in the direction the people identified.

If you plan to change a community, you better be prepared to invest time and money. The Cupertino experience validates for me that community involvement and change does not happen quickly or easily. The Cupertino project had hours and hours of focus-group discussions, interviews, community meetings, reporting back, leadership training, and so on. In order to have any chance to produce fundamental change in the city's culture, I personally feel that these kinds of efforts need to be on-going for a minimum of three years. The more likely scenario is that it will take five years or longer.

In this era of cell phones, Internet, e-mail, and other technological advances in communication, face-to-face communication continues to be the most effective and powerful method for strengthening community. I believe that communities will not survive as healthy places to live and work without face-to-face communication. If we try conduct the public's business using only mediated channels of communication, we will drive out the sound of human voices; we will disconnect the human infrastructure of a community and thus become increasingly isolated from one another. My father, Carl Linder, writes in his monthly column for *Lutheran Partners* (March/April 1999) magazine: "We are becoming individual parts of a huge mobile, each living in his or her own loneliness, struggling with the winds of life in our own circles of existence and wondering why we are lonely, why we don't trust each other, and why it feels as though the fabric of society is unraveling." The Cupertino Project is one example of what we must do to prevent this from happening in our communities.

SUGGESTIONS FOR IMPROVEMENT

I would suggest a couple of changes to improve the project. Along with the participants invited through phone calls and personal contacts, I would also try to engage community organizations and institutions. I would have individual conversations and focus groups with the faith community, service organizations, neighborhood associations, business organizations, and so on. Even though this would make the project more complicated, it has two major benefits. First, it would help determine if the issues that surfaced in the focus groups are the same or different than the issues identified by "active" members of the community, as represented in existing organizations and institutions. Second, if the recommended actions coming out of the process are to become reality, they need the support of diverse groups of leaders. At a minimum, the process should neutralize opposition through involvement. I realize this is a delicate balance between needing to hear new voices while including and respecting those who are active.

Although it worked to not be officially sponsored by the local government, I think the process would be even more effective if the PDC was invited in by a coalition of government, business, church, and community organizations. I would suggest that the group spend time securing that up-front support. This way when the PDC uses citizen volunteers to go into the field they can do so as representatives of an independent, nonprofit organization invited by a coalition of community leaders to examine community issues. Given the PDC's limited resources, it is important that they have volunteers who can go into a community where there is openness to the process and desire to build a better community through public participation and action.

LINKS TO THE CITY OF SAN JOSE

I feel the results of the Cupertino Project validate the direction we are trying to go in the City of San Jose, where I am the Director of the Parks, Recreation and Neighborhood Services Department. Our department conducts many community meetings, guides numerous community endeavors, and organizes community organizations. We strongly believe that the days of the public hearing as the best form of democratic participation are over. Public hearings are isolated "talking-at" forums, with the public talking at the elected officials and/or the elected officials talking at the public. Public hearings do not involve the community at a sufficiently deep level of engagement. We believe that government must encourage interactive dialogue around heartfelt issues that leads to community action. We believe that people, given the opportunity, will do the right thing. We feel that opportunities are best provided through ongoing dialogue, information, and education. Perhaps the biggest obstacle to genuine democratic participation is cynicism and despair.

Democracy cannot flourish if the only methods of participation we have available are public hearings and elections. People will own their neighborhoods and their communities if they are involved, have some power, and are acknowledged and celebrated. Government officials must not fear an active public. We will only benefit. I thank the Public Dialogue Consortium for its excellent example of democracy in action.

IV

KEEPING THE CONVERSATION ALIVE

11

REJOINDER

As the author of Parts I and II of the book I was in many ways constrained by my own perspective and position in the Cupertino Project. As I wrote I could hear the ever-present voices of my PDC colleagues and the project participants, but the words that ultimately came out and made it onto the page (except for the quotes) were my own, a product of my experiential filters and linguistic abilities. The responses of the contributors in the preceding chapters demonstrate how a singular voice or perspective can be expanded through conversational exchange. Having read their responses, I now find myself more energized and enthusiastic about the possibilities of public dialogue than I was before writing the book. I look to my PDC colleagues with a renewed sense of pride, noting points of accomplishment and recognizing ways to improve the community dialogue process. At the same time, I also find myself questioning and reinterpreting decisions and actions that once seemed so clear and certain. In sum, the responses of the contributors were all that I hoped they would be, and more.

In an attempt to continue the conversation, I have chosen to respond to the contributors by drawing out points of similarity and difference and placing them into three categories: (a) those that affirm and extend the work of the PDC and the community dialogue process; (b) those that critique and challenge the decisions, choices, and actions taken in the project; and (c) those that offer lessons for improving community dialogue processes. A qualification is in order here. By searching out themes and reducing them to categories we are sure to lose some of the richly textured details that characterize the contributions. Some questions and criticisms will go unanswered and unchallenged. I hope to compensate for what is lost, however, by weaving the contributions together in a way that retains some distinctiveness while drawing out points of comparison.

AFFIRMING AND EXTENDING THE DIALOGUE PROCESS

In several different ways, all the responses confirm the notion of public dialogue and corroborate the basic principles and assumptions of the Cupertino Project. We can find instances, for example, in which each of the contributors utilizes terms and concepts that fit within the grammar of the PDC. Their descriptions and evaluations of the project are reflected back to us in an intelligible and recognizable form; they demonstrate insight and understanding of the community dialogue process and what we in the PDC were trying to accomplish. By the same token, the contributors have added their own unique perspectives, tweaking our language, principles, and assumptions enough to extend the dialogue process into new territory. There are at least four areas where the responses affirm, enrich, and extend the community dialogue process and the Cupertino Project.

MARKERS OF SUCCESS

The Penman and Chang interviews are the most explicit in describing how the project achieved a number of stated goals and objectives. Each includes ample evidence to conclude that the once undiscussible diversity issue became the focus of extensive public attention and conversation. Several of the project participants who were interviewed also recognized the need to include community members who held different positions and had conflicting opinions on the issues. Michael Chang, for example, talked about the efforts that were made to include "those people who have the most problems with cultural change," and the benefits that derived from keeping these people "in the loop." Moreover, the interviewees noted that the dialogue process was not designed to "change anyone's mind," but that it did in fact allow people to "find common ground" around "an issue of mutual interest" to all members of the community.

Along with the Penman and Chang interviews, Linder highlights how the dialogue process created transformation and change in the community. A seasoned public administrator, Linder initially thought that the project would turn out to be "just another exercise in 'feel good' dialogue." As the project unfolded, however, he found that the discussions surrounding cultural and racial diversity did indeed produce meaningful results. "People felt an ownership in the city's future," and an "on-going process for change" became implemented "in the local government, in the local community, and the local public schools." Similarly, Penman's interviewees recognized the importance of institutionalizing the public dialogue process. As one of them observed, the city now has "a way to handle" the differences that arise over cultural and racial issues.

ADVANCING PARTICIPATORY DEMOCRACY

Along with Linder and the Chang interview, Salmon and Hiatt emphasize the need for new forms of citizen involvement as a way to reinvigorate democratic participation. They describe how the industrial revolution led government employees to become "expert planners and policymakers," thus diminishing the role of citizens in public decision making. "There is a healthy renegotiation of relationships underway," they say, which is leading to "decision-making partnerships" and the "reciprocal transformation of community and government." By situating the Cupertino Project within this larger paradigm shift, the authors have extended the reach and influence of public dialogue beyond the single case study example presented in this book.

There is also recognition among the contributors that public dialogue processes must be flexible enough to adapt to the needs of different communities. The project that developed in Cupertino, for example, was in response to the unique circumstances surrounding the influx of Chinese immigrants. Yet as Salmon and Hiatt note, the efforts to promote public dialogue in Clark County, Nevada, rely on a different approach and a different set of topics because of the unique characteristics of that community. We believe that the flexibility inherent in public dialogue is a critical feature in the paradigm shift to participatory forms of democracy and decision-making partnerships. All initiatives within this emerging paradigm will, of course, share a common set of principles and values, such as fostering collaboration, promoting skill-building, and the like. Dialogue is useful as a community-building process, however, precisely because it can be implemented in any number of different ways depending on the issues, the participants, and the unique needs of the community.

THEORY, METHODOLOGY, AND COMMUNICATION PRACTICE

Three of the contributors comment directly on the methodological practices that undergird the work of the PDC and the Cupertino Project. Of these, two affirm our theoretical focus, the other challenges it.

Stewart introduces a theoretical vocabulary that most clearly resonates with our own. He accurately describes the project as falling within the domain of "praxis" (or practical theory) and carefully explains how the PDC works to advance a form of knowledge called "phronesis" (or practical wisdom). Not surprisingly, these terms appear in Chapter 2 in which I describe the PDC methodology and theoretical orientation (Stewart's contribution is referenced in the chapter as well). Given that we speak the same language and share many of the same assumptions, it is not surprising that Stewart provides the most thorough and far-reaching account of the theory and methodology used to guide the Cupertino Project.

Roth, Stains, and Chasin also articulate a theoretical and methodological framework that aligns with our own, yet it is more subtle, less academic, and more closely tied to communication practice than the Stewart response. For example, the authors identify several areas of commonality between their group, the Public Conversations Project, and the PDC. Both seek to foster "dialogue on controversial matters" and to design projects that are "evolving, collaborative, and emergent." At the same time, they also consider differences between the two groups, most notably that the PCP facilitates private conversations on public issues, whereas the PDC facilitates public conversations on public issues. The authors go on to say, however, that these are differences of practice, not aim. Similar to Salmon and Hiatt, Roth et al. show us that the theory and practice of public dialogue is not a uniform process. Although emerging out of a common set of principles, dialogue is practiced in a variety of different ways.

Halualani's response is conceptually and pragmatically interesting, in part, because it takes us out of our theoretical comfort zone. Because her contribution comes in the form of critique, I discuss it more fully in the next section.

CRITIQUING AND CHALLENGING THE DIALOGUE PROCESS

The contributors were invited to render critical evaluations of the project, and many of them did indeed employ the language of critique. How these claims are offered and how I respond to them is vitally important if we are to sustain this conversational exchange within a dialogic frame. We are sure to fall out of the dialogue, for example, if we treat points of difference and disagreement as battle lines in a war to determine who is right and who is wrong. If we approach our differences as an opportunity to enrich and expand the conversation, on the other hand, we will be in a much better position to balance competing tensions and stay in the dialogue. Fortunately, the contributors have given me the gift of constructive criticism (there is no malice or attribution of blame), which in turn has paved the way for a dialogic response.

EXPANDING THE CIRCLE OF PARTICIPATION

In one way or another, all of the "outside" contributors criticize the selection of participants and recommend that more diverse groups of people be involved in the project. Roth et al., for example, suggest that we expand the range of people to include the "uninvolved majority." "Outlying voices," they write, "often represent perspectives that are enormously enriching to the centrally involved group." Halualani notes the absence of "Chinese, Asian Pacific, and other cultural residents," and offers several practical suggestions for attracting more diverse constituencies into the dialogue process. Stewart recognizes the "selection biases" inherent in the project and insightfully recommends that project participants, not the PDC, "brainstorm ways to involve an even more diverse group of Cupertino residents." Salmon and Hiatt tacitly acknowledge that the project did not include a "representative cross-section of the public," but they view this as a problem inherent in all voluntary community projects that rely on self-selection processes. Finally, Linder notes that the project needs to garner the support and participation of "diverse groups of leaders" if it to have any lasting impact on the community.

These criticisms are familiar to us. From the beginning of the project we struggled with the tension between needing to recruit a broad and diverse group of participants and the inability or unwillingness of many Cupertino residents to volunteer because of time constraints or lack of interest. The lack of resources was also a limiting factor. To attract nonactive, disenfranchised residents into a volunteer community project takes considerable time and effort. Given our constraints and limitations, it is not surprising that many of the participants who ended up volunteering in Phases I and II were "active residents" with some history of civic engagement. This trend continued in Phase III when the city council made a conscious decision to enlist the support and participation of "community leaders."

In Phase IV, however, a fundamental shift in the composition of the project participants took place. As the range of activities expanded into different segments of the community, the project attracted a number of "new" residents who had little or no previous experience participating in civic events. Despite this modest success, we recognize, along with the contributors, that the majority of Cupertino residents did not participate in the project, and those that did tended to be active members of the community.

The question of the ethnic make-up of the project participants is much less certain. We disagree with Halualani's observation that Chinese, Asian Pacific, and other cultural residents were absent from the project. We would point to several examples from Part II of the book in which individuals from these groups were identified as such. However, her suggestion that we differentiate between "new Asian immigrants" and "Asian residents who first settled in Cupertino in the 1970s and 1980s" is extremely useful. Many of the Asians who participated in the project fell into the latter category, having lived in Cupertino for a number of years. Some of them, such as Michael Chang and members of the Asian American Parents Association, were active members of the community. Obviously, these Asian residents assume a different place and have different perspectives compared to those who immigrated to the city within the past few years. Expanding the circle of participation is absolutely critical, as Halualani states, if we are to capture "the differently positioned interests within the Cupertino community." Later in this rejoinder I discuss one potentially useful approach for accomplishing this important goal.

WHERE ARE THE EXPERIENCES OF THE PARTICIPANTS?

Roth et al. and Halualani raise questions about the nature of personal-private-lived experience and its role in the public dialogue process. This is clearly the central theme of the Roth et al. response. The authors question whether the interview protocol used in the focus-group interviews was sufficient enough to elicit experiential responses from the participants, and they note that the ideological statements heard in the earlier phases of the project might have come about because the people making them were not speaking from personal experience. Wanting "to hear the voices of the people in the community," the authors develop a series of provocative questions designed to call forth the rich details and experiences of community members and the dialogue facilitators. Similarly, Halualani asks that our research approach focus on the "private experiences" and "lived stories" of community members. This approach, she suggests, can help us gain insight into how Cupertino residents perceive notions of "community" and "participation" in "culturally specific ways."

On one level, these criticisms speak more to the choices I made as author in writing and presenting the project than any particular feature of the PDC methodology. The key point I want to emphasize here is that participants did indeed share their experiences and stories throughout the course of the Cupertino Project. In the focus-group interviews, for example, the first two questions (see Table 3.2) were designed specifically to elicit narrative responses. In most cases they did. When a response was given in the form of an opinion rather than a personal statement, the PDC facilitators would typically ask a follow-up question like, "What in your background or experience might have led you to this opinion?"

It has been several years since the focus-group interviews, yet I can still clearly recall some of the wonderfully rich stories that were told. There was the long-time resident who vividly described the shacks and run-down buildings where Mexican farm workers used to live when Cupertino was an agricultural, farming community. "I think it's important to remember that Cupertino has always had diversity," he said, "and some of that past diversity had an ugly side to it." Another is the more recent immigrant who described the intense pressure he felt as a young student competing with others in the Japanese school system. "Having been through that," he said, "it's hard for me to feel much sympathy when I hear people complain about the emphasis on scholastics in the Cupertino schools."

Other stories from other activities and events readily come to mind. Although interesting and certainly useful, I elected not to foreground these personal experiences in my descriptions and analyses of the project. The decision was made in terms of the inevitable trade-off between what to include and what not to include. If it is indeed an error of omission, then I am the one responsible for it.

On another level, there are aspects to the criticisms that suggest that the PDC's approach to personal experience is different from what Roth et al. and Halualani recommend. Although we do seek to elicit stories and personal experiences, we do so not as an endpoint but as a way to create opportunities for something else to happen. For us, sharing personal experience is a way to open a space for people to extradite themselves from repetitive and perhaps even polarized patterns of communication. As such, we never focus on a single individual experience, but rather on the way in which multiple stories told by members of a community connect together. By collectively telling their stories, residents can begin to attend to the meanings that they are collectively constructing around an issue and how these various social constructions impact their community.

We strongly believe that this story-telling process enhances deliberation and creates opportunities for shared decision making and the development and implementation of common action plans. (It also helps explain why I focused more on outcomes than experiences in my description of the project.) I sense that Roth et al. and Halualani also approach personal experiences and stories as an opportunity to gain access and insight into other processes. It is less clear whether they would tie experience so closely to pragmatic, decision-making outcomes as we do in the PDC. For example, given Roth et al.'s focus on private "off-the-record" conversations, it is hard to imagine them foregrounding public decision-making processes at the expense of personal experience.

CONNECTING TO LARGER DISCOURSE STRUCTURES

Halualani's suggestion that we interpret participants' discourse in light of larger historical, political, and economic forces is a particularly challenging critique because, as noted earlier, it represents a fundamental shift in our theoretical focus. As communication practitioners, we are committed to facilitating public dialogue in the local spaces that people occupy as they engage in face-to-face interaction. This interpersonal orientation is clearly reflected in the communication techniques and practices (appreciative inquiry, systemic questioning, reflecting) we have developed and adapted from other practitioner groups. When we design and facilitate public events, as we did in Cupertino, our first instinct is to encourage participants to attend closely to the communicative actions (listening, speaking, etc.) they perform together. We want people to recognize that how they act together in the small spaces of their conversation determines what it is that they construct together.

Having said this, we fully agree with Halualani's central claim that larger "discursive, historical, political, and economic forms" prefigure the issues we talk about, and how we talk about them. Whenever people open their mouths to speak, no matter the context, they act into patterns of communication that have already been created for them and, often without realizing it, they perpetuate, for good or bad, the interests that are embedded in those patterns. It is interesting that Halualani recommends that the PDC expand its focus to include these larger discourses, yet our response has been to move in the opposite direction. Working at the local level, we want participants to create their own patterns of communication from the bottom up, to break away from the larger discourse structures that permeate public communication today. We base this on the assumption that people will be unable to engage in dialogue if they are speaking and listening in ways that simply reproduce dominant patterns of communication.

The primary reason why the PDC focuses on interpersonal contexts, as opposed to larger discourse structures, is because it gives us the best chance to have an impact and make a difference. Communication practitioners and action researchers cannot realistically change discourse structures that are deeply embedded in our social institutions. (They have been constructed over extended periods of time through continued use and are thus highly resistant to large-scale change.) What practitioners and researchers can do, however, is foster transformation in the communication patterns of small groups and local communities. It is also important to remember that larger discourse structures do not speak for themselves. They are always enacted in situated contexts, in the way people relate to one another as they act into and out of these contexts. The extent to which macro discourse structures shape social meaning and action, then, is dependent at some fundamental level on how they are negotiated in face-to-face encounters, in the kinds of communication events we facilitated and studied in this project.

What we find most useful about Halualani's critique is that she recognizes ways to use macro discursive forms to bring about local change. This opens up new possibilities for us. Instead of seeing discourse structures as an impediment to dialogue, perhaps we can follow Halualani's suggestion and figure out ways to incorporate them into the community dialogue process. For example, I can imagine an activity in which participants in small-group contexts and large public events discuss the historical, political, and economic articulations of an issue, and then reflect on how these articulations impact the community's abilities to achieve shared understanding, make collective decisions, and otherwise improve conditions in their local situation. The important learning here is that larger discourse structures can be used pragmatically in interpersonal encounters to bring about community change at the local level.

LESSONS LEARNED

To engage in dialogue is to engage in a learning conversation. As we reflect back to others what we hear them saying, and as others do the same for us, we come to a deeper understanding of who we are, what we do, and what we hope to achieve. We are indebted to the contributors for their thoughtful responses, for reflecting the Cupertino Project

back to us so that we might learn from our actions and improve the way
we conduct community dialogue processes in the future. Our hope is
that this exchange was mutual, that the contributors learned something
as well. We also hope that practitioners, academics, public officials, and
others can benefit from our experiences working in Cupertino and our
subsequent exchange with the contributors. In what follows I identify
some of the more important learnings that resulted from our exchange,
and in doing so offer suggestions to others who are interested in facilitating community dialogue projects.

START THE TRAINING AND INSTITUTIONALIZATION PROCESS EARLIER

In their questions to the facilitators, Roth et al. ask us to reflect on the
actions we would avoid and the actions we would do more of in the
future. The single most important change we would make is to begin the
training and institutionalization process earlier. As noted in Part II of the
book, those of us in the PDC designed and facilitated events and activities during the first two phases of the project. Although we began training community members in facilitation skills in the third phase, it was
not until the fourth phase that we focused most of our attention and
efforts on creating a social infrastructure for sustaining the dialogue
process. If we were able to go back and start the project again (if only!),
we would begin at the very outset by recruiting a core group of community members and training them in communication facilitation skills. We
would then proceed to consult closely with this group in planning the
phases of the project, designing events, and conducting trainings for
other community members.

Such an approach offers several advantages. First, it speaks
directly to the observation made in the Penman interviews and Chang
interview that the dialogue process in Cupertino moved too slowly. This
was not framed as a criticism by all of the project participants (Penman
herself states that given the circumstances, "the slower the better"), but
it does raise questions concerning the pace and timing of the project.
Who decides when it is necessary to proceed slowly and when the community is ready to move ahead? For better or worse, these decisions
were made initially by the PDC team in consultation with the city manager. By enlisting a group of community members as co-researchers earlier in the process, as Roth et al. suggest, the project might very well
have followed a different timetable. In this regard, it is interesting to
note that once city council and 5Cs members became involved in planning activities and events, the institutionalization process quickened
considerably.

Another advantage to starting the training and institutionalization process earlier is that it would have allowed us to be more strategic
in recruiting diverse stakeholders into the project. In the first two phases
of the project the PDC recruited all of the participants one at a time via
phone calls and mailings. With few resources and little support from the
city, we were fortunate to get the number and range of participants that
we did. We were also fortunate that as the 5Cs developed a number of
"nonactive" and ethnically diverse residents stepped forward to join the
group.

Looking back, we now realize that we should have been more
systematic in these efforts, relying less on sheer persistence and luck and
more on the identification of key stakeholder groups and organizations.
In line with Linder's suggestion, we would spend more time up-front
securing support from a "coalition of government, church, business, and
community organizations," including, as Halualani suggests, Asian
groups and organizations. We would then invite volunteers from these
organizations to join the initial core group of community members. By
acting as "mediating agents," to use a term from Salmon and Hiatt,
these volunteers would not only bring the interests and perspectives of
their groups forward into the larger project, they would also bring their
communication training and skills back to their respective organizations.
Moreover, we would expect that these individuals would be in an ideal
position to recruit new participants into the project, thus ensuring
greater diversity and a broader circle of participation.

FACILITATORS: DON'T BE TOO QUICK TO LEAVE

Throughout the project we worked from assumption that our services as
facilitators would no longer be needed once a social infrastructure was
in place and enough community members had capacities for practicing
public dialogue. We were apparently far too idealistic in predicting
when this would happen. As noted at the end of Chapter 6, the PDC is
still working in Cupertino as of this writing, with commitments from the
council to continue for at least another year. We never would have imagined we would still be working in Cupertino this long after the project
started.

This development, however, was wisely foreshadowed by some
of the contributors. Stewart and Linder, for example, both suggest that
we underestimated the amount of time it would take to accomplish the
goals of the Cupertino Project. It will "take years of concerted efforts,"
writes Stewart, because "the transformation that this project promises"
is directly at odds with powerful "anti-dialogic" forces within American
society. He cautions us "not to bow out too early." Similarly, Salmon

and Hiatt state that "the need for trainers may evaporate as communication skills are learned, but the need for external facilitators may continue." This leads to another important lesson learned. Instead of rushing to find the right moment to remove ourselves from the community dialogue process, we should instead be looking at how the contexts of the project evolve and how we can best change our role and ways of working to fit the changing needs of the community.

NEVER UNDERESTIMATE STAFF SUPPORT

Salmon and Hiatt provide insight into the importance of staff support, something we learned first hand when the city hired Laura Domondon Lee as the community relations coordinator. Her presence and expertise had a tremendously positive effect on the dialogue process. In fact, it was one of the contributing factors that accounted for the growth and accelerated pace of the project in Phase IV. Obviously, staff play a central role in disseminating information, scheduling meetings, and coordinating activities, efforts which are especially critical in community-wide projects that involve large numbers of people. Beyond that, Salmon and Hiatt also discuss the contribution of staff support in terms of their role as "mediating agents." "Staff are apt to know the issues of both elected officials and citizens, and they play a significant part in the facilitation and institutionalization of participatory decision making."

One of the ways that we sought to enhance Lee's role as mediating agent in Cupertino was to involve her directly in the facilitation training programs, both as teacher and student. She also worked closely with us in learning how to summarize and analyze information from the various events and activities and how to feed these results back to project participants. Following the lead of Salmon and Hiatt, we would strongly suggest to other practitioners that they include staff as co-researchers in community dialogue projects.

BRIDGING THE THEORY-PRACTICE DICHOTOMY

As noted earlier, several of the contributors comment on the theoretical and methodological practices used by the PDC in the Cupertino Project. In addition to evaluating our approach, it is noteworthy that the outside contributors also demonstrate how they link theoretical concepts to their own professional activities and practical endeavors. For example, Roth et al. and Salmon and Hiatt show us how their efforts to design conversational structures and community-building programs are grounded in sophisticated models of dialogic communication and the "reciprocal transformation of community and government." The two academic contributors, Halualani and Stewart, work from the other side. While advancing complex notions of communication theory, they both go to great lengths to connect these ideas to the concrete world of practical action. Whether they stress the theory behind the practice or the practice behind the theory, the contributors remind us that there can be no clear separation between the two. We firmly believe that the future of public dialogue lies within the realm of practical theory (see Chapter 2), in bridging the traditional concerns of academics with the pragmatic demands of the public sector in order to improve the quality of social life.

KEEP THE FAITH, TRUST THE PROCESS: SOME PRACTICAL ADVICE

Several of the outside contributors recognize that a community dialogue project like the one in Cupertino requires a good deal of commitment, faith, trust, and courage. There must be a commitment to the ideals of participatory democracy and self-government; faith in the constructive power of public dialogue to bring about these ideals; trust in community dialogue processes and in the people who participate in them; and the courage to risk failure and persevere when faced with what appear to be insurmountable obstacles. Public dialogue projects are not likely to succeed if any of these values are in short supply. Although this might seem a bit daunting, we have learned that there are a few things that facilitators can do to help them get started on the right track and to keep them from losing their focus and becoming discouraged.

First, we suggest that community dialogue facilitators and researchers work as a team. It is hard to imagine how any single individual could have conducted the Cupertino Project, and, even if they could, we suspect that the quality of the work would have suffered. It is important that the team be composed of people with different perspectives, skills, and areas of expertise, yet it is also essential that members share core values concerning the ideals of democracy, public dialogue, and the like.

Second, the team should focus initially on collaboration and building relationships with people in the community. By engaging in dialogue and interpersonal contact with community members at the very outset, the facilitators can help establish the kind of open and honest relationships that will allow them to deal productively with conflict and differences that are sure to arise later in the project.

Third, as noted earlier, begin by working with a small cohort group of volunteers from different stakeholder groups in the community who are willing, able, and committed. Facilitators will inevitably experience opposition at some point in the project, but it makes little sense to seek out these difficult cases in the beginning. If you begin with those who will be ambassadors, it will much easier and more productive when it comes time to reach out to the resistors.

Fourth, start small by designing events and activities that are likely to produce some modest level of success. The key here is to first give people a positive experience with public dialogue—what it is, what it can do—and then to work with these people to expand the possibilities into other areas of the community (schools, faith-based institutions, service organizations, etc.). We have found that dialogue sells itself. Once people experience this form of communication they are likely to want more and to seek out additional opportunities to practice it.

Fifth, be flexible, realistic, and patient. As the dialogue process expands and more people join the project it will almost certainly move in directions that the participants and the facilitators did not envision (or perhaps even agree with!). Dialogue processes are inherently "messy, imprecise, changing, and unpredictable," as Stewart notes. Facilitators must be able to work comfortably and effectively with what is often a chaotic and paradoxical process. Moreover, they need to be able to teach other project participants to be comfortable as well.

Finally, we encourage other public dialogue facilitators to seek outside consultations by inviting others to observe and critique their projects. As Linder notes, these evaluations will be most helpful if they are conducted at various points in the process, not just at the end. We also recommend that a variety of consultants be used. Although some of these people should be similar in background to the facilitating team, it is vital to include others who have different perspectives, interests, and competencies. Outside consultants are especially helpful when the facilitating team is "stuck," when they are so enmeshed in the project that they have difficulty stepping away and looking at it from a fresh perspective. The PDC benefited immensely from the feedback we received from consultants on the Cupertino Project, just as we did from this exchange with the contributors.

REFERENCES

1998: A look back. (1999, January 6). *Cupertino Courier*, p. 1.

Allport, G. (1958). *The nature of prejudice*. New York: Doubleday.

Andersen, T. (1992). Reflections on reflecting with families. In S. McNamee & K. J. Gergen (Eds.), *Therapy as social construction* (pp. 54-68). London: Sage.

Aristotle, (1941). *Nicomachean ethics* (W. D. Ross, Trans.). In *Basic Works* (R. McKeon, Ed.). New York: Random House.

Bachrach, P., & Bostwinick, A. (1992). *Power and empowerment: A radical theory of participatory democracy*. Philadelphia: Temple University Press.

Barber, B. (1984). *Strong democracy: Participatory politics for a new age*. Berkeley: University of California Press.

Barber, B. (1997). Foreword. In G. Reeher & J. Cammarano (Eds.), *Education as citizenship* (pp. ix-xiv). Latham, MD: Rowman & Littlefield.

Barber, B. (1998). *A place for us: How to make society civil and democracy strong*. New York: Hill and Wang.

Barrett, W. (1978). *The illusion of technique: A search for meaning in a techno-logical civilization.* Garden City, NY: Anchor Press.

Bateson, G. (1972). *Steps to an ecology of the mind.* New York: Ballantine.

Battistoni, R. M. (1997). Service learning as civic learning: Lessons we can learn from our students. In G. Reeher & J. Cammarano (Eds.), *Education as citizenship* (pp. 31-49). Latham, MD: Rowman & Littlefield.

Bernstein, R. J. (1983). *Beyond objectivism and relativism: Science, hermeneu-tics, and praxis.* Philadelphia: University of Pennsylvania Press.

Bernstein, R. J. (1992). *The new constellation: The ethical-political horizons of modernity/postmodernity.* Cambridge, MA: MIT Press.

Berman, D. R. (1994). *State and local politics* (7th ed.). Madison, WI: Brown and Benchmark.

Briand, M. K. (1999). *Practical politics: Five principles for a community that works.* Urbana: University of Illinois Press.

Buber, M. (1958). *I and Thou* (R. G. Smith, Trans.). New York: Scribner.

Bunker, B. B., & Alban, B. T. (1997). *Large group interventions: Engaging the whole system for rapid change.* San Francisco: Jossey-Bass.

Burns, J. M., Peltason, J. W., & Cronin, T. E. (1987). *State and local politics: Government by the people.* Englewood Cliffs, NJ: Prentice-Hall.

Carr, W. (1995). *For education: Toward a critical educational theory.* Oxford: Open University Press.

Chasin, R., Herzig, M., Roth, S., Chasin, L., Becker, C., & Stains, R. R. (1996). From diatribe to dialogue on divisive issues: Approaches drawn from family therapy. *Mediation Quarterly, 13,* 323-344.

Cissna, K. N., & Anderson, R. (1994). Communication and the ground of dialogue. In R. Anderson, K. N. Cissna, & R. C. Arnett, (Eds.), *The reach of dialogue: Confirmation, voice, and community* (9-30). Cresskill, NJ: Hampton Press.

Collins, N. (1996a, December 4). City mulls law to encourage use of English on store signs. *Cupertino Courier,* p. 10.

Collins, N. (1996b, December 25). Owners say Asians signs simply good for business. *Cupertino Courier,* p. 7.

Cooperrider, D., Barrett, F., & Srivastva, S. (1995). Social construction and appreciative inquiry: A journey in organizational theory. In D. M. Hosking, P. Dachler, & K.J. Gergen (Eds.), *Management and orga-nization: Relational alternatives to individualism* (pp. 157-200). Aldershot, England: Avebury.

Crawford, D., & Bodine, R. (1996). *Conflict resolution education* [NCJ 160935]. Washington, DC: U.S. Department of Justice and U.S. Department of Education.

Creswell, J. W. (1998). *Qualitative inquiry and research design: Choosing among five traditions.* Thousand Oaks, CA: Sage.

Cronen, V. E. (1995a). Coordinated management of meaning: The consequentiality of communication and the recapturing of experience. In S. Sigman (Ed.), *The consequentiality of communication* (pp. 17-65). New York: Erlbaum.

Cronen, V. E. (1995b). Practical theory and the tasks ahead for social approaches to communication. In W. L. Hurwitz (Ed.), *Social approaches to communication* (pp. 217-242). New York: Guilford.

Cronen, V., & Lang, P. (1994). Language and action: Wittgenstein and Dewey in the practice of therapy and consultation. *Human Systems, 5,* 5-43.

Cronk, M. (1997a). Cupertino tackles diversity head-on. *San Jose Mercury News,* pp. 1B, 4B.

Cronk, M. (1997b). Cupertino campaign waged on a high plane. *San Jose Mercury News,* pp. 1B-2B.

Cupertino Community Guide and Business Directory. (1998). Cupertino: Cupertino Chamber of Commerce.

Dewey, J. (1927). *The public and its problems.* Athens, OH: Swallow Press.

Dryzek, J. S. (1990). *Discursive democracy: Politics, policy, and political science.* Cambridge: Cambridge University Press.

Ellinor, L., & Gerard, G. (1998). *Dialogue: Rediscover the transforming power of conversation.* New York: Wiley.

Elmore, R. F. (1991). Foreword. In C. R. Christensen, D. A. Garvin, & A. Sweet (Eds.), *Education for judgment: The artistry of discussion leadership.* Cambridge, MA: Harvard Business School Press.

Enders, S. (1998, August 19). Angus steps up to community officer role. *Cupertino Courier,* p. 5.

Freeman, S. A., Littlejohn, S. W., & Pearce, W. B. (1992). Communication and moral conflict. *Western Journal of Communication, 56,* 311-329.

Gastil, J. (1993). *Democracy in small groups: Participation, decision making, and communication.* Philadelphia: New Society Publishers.

Gastil, J., & Dillard, J. P. (1999). The aims, methods, and effects of deliberative civic education through the National Issues Forums. *Communication Education, 48,* 179-192.

Goode, J., & Schneider, J. A. (1994). *Reshaping ethnic and racial relations in Philadelphia.* Philadelphia: Temple University Press.

Gramsci, A. (1971). *Selections from the prison notebooks* (Q. Hoare, Ed., & J. Nowell Smith, Trans.). New York: International Publishers.

Green, J. O. (1984). Evaluating cognitive explanations of communicative phenomena. *Quarterly Journal of Speech, 70,* 241-254.

Greenwood, D. J., & Levin, M. (1998). *Introduction to action research: Social research for social change.* Thousand Oaks, CA: Sage.

Grossberg, L. (1996). History, politics and postmodernism: Stuart Hall and cultural studies. In D. Morley & K. Chen (Eds.), *Stuart Hall: Critical dialogues in cultural studies* (pp. 151-173). London: Routledge.

Gutmann, A., & Thompson, D. (1996). *Democracy and disagreement.* Cambridge, MA: The Belknap Press of Harvard University Press.

Habermas, J. (1970). Toward a theory of communicative competence. *Inquiry, 13,* 360-375.

Habermas, J. (1984). *The theory of communicative action I: Reason and the rationalization of society.* Boston: Beacon.

Hall, S. (1979). Race, articulation and societies structured in dominance. In UNESCO, *Sociological theories: Race and colonialism* (pp. 305-345). Paris: UNESCO.

Hammond, S. A., & Royal, C. (Eds.). (1998). *Lessons from the field: Applying appreciative inquiry.* Plano, TX: Practical Press.

Heron, J. (1996). *Co-operative inquiry: Research into the human condition.* Sage: London.

Hickson, M. (1996). Rethinking our rethinking retrospectively: A rejoinder to Spano. *Basic Communication Course Annual, 8,* 97-107.

Hickson , M. (1998). Theory and pedagogy in the basic course: A summary from Spano and Hickson. *Basic Communication Course Annual, 10,* 125-132.

Ku, M., & Marino, P. (1998, September 30). At the crossroads: A quickly shifting demographic causes tension, discussion. *Cupertino Courier,* pp. 12-13.

Lappé, F. M., & Du Bois, P. M. (1994). *The quickening of America: Rebuilding our nation, rebuilding our lives.* San Francisco: Jossey-Bass.

Lindlof, T. R. (1995). *Qualitative communication research methods.* Thousand Oaks, CA: Sage.

Lowe, L. (1996). Immigration, citizenship, racialization: Asian American critique. In L. Lowe (Ed.), *Immigrant acts: On Asian American cultural politics* (pp. 1-36). Durham, NC: Duke University Press.

Marino, P. (1997, October 8). Voters put diversity on the agenda. *Cupertino Courier,* pp. 7-8.

Mathews, D. (1994). *Politics for people: Finding a responsible public voice.* Urbana: University of Illinois Press.

McNamee, S., & Gergen, K. J. (1999). *Relational responsibility: Resources for sustainable dialogue.* Thousand Oaks, CA: Sage.

Mehta, J. (1996, February 28). Can the public influence what the city should be? *Cupertino Courier,* p. 7.

Middleton, D., & Edwards, D. (1990). Introduction. In D. Middleton & D. Edwards (Eds.), *Collective remembering* (pp. 1-22). London: Sage.

Morgan, D. L. (1997). *Focus groups as qualitative research* (2nd ed.). Thousand Oaks, CA: Sage.

Osborn, M., & Osborn, S. (1991). *Alliance for a better public voice: The communication discipline and the National Issues Forums.* Dayton, OH: National Issues Forums Institute.

Owen, H. (1992). *Open space technology: A user's guide*. Potomac, MD: Abbott.

Owen, W. F. (1984). Interpreting themes in relational communication. *Quarterly Journal of Speech, 70*, 274-286.

Page, B. I. (1996). *Who deliberates? Mass media in modern democracy*. Chicago: University of Chicago Press.

Parker, W. C. (1996). Advanced ideas about democracy: Toward a pluralist conception of citizen education. *Teachers College Record, 98*, 104-125.

Pearce, W. B. (1989). *Communication and the human condition*. Carbondale: Southern Illinois Press.

Pearce, W. B. (1994). *Interpersonal communication: Making social worlds*. New York: Harper Collins.

Pearce, W. B., & Cronen, V. E. (1980). *Communication, action, and meaning: The creation of social realities*. New York: Praeger.

Pearce, W. B., & Littlejohn, S. W. (1997). *Moral conflict: When social worlds collide*. Thousand Oaks, CA: Sage.

Pearce, W. B., & Pearce, K. A. (2000). Combining passions and abilities: Toward dialogic virtuosity. *Southern Communication Journal, 65*, 161-175.

Pearce, W. B., & Pearce, K. A. (in press). Extending the theory of the coordinated management of meaning ("CMM") through a community dialogue process. *Communication Theory*.

Penn, P. (1982). Circular questioning. *Family Process, 21*, 267-280.

Putnam, R. (1995). Social capital and the prosperous community. *Wingspread Journal, 17*, 35-42.

Reason, P. (1994). Three approaches to participative inquiry. In N. K. Denzin & Y. S. Lincoln (Eds.), *Handbook of qualitative research* (pp. 324-339). Thousand Oaks, CA: Sage.

Selvini, M. P., Boscolo, L., Cecchin, G., & Prata, G. (1980). Hypothesizing, circularity, neutrality: Three guidelines for the conductor of the session. *Family Process, 19*, 3-12.

Shotter, J. (1993). *Conversational realities: Constructing life through language*. London: Sage.

Shotter, J., & Gergen, K. J. (1994). Social construction: Knowledge, self, others, and continuing the conversation. In S. A. Deetz (Ed.), *Communication yearbook 17* (pp. 3-33). New Brunswick, NJ: Transaction.

Spano, S. (1995, February). *Cognitive explanations of interpersonal communication: Review, critique, and alternative perspective*. Paper presented at the annual meeting of the Western States Communication Association, Portland, OR.

Spano, S. (1996). Rethinking the role of theory in the basic course: Taking a "practical" approach to communication education. *Basic Communication Course Annual, 8*, 74-96.

Spano, S. (1998). Delineating the uses of practical theory: A reply to Hickson. *Basic Communication Course Annual, 10*, 105-124.

Spano, S., & Calcagno, C. (1996). Adapting systemic consultation practices to public discourse: An analysis of a public conflict episode. *Human Systems, 7*, 17-43.

Stewart, D. W., & Shamdasani, P. N. (1990). *Focus groups: Theory and practice*. Newbury Park, CA: Sage.

Stewart, J., & Logan, C. (1998). *Together: Communicating interpersonally* (5th ed.). New York: McGraw-Hill.

Stocking, B. (1999, April 15). Cupertino adjusts to influence of immigrants. *San Jose Mercury News*, pp. 1A, 14-15A.

Strike, K. A. (1994). On the construction of public speech: Pluralism and public reason. *Educational Theory, 44*, 1-26.

Stringer, E. T. (1996). *Action research: A handbook for practitioners*. Thousand Oaks, CA: Sage.

Survey of residents. (1998, March). *Cupertino residents satisfaction survey*. Godbe Research & Analysis. Unpublished report.

Survey of residents. (2000, May). *Cupertino residents satisfaction survey*. Godbe Research & Analysis. Unpublished report.

Tannen, D. (1998). *The argument culture: Moving from debate to dialogue*. New York: Random House.

U.S. Department of Justice. (1998). *Guidelines for effective human relations commissions*. Washington, DC: Community Relations Service.

Watzlawick, P., Bevin, J. H., & Jackson, D. J. (1967). *Pragmatics of human communication*. New York: W. W. Norton.

Weisbord, M. R., & Janoff, S. (1995). *Future search*. San Francisco: Berrett-Koehler.

Wittgenstein, L. (1953). *Philosophical investigations* (G. E. M. Anscombe, Trans.). New York: MacMillian.

Yankelovich, D. (1991). *Coming to public judgment: Making democracy work in a complex world*. Syracuse, NY: Syracuse University Press.

AUTHOR INDEX

SUBJECT INDEX

283